Cambridge IGCSE™

Information and Computing Technology

Second Edition

David Watson
Graham Brown

This text has not been through the Cambridge International endorsement process. Any references or materials related to answers, grades, papers or examinations are based on the opinion of the author(s). The Cambridge International syllabus or curriculum framework, associated assessment guidance material and specimen papers should always be referred to for definitive guidance.

The Publishers would like to thank the following for permission to reproduce copyright material.

Acknowledgements

Every effort has been made to trace all copyright holders, but if any have been inadvertently overlooked, the Publishers will be pleased to make the necessary arrangements at the first opportunity.

Photos reproduced by permission of: **p.21** (top to bottom) Phonlamaiphoto/Adobe Stock, Amnach kinchokawat/123RF, Kaspars Grinvalds/Adobe Stock, Murat BAYSAN/Fotolia, Geppe/Adobe Stock; **p.34** Sheval/Alamy Stock Photo; **p.129** JFL Photography/Adobestock.

Although every effort has been made to ensure that website addresses are correct at time of going to press, Hodder Education cannot be held responsible for the content of any website mentioned in this book. It is sometimes possible to find a relocated web page by typing in the address of the home page for a website in the URL window of your browser.

Hachette UK's policy is to use papers that are natural, renewable and recyclable products and made from wood grown in well-managed forests and other controlled sources. The logging and manufacturing processes are expected to conform to the environmental regulations of the country of origin.

Orders: please contact Hachette UK Distribution, Hely Hutchinson Centre, Milton Road, Didcot, Oxfordshire, OX11 7HH. Telephone: +44 (0)1235 827827. Email education@hachette.co.uk. Lines are open from 9 a.m. to 5 p.m., Monday to Friday. You can also order through our website: www.hoddereducation.com

ISBN: 978 1 3983 1852 6

© David Watson and Graham Brown 2022

First published in 2017.
This edition published in 2022 by
Hodder Education,
An Hachette UK Company
Carmelite House
50 Victoria Embankment
London EC4Y 0DZ

www.hoddereducation.com

Impression number   5 4 3 2 1

Year   2026 2025 2024 2023 2022

All rights reserved. Apart from any use permitted under UK copyright law, no part of this publication may be reproduced or transmitted in any form or by any means, electronic or mechanical, including photocopying and recording, or held within any information storage and retrieval system, without permission in writing from the publisher or under licence from the Copyright Licensing Agency Limited. Further details of such licences (for reprographic reproduction) may be obtained from the Copyright Licensing Agency Limited, www.cla.co.uk

Cover photo © Julien Eichinger - stock.adobe.com

Illustrations by Aptara, Inc.

Typeset in India by Aptara, Inc.

Printed in Spain

A catalogue record for this title is available from the British Library.

Contents

Introduction iv

Section 1 Theory
1. Types and components of computer systems 1
2. Input and output devices 10
3. Storage devices and media 24
4. Networks and the effects of using them 32
5. The effects of using IT 45
6. ICT applications 51
7. The systems life cycle 81
8. Safety and security 93
9. Audience 107
10. Communication 112

Section 2 Practical
11. File management 124
12. Images 128
13. Layout 131
14. Styles 134
15. Proofing 137
16. Graphs and charts 140
17. Document production 144
18. Databases 148
19. Presentations 156
20. Spreadsheets 159
21. Website authoring 167

Practice Paper 1: Theory 181

Answers to exam-style questions 188
Answers to Practice Paper 1 204
Index 209

Introduction

Welcome to the *Cambridge IGCSE™ Information and Communication Technology Study and Revision Guide Second Edition*. This book has been written to help you revise everything you need to know for your ICT examinations, alongside the *Cambridge IGCSE Information and Communication Technology Third Edition* Student's Book. Following the new ICT syllabus (first exams in June 2023), it covers all the key content along with sample questions and answers and exam-style practice questions. A sample practice paper 1 is at the end of this book, with sample practice papers 2 and 3 (and their source files) online at https://www.hoddereducation.co.uk/cambridgeextras. These practice papers, written by the authors, are slightly longer than the actual Cambridge IGCSE papers to ensure questions covering more of the syllabus can be offered. Red bold words are glossary words. The glossary can also be found online at Cambridge Extras.

How to use this book

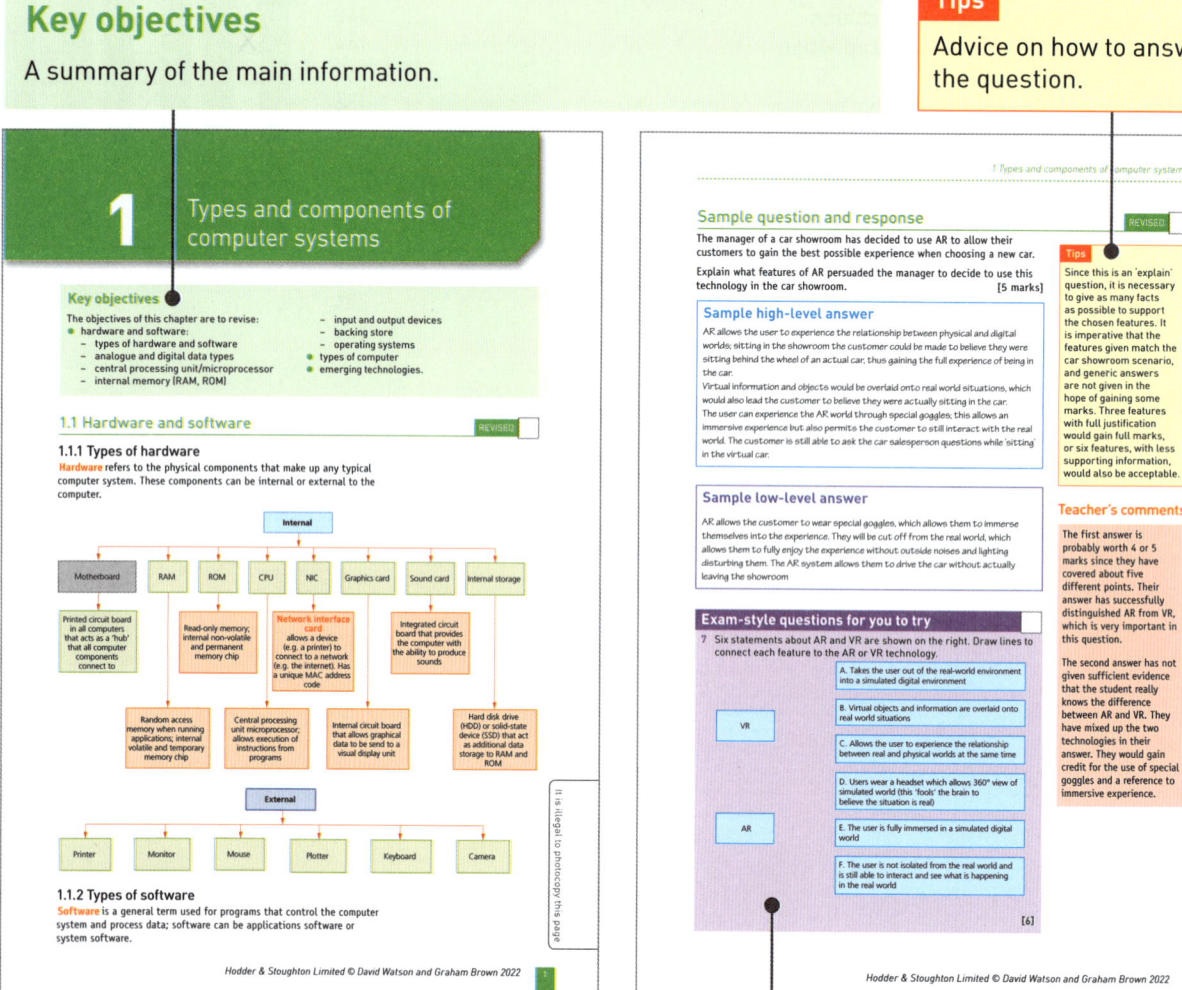

Cambridge IGCSE Information and Communication Technology Study and Revision Guide Second Edition

Sample question and response

REVISED ☐

Exam-style questions with sample student answers to show how the question can be answered. In the Theory section, high-level answers are strong answers while low-level answers require more revision.

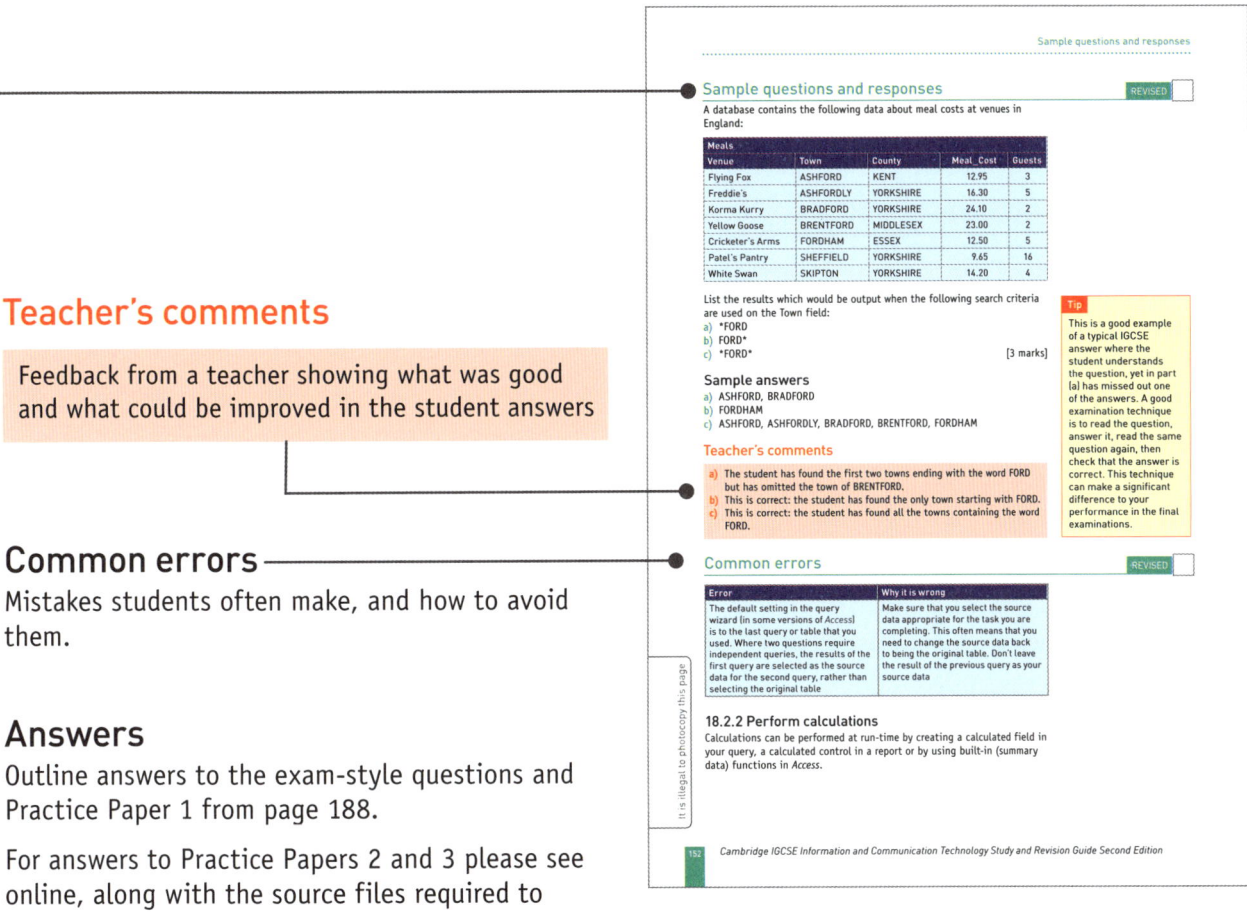

Teacher's comments

Feedback from a teacher showing what was good and what could be improved in the student answers

Common errors

Mistakes students often make, and how to avoid them.

Answers

Outline answers to the exam-style questions and Practice Paper 1 from page 188.

For answers to Practice Papers 2 and 3 please see online, along with the source files required to complete those papers. Where ellipses are used in the practical answer section, the ellipses indicate follow on marks when the first mark has been attained.

Assessment

The information in this section is taken from the Cambridge IGCSE Information and Communication Technology 0417/0983 syllabus for examination from 2023. You should always refer to the appropriate syllabus document for the year of examination to confirm the details and for more information.

There are three examination papers. Papers 2 and 3 assess practical skills using a range of different software applications.

	Paper 1 Theory	Paper 2 Document Production, Databases and Presentations	Paper 1 Theory Paper 3 Spreadsheets and Website authoring
Duration	1 hour 30 minutes	2 hours 15 minutes	2 hours 15 minutes
Marks	80 marks	70 marks	70 marks
Syllabus topics examined	1–21	11–16, 17, 18, 19	11–16, 20, 21

Hodder & Stoughton Limited © David Watson and Graham Brown 2022

v

1 Types and components of computer systems

Key objectives

The objectives of this chapter are to revise:
- hardware and software:
  - types of hardware and software
  - analogue and digital data types
  - central processing unit/microprocessor
  - internal memory (RAM, ROM)
- input and output devices
- backing store
- operating systems
- types of computer
- emerging technologies.

1.1 Hardware and software

REVISED

1.1.1 Types of hardware

Hardware refers to the physical components that make up any typical computer system. These components can be internal or external to the computer.

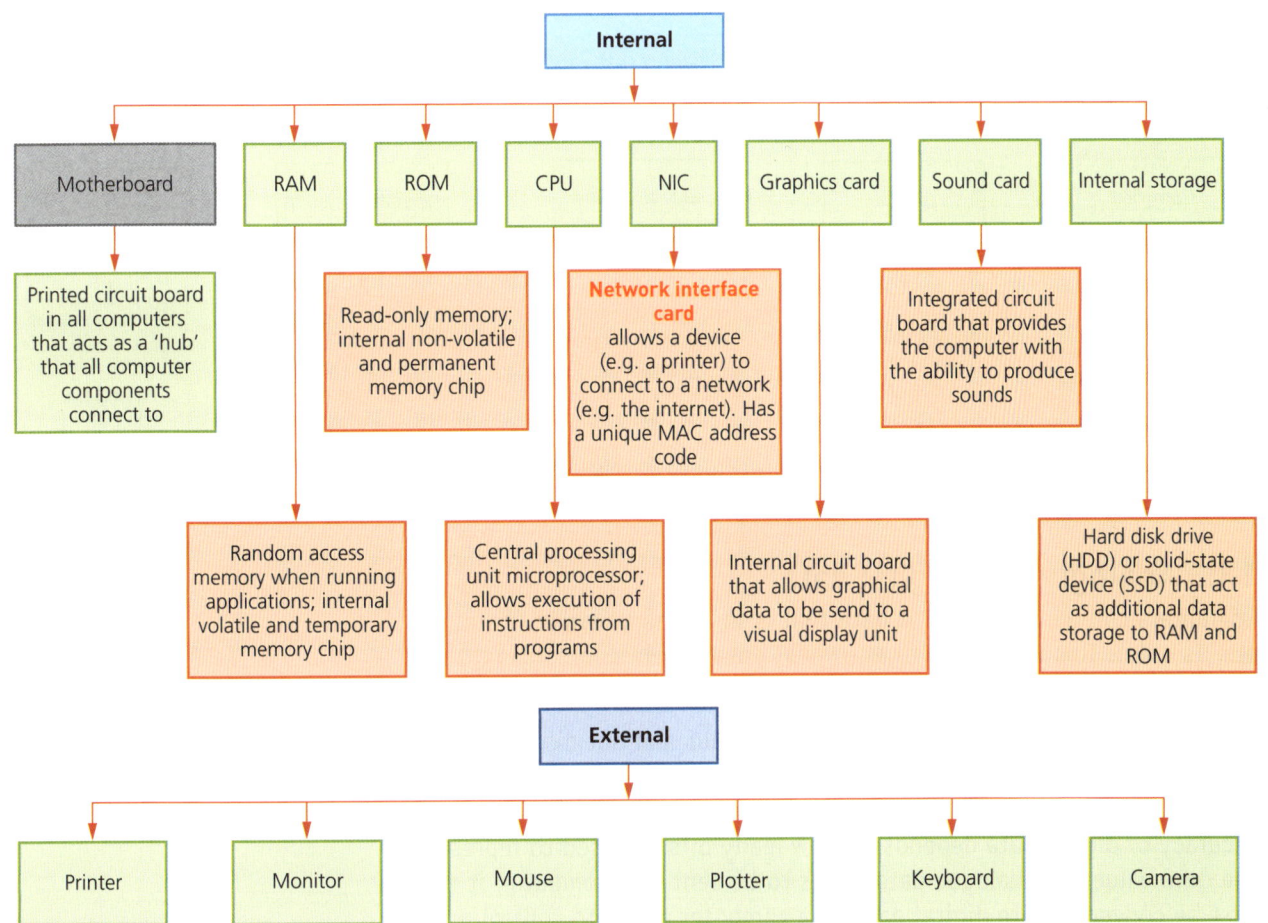

1.1.2 Types of software

Software is a general term used for programs that control the computer system and process data; software can be applications software or system software.

1.1 Hardware and software

Applications software provides the services that the user requires to solve a particular task. **System software** is designed to provide a platform on which all other software can run. Examples of both include:

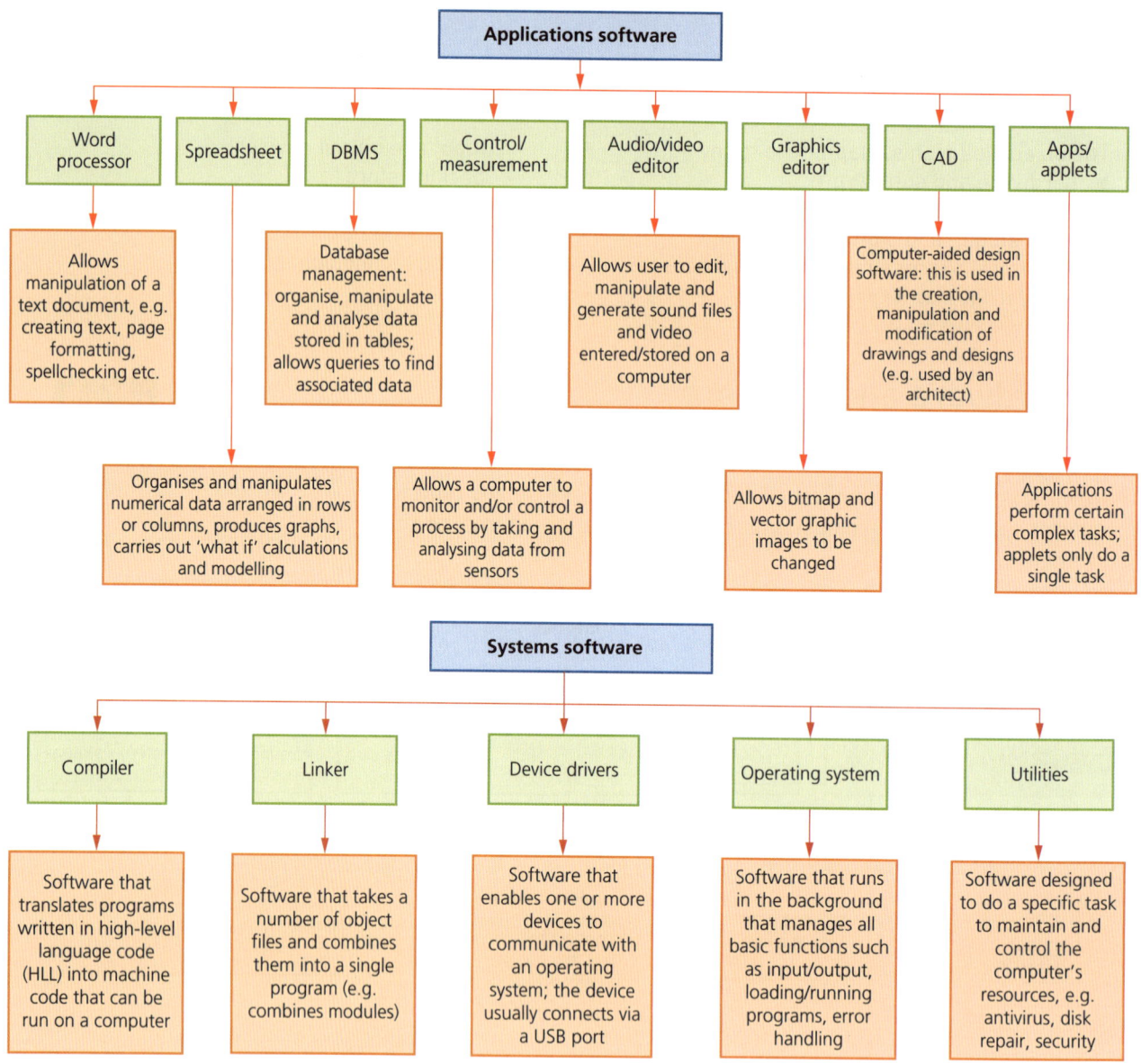

1.1.3 Analogue and digital data

Computers can only understand data that is in a binary format (i.e. 0s and 1s only). This is referred to as **digital data** which is in contrast to **analogue data** found in the real world.

Analogue data is physical data that is continuous and not discrete in nature; it can have an infinite number of values. Digital data is written in binary format; the data is discrete and can only have specific values. The accuracy of digital data depends on how many bits are used to represent the data values. If analogue data needs to be sent to a computer, it must first be converted into digital data. If a computer needs to control a device (for example a motor), then the digital output must be converted into an analogue form. To convert data from analogue to digital requires an **analogue-to-digital converter** and to convert from digital to analogue requires a **digital-to-analogue converter**.

1.2 Main components of computer systems

REVISED ☐

1.2.1 Central processing unit

The **central processing unit (CPU)** is a computer component that interprets and executes commands from computer hardware and software. It is usually part of the motherboard. The main components of the CPU are the control unit and arithmetic logic unit (ALU). It is often referred to as a **microprocessor**.

1.2.2 Internal memory and backing storage

Random access memory (RAM) is an internal memory chip where data is stored temporarily. The contents of RAM are lost when the computer is powered down. **Read-only memory (ROM)** is also an internal memory chip and stores data permanently; the data is retained even when the computer is powered down.

ROM also contains coding known as a **boot file**. This file tells the computer what to do when it first starts up. **Basic input-output system (BIOS)** is also part of this start-up procedure; here BIOS stores computer settings on a **complementary metal oxide semiconductor (CMOS)** chip.

This table summarises the differences between RAM and ROM:

RAM	ROM
Temporary memory so data can be changed	Permanent memory so data cannot be changed
Volatile memory – contents lost when power turned off	Non-volatile memory – contents retained even when power turned off
Can be written to and read from	Can only be read from
Stores data, files, part of operating system currently in use	Used to store BIOS and other start-up data
Can be increased in size to improve computer's performance	

1.2.3 Input and output devices

Input devices allow data to be entered into a computer either manually (e.g. using a keyboard) or automatically (e.g. direct data entry such as QR code readers).

Output devices allow the results of a computer's processing to be shown in a human-readable form (e.g. monitor or printer). Note that some devices can be both input and output (e.g. a touchscreen). Input and output devices are covered in more detail in Chapter 2.

1.2.4 Backing storage

Although main memory is RAM and ROM, data to be kept permanently (that can also be altered) is stored on a backing store. Backing stores are generally either **hard disk drives (HDD)** or **solid-state drives (SSD)**.

Backing storage (usually solid state in modern computers) is used to permanently store data; but it can also be changed, added to or removed by the computer or user. Backing storage can also be hard disk (magnetic) or Blu-ray disc (optical) and it can be either internal or external to the computer.

Data access is slower than for RAM or ROM but backing storage is usually considerably larger (2 TB or 4 TB is not unusual). The cost per byte of storage is also much less for backing storage devices.

> **Tip**
> RAM and ROM are directly addressable (i.e. can be read directly) by the CPU but backing storage is not. The data must be loaded into RAM first before it can be used by the computer.

1.3 Operating systems

REVISED

An **operating system (OS)** is a type of software that enables a computer system to function and allows the user to communicate with the computer by:

- controlling input/output devices and backing storage devices – this usually involves control of data flow
- supervising the loading, running and storage of applications (apps)
- dealing with errors as they occur
- maintaining security
- keeping a computer log of events
- allowing communication between computer and user.

1.3.1 User interfaces

In this part of the computer, we will consider four types of human–computer interface (HCI):

> **Tip**
>
> A GUI is often called a **windows icons menu and pointing (WIMP)** device environment and is used by PCs not equipped with touchscreens. Modern devices, such as notebooks, tablets and smartphones, all use touchscreens and these adopt a post-WIMP environment – this interface allows fingers to be used to carry out tasks such as pinching and rotating, which would be impossible with a mouse.

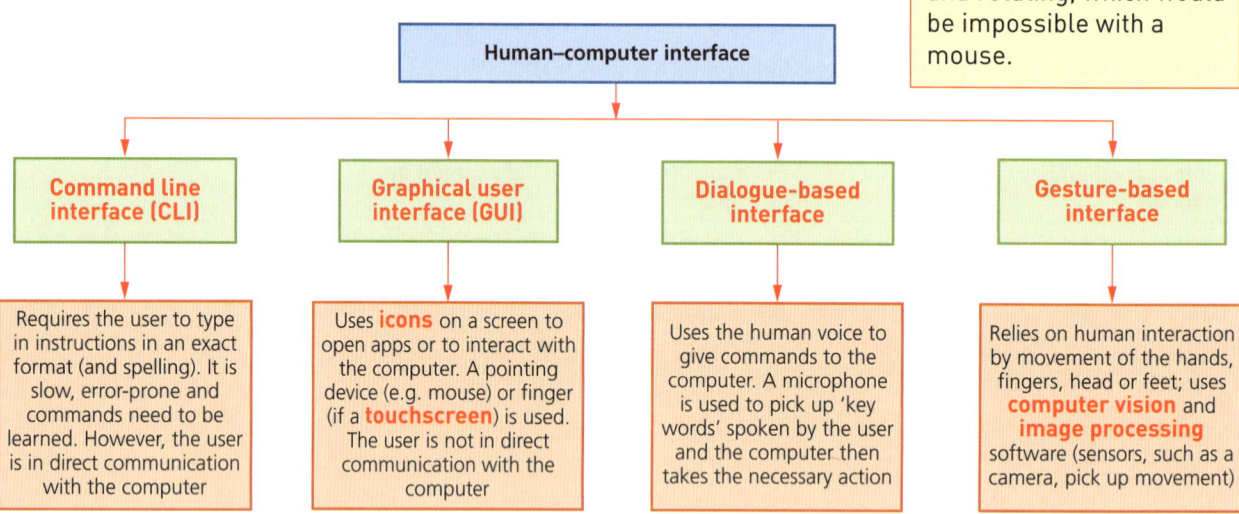

Sample questions and responses

REVISED

a Describe the advantages and disadvantages of using dialogue-based and gesture-based interfaces **[6 marks]**
b Give an example of where each type of interface is used. **[2 marks]**

> **Tip**
>
> This is a 'describe' question so it is necessary to give all the main facts, features and/or characteristics of both types of interface. No comparison of the two types of interface has been asked for. In the second part of the question, it is important that the examples given reflect the list of advantages and disadvantages; they should not be contradictory. Six marks are awarded in the first part; you would be expected to give a minimum of six features. It would be advisable to give three features of each type of interface.

1 Types and components of computer systems

Sample high-level answer

a) Advantages of dialogue based-interfaces:
- when used in a vehicle, there is no need for a driver to take their hands off the steering wheel to increase sound volume in a stereo, for example
- in a home this is very useful for people with disabilities, since many tasks can be carried out by the spoken word only
- it is possible to use this as a security feature, since voice recognition could be used to identify a person.

Disadvantages of dialogue-based interfaces:
- the system is still not that reliable, with many commands not being recognised or needing to be repeated several times (especially if there is background noise)
- dialogue-based interfaces can be quite complex to set up
- the user needs to know which commands can be used.

Advantages of gesture-based interfaces:
- replaces mechanical input devices
- there is no physical contact required
- it is a very natural interface for a human operator; no training is needed to interface with the computer.

Disadvantages of gesture-based interfaces:
- it is possible for unintentional movement to be picked up
- it only works fairly near to the camera or sensor (maximum of 1.5 metres)
- it can be limiting what the gesture-based system will accept (e.g. it may take several attempts to find out exactly what finger movements are recognised).

b) Dialogue-based systems could be used in the home by people with disabilities to do tasks such as close the curtains, switch on the lights (etc.) by simple verbal commands. Gesture-based systems could be used in a vehicle to open/close windows and doors or to alter the heating/air conditioning settings.

Sample low-level answer

a) The advantage of a dialogue-based interface is it allows a person with disabilities to control the opening and closing of curtains without them having to leave their seat. The biggest disadvantage would be verbal commands to control devices could annoy other people in the house.

The advantage of gesture-based interfaces would be in a car where the passenger finds the music too loud; they could gesture to the driver to turn the sound down. This, of course, could distract the driver which is an obvious disadvantage.

b) Dialogue-based interfaces could be used in the house by a person with disabilities to control devices without leaving their seat. Gesture-based interfaces could be used in a car to let the driver know what needs to be altered.

Teacher's comments

The first answer is well-constructed and, if anything, gives too much information. This is fine provided the student doesn't write anything that contradicts any earlier answers. The answers are set out logically which will make it easy for the examiner to pick out salient points and it also logically follows the question.

The second answer is probably only worth about 2 marks in total. The reference to the person with disabilities is repeated in part (b), so credit would only be given once. A second mark could also be awarded for suggesting this type of interface would be useful in a car, even though the scenario given totally misses the point of gesture-based interfaces. The rest of the answer is very vague and not worth any additional marks.

Hodder & Stoughton Limited © David Watson and Graham Brown 2022

1.3 Operating systems

Exam-style questions for you to try

1 Explain the following terms. In each case, give an example to help in your explanation.
   a Input device
   b Output device
   c Dialogue-based interface
   d Gesture-based interface   [8]

2 In the following table, five statements about CLI and GUI have been made. In each case, tick (✓) the appropriate box to show whether the statement refers to a CLI or GUI interface.

Statement	CLI (✓)	GUI (✓)
The user is in direct communication with the computer		
All commands need to be typed in using the correct format		
Needs a complex OS and large memory requirement to operate		
Allows computer configuration settings to be *directly* changed		
Makes use of pointing devices (such as a mouse) or finger (if using a touchscreen)		

[5]

3 Seven statements are shown on the left and seven computer terms are shown on the right. By drawing lines, connect each statement to the correct term.

1. Non-volatile chip that is battery-powered and stores key BIOS data such as the date, time and system requirements	A. RAM
2. Used with touchscreens to allow actions such as pinching and rotating as well as app selection	B. ROM
3. Software used in the creation, manipulation, modification and analysis of drawings and designs	C. CMOS
4. Internal memory chip which can be read from and written to; stores files, data and part of the operating system currently in use	D. CPU
5. Picture or symbols used on screen to represent apps (or applets); when selected, the app will be launched; part of a WIMP system	E. CAD
6. Internal memory chip which stores data permanently; it is non-volatile in nature and is often used to store the computer BIOS	F. Post-WIMP
7. Interprets and executes commands from hardware and software; part of the motherboard; main components are CU and ALU	G. Icon

[7]

Cambridge IGCSE Information and Communication Technology Study and Revision Guide Second Edition

1.4 Types of computer

REVISED ☐

1.4.1 Desktop computers

- **Desktops:** not portable but less expensive than other computer types and usually more powerful for the same cost. More stable internet connection since usually uses wired connectivity.

1.4.2 Mobile computers

There are four categories of mobile computers:

- **Laptop (or notebook):** lightweight, low power consumption, with no trailing wires, takes up less room than a desktop and is easy to work with multimedia systems since it is portable. Similar advantages to tablets but often bulkier (but this is changing with introduction of notebooks).
- **Smartphone:** very small and easy to carry round (always with you), can connect to cellular network and WiFi. Has a long battery life. Small screen size and virtual keyboards can make them difficult to use; relatively small memories and slower data transfer rates.
- **Tablet or phablet:** similar features to smartphones but much larger screen size (can be up to 33 cm); can be used with much larger keyboards built into cases. Slowly taking over from laptops as the preferred portable computing device since they often have similar or better performance.

> **Tips**
>
> In the sample question below, the term 'give' means it is acceptable to write a single sentence to highlight a typical use. In the second part, be brief when giving an example. However, remember your example must match with the use or it won't gain any marks. Note that each use, plus its example, is only worth one mark. This means it is very easy to lose the mark if either your use or the chosen example are too vague or don't match.

Sample question and response

REVISED ☐

Apart from making phone calls and text messaging, give five uses of the smartphone. For each use, give an example to illustrate your answer.

[5 marks]

Sample high-level answer

- In the field of entertainment
  - for example, when streaming videos or music.
- As a camera
  - for example, taking 'on the spur of the moment' photos at an accident since your phone is always with you.
- Internet services
  - for example, using QR codes at an airport or bus station, which allow automatic website connections to tourist attractions, hotels or taxis.
- Telephone banking
  - for example, payment of goods or services at a supermarket or restaurant (no need to carry a credit/debit card with you).
- Remote control of devices
  - for example, devices that contain embedded processors (e.g. an oven) can be controlled by an app via the internet.

Sample low-level answer

Five uses of a smartphone would include:
- accessing the internet
- playing computer games
- using Facebook or Twitter
- playing music
- watching videos

Teacher's comments

The first answer is well-constructed. The student has separated uses from examples; this means they could potentially gain all the marks available for the question. Where only 1 mark is available for use *and* example, both are needed to gain the marks.

In the second answer, the student was unable to distinguish between the use of a smartphone and examples to illustrate the use. Consequently, they could potentially lose all 5 marks! It is possible to join up accessing the internet with playing music/videos and using Facebook giving a maximum of 2 marks. However, you should not use tradenames (Facebook) so this second mark would be at serious risk.

1.5 Emerging technologies

Exam-style questions for you to try

4 Give three advantages and three disadvantages of using smartphones rather than laptop computers. **[6]**
5 Explain the following terms. In each case, also give an example to help in your explanation.
   a Phablet
   b Accelerometer
   c Fast battery drain
   d App store **[8]**
6 Six statements about types of computer are shown in the following table. Tick (✓) the appropriate columns to indicate whether each statement is true or false.

Statement	True (✓)	False (✓)
Desktop computers are easier to upgrade/expand than laptops		
Laptop computers use a touchpad, as part of the keyboard, as a pointing device		
Phablets and tablets require the use of plug-in keyboards to allow them to be used to write emails		
Tablets don't allow the use of Voice over Internet Protocol (VoIP) or video calling		
The built-in cameras on smartphones and tablets can be used to read QR codes		
Desktop computers must use a wired internet connection; they cannot connect to WiFi		

[6]

1.5 Emerging technologies

REVISED

1.5.1 Impact of emerging technologies

Artificial intelligence (AI) is a machine or application which carries out a task that requires some degree of intelligence. There are a number of positive aspects of AI:

- improvements in safety
- improvements in quality
- faster development of products
- autonomous vehicles.

There are also a number of negative aspects of AI:

- can lead to job losses and de-skilling
- technology dependency
- suspicion that machines are 'taking over'.

Extended reality (XR) refers to the combination of real and virtual environments. The most common examples are **augmented reality (AR)** and **virtual reality (VR)**. The table summarises the differences between AR and VR:

Augmented reality	Virtual reality
The user experiences relationship between digital (virtual) and physical (real) worlds	Technology is able to take the user out of the real world into a virtual, digital environment
The user is not isolated from the real world and can still interact and see what is in front of them	The user is fully immersed in the simulated world
The user can experience the AR world through special goggles or via a smartphone/tablet	Users wear a VR headset which gives a 360° view of the virtual world
Virtual data and objects are overlaid	Can be used in medicine/surgery, construction, education and military applications

Sample question and response

REVISED

The manager of a car showroom has decided to use AR to allow their customers to gain the best possible experience when choosing a new car.

Explain what features of AR persuaded the manager to decide to use this technology in the car showroom. **[5 marks]**

Sample high-level answer

AR allows the user to experience the relationship between physical and digital worlds; sitting in the showroom the customer could be made to believe they were sitting behind the wheel of an actual car, thus gaining the full experience of being in the car.
Virtual information and objects would be overlaid onto real world situations, which would also lead the customer to believe they were actually sitting in the car.
The user can experience the AR world through special goggles; this allows an immersive experience but also permits the customer to still interact with the real world. The customer is still able to ask the car salesperson questions while 'sitting' in the virtual car.

Sample low-level answer

AR allows the customer to wear special goggles, which allows them to immerse themselves into the experience. They will be cut off from the real world, which allows them to fully enjoy the experience without outside noises and lighting disturbing them. The AR system allows them to drive the car without actually leaving the showroom

Tips

Since this is an 'explain' question, it is necessary to give as many facts as possible to support the chosen features. It is imperative that the features given match the car showroom scenario, and generic answers are not given in the hope of gaining some marks. Three features with full justification would gain full marks, or six features, with less supporting information, would also be acceptable.

Teacher's comments

The first answer is probably worth 4 or 5 marks since they have covered about five different points. Their answer has successfully distinguished AR from VR, which is very important in this question.

The second answer has not given sufficient evidence that the student really knows the difference between AR and VR. They have mixed up the two technologies in their answer. They would gain credit for the use of special goggles and a reference to immersive experience.

Exam-style questions for you to try

7 Six statements about AR and VR are shown on the right. Draw lines to connect each feature to the AR or VR technology.

VR

AR

A. Takes the user out of the real-world environment into a simulated digital environment

B. Virtual objects and information are overlaid onto real world situations

C. Allows the user to experience the relationship between real and physical worlds at the same time

D. Users wear a headset which allows 360° view of simulated world (this 'fools' the brain to believe the situation is real)

E. The user is fully immersed in a simulated digital world

F. The user is not isolated from the real world and is still able to interact and see what is happening in the real world

[6]

2 Input and output devices

Key objectives

The objectives of this chapter are to revise:
- the characteristics, uses, advantages and disadvantages of:
  - input devices
  - direct data entry devices
  - output devices.

2.1 Input devices

REVISED

An input device is hardware that allows a user to interact with a computer and also allows the computer to collect data. The following table lists a number of input devices together with some of their uses as well as their advantages and disadvantages:

Input device	Uses of input device	Advantages	Disadvantages
Keyboard	• Entering data manually into a computer • Typing in commands to a computer (e.g. PrtScrn, Ctrl+P and so on)	• Well-known method • Easy method of entering data into a computer • Easier to carry out verification checks on data entered	• Difficult to use for people with certain physical disabilities • Slow entry method compared to direct data entry • Can lead to ailments such as **RSI**
Numeric keypad	• At **ATMs** to key in PIN to obtain money • At **POS** terminals in case the barcode on an item fails to scan properly • When using chip and PIN devices to make a card payment	• Faster input method than a standard keyboard when entering numeric data • Easy-to-use input device since it involves fewer keys	• Keys can be small, making input difficult for some people • Order of numbers on keypads is often not intuitive
Pointing device: **mouse**	• Controls the position of an on-screen pointer to allow selections, open/close files and so on	• Faster method to choose on-screen options compared to a keyboard • Only requires a small amount of desk space	• Difficult to use by people with certain disabilities • Can lead to injuries such as RSI • Some surfaces don't work well with mechanical mice (mouse slips on the surface)
Pointing device: **touchpad**	• Similar to mouse but uses a flat panel below the keyboard on a laptop computer	• Same advantages as a mouse • Since it is integrated into a laptop, there is no need to carry a mouse around with you	• Not everyone finds touchpads easy to control and certain actions can be difficult (such as drag and drop)
Pointing device: **trackerball**	• Used in control rooms where desk space is at a premium (and has more accurate control than a mouse) • Used in luxury cars to select functions such as operating the Global Positioning System, allowing use of smartphone and so on	• More accurate positioning of pointer on screen than a mouse • More robust and doesn't need any special surface to work properly • Requires less desk space than a mouse • Less prone than a mouse at causing RSI	• More expensive to buy than a mouse • May require training to use properly since it is a less well-known type of pointing device

Cambridge IGCSE Information and Communication Technology Study and Revision Guide Second Edition

2 Input and output devices

Input device	Uses of input device	Advantages	Disadvantages
Remote control	• Used to control functions on televisions, Blu-ray players, hi-fi equipment and so on	• Can operate from a reasonable distance unlike, for example, a wired mouse • Easy-to-use interface	• Easy to lose the device • Batteries need replacing on a regular basis (an environmental issue) • The remote's infrared signal can be blocked and may not work well if not in direct line of device
Pointing devices: **joystick** and **driving wheel**	• Both are used as input devices to many gaming consoles or **simulators** (e.g. flight simulator or car driving simulator) to mimic actual controls	• More realistic interface than a mouse in many games and **simulations** • Easier and more accurate than a mouse or keyboard to control on-screen movements	• Movement can be too sensitive, making the input device difficult to use in certain applications • Doesn't allow any feedback during a simulation
Touchscreen	• Self-service tills (e.g. at a petrol station) • ATMs to enter PIN, amount of money required and so on • Public information kiosks (e.g. at an airport) • Mobile phones and tablets • Computer-based training	• Fast data entry and easy-to-use interface • It is easy to expand screen size as necessary with no need to change software or entry method • Easier to keep clean since the surface is glass (keypads and keyboards are more difficult to keep clean)	• Limited number of possible choices available • Screens can get very dirty quickly and can cause issues at fast food menu screens, for example, if not cleaned on a regular basis • Screens can get scratched, causing them to malfunction
Scanner	• Scanning in paper documents and photos to be saved in electronic format on a computer • Archiving of valuable old manuscripts • Used to scan in barcodes at a POS using laser or LED scanners	• Converts written text into electronic format, allowing the text to be manipulated by OCR software and used in other documents (using a word processor) • Allows damaged photos and manuscripts to be recovered • When used to read barcodes, the scanner becomes a DDE device (see 2.2)	• Quality of photos and text depends on the scanner resolution • Scanning (particularly colour image scanning) can be a very slow process • If the barcode being scanned is damaged, the scanner can't successfully read it and a backup input method is needed
Digital camera	• Taking photographs or videos • A data capture device (e.g. reading of QR codes or a reversing aid in a vehicle) • In dentistry to photograph teeth for later dental work • Creation of virtual tours around buildings, industrial plants and so on	• Can take many photos compared to a traditional camera (unwanted photos are easy to delete) • No need to develop photos (saving money and also gain immediate feedback about photo just taken) • Easy to store photos on another device or in the cloud	• Need to be computer-literate to use digital cameras effectively • Some artistry is lost since brightness, sharpness, exposure (etc.) can all be altered by software later on • Compression of images when being stored can lead to some loss of quality
Microphone	• Input speech/sound to be used in presentations, special effects, music sampling and so on • As a sensor to pick up sounds (e.g. in an intruder alert system, detection of liquid dripping from pipes) • In video conferencing • Input device for people with disabilities	• Fast input method and useful for people with certain disabilities • Allows the possibility of manipulating sounds in real time • Can be used in voice activation systems improving safety (e.g. verbal commands in a car to operate key functions without the driver taking their hands off the steering wheel)	• Sound files can take up a large amount of memory unless they are compressed • Using verbal input can be inaccurate (e.g. 'how to wreck a nice beach' could be mistaken for 'how to recognise speech', which would be a problem if a microphone was used to input data into a word processor) • In voice activation, you must remember keywords or certain functions of the system can be activated by mistake

2.1 Input devices

Input device	Uses of input device	Advantages	Disadvantages

Analogue sensors	• Measure physical data from the environment and send it to a computer
	• Many sensors exist:
	  – temperature (greenhouse environment)
	  – pressure (intruder alert system)
	  – light (control of street lighting)
	  – sound (intruder alert system)
	  – humidity (monitor the atmosphere in a chip manufacturing process)
	  – pH (monitor acidity levels in a chemical process)
		• Readings taken are more accurate than manual methods
		• Readings taken continuously (no vital readings would be missed)
		• Possible to take readings in places hazardous to humans or when severe weather causes risks to human life
		• Data gathering is automatic so it can be automatically sent to a computer
			• Faulty readings can lead to spurious results, which can be dangerous (e.g. sensors used in monitoring/controlling functions in an aeroplane)
			• Most sensors are analogue, which means they require conversion to digital using an **ADC**

Light pen	• Selecting objects on a CRT screen • Used with **CAD**/CAM software on a CRT screen	• Have greater accuracy than touchscreens • Very small devices (useful where space is an issue) • Very easy input device to use	• Problems of 'lag' when moving the pen on screen (especially if the screen is not clean) • Currently only work with CRT screens • Very dated technology

Sample questions and responses

REVISED

Name a suitable input device for each of the following applications. Give an advantage and a disadvantage of your chosen device in each case. A different device needs to be chosen for each application:

a) street lighting in a town where the lights are turned on automatically when it turns dark and are switched off again when it becomes light.
b) a 'smart house' where the opening/closing of windows, turning lights on/off and operating other devices (such as a television) is done by voice command.
c) simulation of an aircraft cockpit which needs to be as realistic as possible.
d) selection and control of icons (e.g. representing pumps) on a large screen in the control room of an oil refinery plant. **[12 marks]**

> **Tip**
> The question only asks for a named device; do not give any unnecessary descriptions. For advantages and disadvantages, ensure your answers refer to the scenario given and don't use generic examples. Think about your answer carefully to ensure you don't choose the same device for two applications; for example, choosing sensors for applications (a) and (b) would lose you all the marks for part (c).

Sample high-level answer

a) **Device:** light sensor
   Advantage: allows for automatic control of the street lights, therefore there is no need to manually switch them on/off; allows 24-hour control irrespective of the time of day or the weather.
   Disadvantage: unless set up properly, lights would come on and off during heavy cloud cover during the day causing constant on/off; light sensors are analogue devices requiring the use of an additional ADC to convert input to digital; sensors also need regular maintenance to operate correctly.

b) **Device:** microphone
   Advantage: a person with disabilities can easily control the operation of devices in the home from their seat without the need to physically open/close windows and so on.
   Disadvantage: can be expensive to set up initially; a dependence on technology is always a big risk, for example what happens if the system breaks down?

2 Input and output devices

c) **Device:** joystick
Advantage: gives a fairly realistic control of an aircraft interface; it is an easy input device to operate.
Disadvantage: movement of a joystick can be too sensitive, reducing the realism or leading to unwanted results; an expensive interface would be needed for actual realism since the joystick doesn't feed back in a simulation.

d) **Device:** trackerball
Advantage: space is at a premium in a control room (for safety reasons, desks need to be uncluttered), therefore a trackerball is a better option than, say, a mouse or a keyboard; they are a very robust device and can handle rough treatment by the operators; they have more accurate control of the on-screen process parameters.
Disadvantage: often requires training to gain maximum benefit of the device since operators would only be used to using a mouse or touchscreen before.

Teacher's comments

The first answer would probably gain the full 12 marks as each device has been correctly identified and the advantages and disadvantages refer to the actual application and are not generic.

The second answer would only gain about 5 marks. Devices (a), (c) and (d) would just about gain 3 marks; the second device is far too vague and is also a repeat of sensors as an input device. Part (b) advantage and part (d) disadvantage would also gain 2 marks since they are just enough – the answers are weak but not wrong. The rest of the advantages and disadvantages are either incorrect or much too vague to gain any marks.

Sample low-level answer

a) **Device:** light sensor
Advantage: inexpensive item with low maintenance.
Disadvantage: may break down in use.

b) **Device:** sound sensor
Advantage: a person with disabilities doesn't need to move.
Disadvantage: can pick up other sounds and not work properly.

c) **Device:** steering wheel
Advantage: can control an aircraft as in real life.
Disadvantage: aeroplanes don't use steering wheels.

d) **Device:** touchscreen
Advantage: easy-to-use interface.
Disadvantage: screen becomes dirty.

Exam-style questions for you to try

1 A water purification plant needs to check acidity levels and oxygen levels in the water. This process is controlled from large LCD screens in a control room.
A list of possible input devices is given in the table below. Select which input devices would be suitable for this pollution monitoring plant and its control room.

Input device	Tick (✓) if suitable device
Microphone	
pH sensor	
Keypad	
Oxygen gas sensor	
Touchscreen	
Joystick	
Remote control	
Light pen	
Trackerball	

[4]

2 Describe applications for each of the following input devices. Justify your choice of device in each case:
  a Driving wheel   c Touchscreen
  b Microphone   d Digital camera   [8]

Hodder & Stoughton Limited © David Watson and Graham Brown 2022

2.2 Direct data entry devices

REVISED

Direct data entry (DDE) devices are used to input data into a computer without the need for very much, if any, human interaction. For example, barcode readers are DDE devices and the only human intervention is to point a reader/scanner at the barcode. The data collection and transfer to a computer is done automatically. The following table lists a number of DDE devices together with a description and some of their uses as well as their advantages and disadvantages:

DDE device	Description of device	Uses	Advantages	Disadvantages
Magnetic stripe reader	Reads information on **magnetic stripes** on the back of a card, for example a debit or credit card, which holds data such as account number, sort code, expiry date and start date. It does *not* hold the PIN	• On credit/debit cards for use at ATMs or POS terminals • Security cards to allow entry to a building, hotel room and so on	• Faster data entry than using a keyboard or keypad • Error-free (no typing) • Information is more secure: the data isn't held in human-readable format • Physically robust system	• If the magnetic stripe is damaged, the information cannot be read • Reader needs to be in close contact with card • Data may not be human-readable but certain devices can read and clone data on the magnetic stripe
Contactless debit card readers	A read-only RFID chip is embedded in the card, containing data such as PIN, account number, sort code, expiry date and so on A radio frequency reader can read the chip from a few centimetres away	• Debit cards – allow customers to pay for items (up to a certain amount) without the need to enter a PIN	• Faster transaction as no need to enter a PIN • Uses 128-bit encryption • No need for a customer to remember their PIN • Retailers now don't have access to customers' credit card/debit card information	• It is possible to monitor contactless transactions if someone near you is using an RFID reading device • The maximum transaction is limited to a small value
Chip and PIN reader	The credit/debit card is inserted into the device and the embedded chip is read. A PIN is then entered that should match the PIN stored on the chip before the transaction can take place	• To make payments at garages, restaurants, travel agents and so on • The card reader uses an internet link (usually WiFi) to contact the card-issuing bank when making a transaction	• More secure than contactless payments (needs a PIN) • The limit on spending is much higher than for contactless methods	• If the PIN is accessed by a third party, the chip and PIN system is very insecure (cards can be cloned using devices attached to ATMs) • The lack of an upper limit can cause problems if a stolen card is used before it is reported stolen

Cambridge IGCSE Information and Communication Technology Study and Revision Guide Second Edition

2 Input and output devices

DDE device	Description of device	Uses	Advantages	Disadvantages
Radio Frequency Identification (RFID) readers	Use radio waves to read and capture information stored on a tag. The tag is made up of a microchip and an antenna. (Note: passive tags use the reader's radio wave energy to relay back information)	• Livestock tracking on a farm • Retail (unlike barcodes, there is no need to scan – the tag is automatically read from a distance) • Security (RFID tags attached to goods allow supermarkets to check if articles are being removed from the store without payment) • Admission passes, for example at a theme park to gain access to rides and events • Libraries (to track books out on loan)	• Tags can be read from a reasonable distance • Very fast read rate (it takes less than 100 milliseconds to respond) • Allows bi-directional data transfer (data can be sent in both directions) • Allows bulk detection/reading to occur (several tags can be read at the same time) • Unlike barcodes, it is difficult to copy or alter the data stored on RFID tags	• Tag collisions can occur (where data from two or more tags overlap) • Radio waves can be blocked or jammed which means the data can't be read • It is possible to hack into transmitted data and read or change it • The system is more complex and more expensive than barcode readers
Optical mark recognition (OMR)	Can read marks written in ink or pencil on a pre-printed form either by joining dots or filling in a lozenge	• Reading questionnaire responses • Automatic marking of multi-choice exam papers • Automatic counting of voting choices in an election	• Fast method of data input (documents can be loaded into a hopper and read automatically) • More accurate than entering the data using a keyboard (removes risk of typing errors) • Faster to fill in a form than if using OCR	• Needs expensive and complex forms • Forms need to be carefully designed to capture required data (OMR limits the amount of data that can be captured) • Problems occur if the form is not filled in correctly (often instructions on how to fill out the form need to be given)
Optical character recognition (OCR)	Converts text on hard copy documents into an electronic format. The data can then be processed and used, for example in a word processor	• Processing of passports and ID cards at an airport security desk • Converting handwritten text into a computer-usable format • Automatic number plate recognition to identify cars when entering, for example, car parks • Digitisation of valuable, ancient documents and books	• Much faster data entry than manually keying in data using a keyboard • More accurate and less error-prone than manual data entry methods • If used in questionnaires, allows customer to expand on answers (unlike OMR where a customer is limited to answering a set questions)	• The system can't always read certain handwriting styles • Scanning of documents isn't always 100% accurate • A complex and expensive system

2.2 Direct data entry devices

DDE device	Description of device	Uses	Advantages	Disadvantages
Barcode readers	Reads **barcode** labels on items Barcodes are read by a laser or LED scanner/reader which scans the thickness of the dark and light lines and converts the data into a digital format	• In supermarkets on products, enabling automatic product information, pricing and automatic re-ordering of items; they also allow for itemised billing • In libraries to track books out on loan • Safety records of equipment, for example in an office (e.g. recording the last time an electrical safety check was carried out)	• Faster checkouts and fewer errors than typing in prices using a keypad • Allows for automatic stock control in many applications, such as in a supermarket, allowing for 'just-in-time' stocking of items • A well-tried and trusted technology	• Not totally foolproof, barcodes can be altered or swapped by someone • Barcodes are more easily damaged than RFID tags or magnetic stripe cards • If damaged or torn, barcodes may not be successfully scanned
Quick response (QR) code readers	QR codes are made up of a matrix of dark squares on light backgrounds QR codes are able to store large amounts of information/data; the codes can be read by the camera built into a smartphone or tablet	• In advertising, the QR code can contain phone numbers, physical addresses, website addresses and so on • Can contain weblinks that are automatically activated when the codes are scanned in • Can store WiFi authentication details (e.g. passwords and type of encryption being used) • In **augmented reality** (e.g. in a car showroom) • Can establish **virtual online stores** (the QR code is scanned by the customer's phone and the goods are automatically delivered to their home)	• QR codes can store much more information/data than barcodes • Fewer errors than using barcodes, since QR codes allow the use of built-in error-checking procedures • Easier to read than barcodes, they don't need expensive scanners and can be read by a smartphone/tablet camera • QR codes can be encrypted which makes them more secure than barcodes	• There is more than one QR code format • QR codes can be used to store malicious codes (known as **attagging**). When the QR code is scanned, the user is sent to a bogus website or even unwittingly downloads malware

Sample question and response

REVISED

VISIT WHITEPOOL

Visit our local attractions. Need help? Call 0800 1111 11000

The local bus station and railway station at a popular holiday resort use posters containing QR codes that give arrivals important information about amenities and attractions in the local area.

Describe how a holidaymaker can use their smartphone to find out information about local attractions in the area using this poster.

[5 marks]

2 Input and output devices

Sample high-level answer
- the holidaymaker points their smartphone at the QR code on the poster(s)
- an app on their smartphone processes the image taken by the camera
- browser software on the smartphone automatically reads the data about the holiday resort generated by the app
- the user will then see either information about local attractions and possible phone numbers or they will be sent a link to a website where they will find useful information about various attractions at the holiday resort
- the user will also be able to buy tickets online to allow them to visit theatres, museums and so on without the need to queue
- entry passes will be sent to the holidaymaker's smartphone (probably in the form of a barcode or QR code).

Sample low-level answer
The holidaymaker would use their smartphone and photograph the QR code. The QR code may contain weblinks, which take the user to the holiday resort's website. The user would type in this website on their phone and get the information they want. They could also use their smartphone to call the number on the poster at the bus station or railway station.

Tips
As a 'describe' question, a full description of the process of how the smartphone and QR code would be used by the holidaymaker is expected. The answer should be as detailed as possible and make references to the given scenario rather than giving generic responses. Five marks will be awarded so you need to make at least five valid points for a strong answer.

Teacher's comments
The first answer would probably gain full marks, but they may be marked down for use of bullet points since this is a description (and usually requires sentences). They would, however, still gain at least 4 of the 5 marks since their answer is very thorough.

The second answer is very brief and only worth 1 or 2 marks: 1 mark for mention of the use of a camera (in a smartphone) to record the QR code and 1 mark (probably) for phoning the holiday 'hot line' since a phone number was given on the poster which means the student is technically correct. The rest of the answer was worth no marks.

Exam-style questions for you to try

3. Which five computer terms and devices are being described below?
    a. A matrix of filled-in dark squares on a light background; the matrix is read by the built-in camera in a smartphone or tablet.
    b. A device that can read marks written in pen or pencil; the pen or pencil marks must be made in predetermined positions.
    c. A device that converts a photograph or document into a computer-readable format.
    d. A device used to control the operation of other electronic devices using infrared signals.
    e. Direct data entry device that uses radio waves to read and capture information stored on an electronic tag. [5]
4. a. Explain how barcodes could be used in a library to track books that are out on loan. [4]
    b. Another library uses RFID tags to track books on loan. Describe the relative advantages and disadvantages of using RFID tags compared to the method you described in part (a). [4]
5. Seven applications are given below. Tick (✓) the appropriate column to indicate the best DDE device for each of the applications.

Application	OCR	OMR	QR reader
Reading the number plate on a vehicle entering a pay car park			
Reading and counting the voting slips in an election			
Reading the data on a passport at an airport security desk			
Used in augmented reality at a car showroom to give the customer an immersive experience			
Reading embedded website addresses written in a matrix code on an advertising poster			
Digitisation of ancient books and manuscripts			
Marking multi-choice exam questions automatically			

[7]

Hodder & Stoughton Limited © David Watson and Graham Brown 2022

2.3 Output devices

The following table lists a number of output devices together with some of their uses as well as their advantages and disadvantages:

Output device	Uses of output device	Advantages	Disadvantages
monitor: **cathode ray tube (CRT)**	• In specialist areas, in applications such as CAD where a light pen is used to draw and select items on a large CRT screen	• They have a very large viewing angle • CRT monitors allow the use of light pens	• CRT monitors are heavy when compared to modern LCD screens • They tend to run very hot posing a fire risk • They consume considerably more power than LCD screens • CRT screens can flicker, causing headaches and eye problems
monitor: • liquid crystal display (LCD screens are made up of tiny liquid crystals backlit using LEDs) • light emitting diode (made up of a matrix of tiny LEDs)	• LCD: – The main output device for computers, tablets, laptops and smartphones – Where touchscreen technology is required, LCD screens are used • LED: – Generally used in large outdoor displays	• LCD: – Very efficient, low power consumption – Very lightweight and very thin screens – Don't suffer from image burn-in – Don't suffer from a flickering image – Very sharp image resolution – Very low electromagnetic screens compared to CRT • LED: – No motion lag/ghosting – No need for backlighting since LEDs produce their own light – Low power consumption – LEDs have a very long life – Screens can be any size	• LCD: – Colour and contrast from various viewing angles can be inconsistent – Suffer from some motion blur/image ghosting – Possible to have weak pixels that can show as either black (all fully off) or white (all fully on) dots on the screen – Need backlighting (LCDs don't produce their own light) – this can lead to variable illumination • LED: – More expensive than LCDs – Can suffer from colour shift (e.g. white can become yellowed) due to age and temperature – Contrast ratios are not consistent
Touchscreen (acting both as input and output device)	• Smartphones and tablets • ATMs (supplying cash and other bank facilities) • Ticket collection machines (at railway/bus stations, theatres, cinemas, etc.) • Information kiosks (at museums, airports, galleries, etc.)	• Faster data entry than a keyboard/keypad • Easy method to use and less error-prone since no typing is involved • Easy to keep screen clean (unlike keyboards) since the surface is glass • They allow multi-touch functions (such as zoom in/out, rotation, etc.) • No physical switches or buttons allowing interfaces to be more creative/intuitive	• Screens can become scratched and dirty, leading to poor performance or malfunction • As there is no 'mechanical interface', it is sometimes difficult to know if a user's action has registered. (Note: latest systems have 'haptic' feedback e.g. buzzing – but this is outside the syllabus)

2 Input and output devices

Output device	Uses of output device	Advantages	Disadvantages
Multimedia projectors (take computer output and enlarge it to be projected onto a screen or white wall)	• Training presentations (large screen makes it easy for a large number of people to take part) • Advertising, for example at a shopping mall • Home cinema systems (projecting image from DVD/Blu-ray, television, mobile phone and so on)	• Enables many people to see a presentation • Avoids the need for several networked computers since a computer output can be seen on one large screen • Space saving – projectors can be mounted on the ceiling, for example	• Images can be a bit fuzzy and colours faded or incorrect shade • Expensive items to purchase and maintain • Setting up projectors can be difficult • A darkened room is usually needed • Need a separate audio system (which can add to the costs and complexity of setting up)
Laser printer (uses a rotating drum, dry ink (toner) cartridges and electrostatic printing)	• Where low noise required (e.g. in an office) • When fast, high-quality, high-resolution printing is needed (e.g. a large print run)	• Faster printing than an inkjet printer for large print runs • Quality of the printing is high and these printers can handle small fonts and fine lines better than an inkjet • Toner cartridges last for a long time • The paper trays have much greater capacity than inkjet printers	• Can be expensive to run (especially colour printers) since the toner cartridges and maintenance are expensive • Produce ozone gas and volatile toner particles (which can be harmful to people in an office, for example) • Unlike inkjet printers, they can't handle a variety of printing materials (any material that is heat sensitive can't be used) • Larger and heavier than inkjet printers
Inkjet printer: (use **thermal bubble** or **piezoelectric** technology; use four or five small wet ink cartridges and stepper motors to feed the paper)	• Where a low-volume print run is needed (e.g. a one-off photograph) • Good for high-quality colour printing (e.g. they have a photo quality option which enhances photos) • Useful when an 'unusual' printing medium is used (e.g. printing logos on T-shirts (cloth))	• Low start-up costs • Can handle many types of paper (e.g. cardboard) and other materials (e.g. as plastics, cloth, photo paper, etc.) • Cheaper to buy than laser printers • The ink cartridges can be refilled • Smaller footprint and lighter than a laser printer • Don't produce ozone gas or ink particulates	• Inkjet ink is very expensive • Not suited for long print runs since they have very small paper trays and the ink cartridges don't last long • The paper fastness of the ink isn't good; for example, a highlighter pen can't be used on the printed sheets since the ink will 'dissolve' • Need regular head cleaning to prevent the head clogging up with ink (a process which uses a lot of ink) • Not as durable as laser printers
Dot matrix printer (a type of impact printer that uses an inked ribbon (like an old typewriter) and a printhead containing an array of pins)	• Useful in places where the atmosphere is damp or dusty (e.g. a factory floor) • Can be used in places where their noise is not an issue (e.g. in a workshop) • Useful if the print run requires multi-part stationery (i.e. carbon copies) or continuous stationery – for example, when producing thousands of wage slips during a night run	• Can be used in an environment that would be harmful to a laser or inkjet printer • Carbon copies (multi-part) can be made (very useful when producing wage slips where the impact head prints on the inside of a folded paper and not on the outside, thus keeping information confidential) • Very cheap to run and maintain • Very good for long print runs since they can use continuous stationery (which can be 2000 continuous perforated sheets)	• Very noisy in operation • Expensive to buy initially • Very slow at printing • Very limited colour printing options (some 4-coloured ribbons exist, but the colour range is very limited) • Printing is generally of very poor quality • The technology is very outdated; the printers are only suitable where laser or inkjet are not suitable

Hodder & Stoughton Limited © David Watson and Graham Brown 2022

2.3 Output devices

Output device	Uses of output device	Advantages	Disadvantages
(graph) **plotters** (use pens to draw lines on very large sheets of paper or plastic)	• Producing architectural drawings and product blueprints • Producing engineering drawings • Drawing animation characters for the film industry	• Very high-quality drawings • Can produce large monochrome and colour drawings to a high accuracy • Can print on a variety of materials (e.g. aluminium, cardboard, plastic, cloth, steel, wood) as well as paper • Not expensive to run	• Very slow printing • Expensive equipment to purchase initially (although running costs are relatively low) • Need a very large physical footprint
3D printer (uses **additive printing** technology where a solid object is built up in very thin layers (typically <0.1 mm thick) – makes use of adapted inkjet or laser printer technology)	• Making prosthetic limbs, which are unique to each person • Making bespoke items to allow for reconstructive surgery based on exact scans of the patient's anatomy • Making precision parts for industry (e.g. in aerospace) • Fashion and art; allows for new creative ideas • Making parts for items no longer in production (e.g. vintage cars)	• Easier to produce prototypes that work (it is also much quicker and less expensive than making a real part) • Although expensive, it is still cheaper than making a product in the conventional way • Many medical benefits, such as producing artificial organs and so on • It is good for the environment: keeping items working for longer by making bespoke parts reduces the 'throw away' mentality	• Counterfeit items are easier to produce using 3D printing • Can lead to illegal activity (e.g. production of dangerous items based on blueprints found online) • Printing is a slow process • Potential for job losses as 3D printing can replace certain skills • Use of 3D printers is very expensive
Speakers or **loudspeakers** (convert electric signals to sound)	• Sound in multimedia presentations • Act as an interface with devices for people with certain disabilities (e.g. people with visual impairment) • Playback of music files • Audible warnings in systems being computer-controlled (e.g. nuclear power station safety systems)	• Sounds add an extra dimension to a presentation making it more interesting and informative • Useful when helping people with disabilities where a microphone/speaker combination affords a workable interface with devices • A well-tried technology	• Speaker output can be very annoying in the office environment • Expensive if high quality sound is required
Actuators (used in control applications)	• Control motors, pumps, switches and so on • Allow a computer to control physical devices by using a **DAC** interface	• Allow automatic control of many devices • Relatively inexpensive technology	• Require the use of a DAC interface if digital devices are sending signals to actuators • An additional device in the system that could go wrong

2 Input and output devices

Sample question and response

REVISED

Name the following output devices and give a suitable application for each device.

Output device image	Name of output device	Suitable application
(3D printer)		
(speakers)		
(touchscreen)		
(inkjet printer)		
(graph plotter)		

Tips
Look carefully at the pictures of the devices since it can be easy to confuse them. A brief description of an application that would use this output device is required – don't give a lot of detail since it only carries one mark. However, it is vital that your application matches the device. You shouldn't use the same application more than once.

[10 marks]

Sample high-level answer

Device 1: 3D printer — Application: making parts for a vintage vehicle which can no longer be bought.

Device 2: (loud) speaker — Application: in a presentation (in the form of spoken word or music).

Device 3: touchscreen — Application: information kiosk at an airport allowing passengers to select options using their finger.

Device 4: inkjet printer — Application: produce a one-off high quality colour photograph.

Device 5: (graph) plotter — Application: making large engineering drawings or blueprints.

Teacher's comments
The first answer would gain full marks since each device has been correctly identified. The applications given are also correct and the student has given just enough information.

Hodder & Stoughton Limited © David Watson and Graham Brown 2022

21

2.3 Output devices

Sample low-level answer

Device 1: 3D printer   Application: making parts that move.
Device 2: speaker   Application: producing sound.
Device 3: monitor   Application: showing output on a screen.
Device 4: printer   Application: producing hard copy output on paper.
Device 5: plotter   Application: making large drawings of houses.

Teacher's comments

The second answer would only gain 4 marks. The answer 'monitor' isn't enough since the image is clearly a touchscreen (monitor); the answer 'printer' is not enough and would gain no marks. However, since none of the answers are actually wrong, the student could still gain the application marks. The first four answers given are *not* applications; they are simply describing what type of output is given by the device. However, the last application is probably just enough to get the mark.

Exam-style questions for you to try

6 A company manufactures parts for cars. The factory is a very noisy, dirty environment. Each part needs to be labelled at each stage of the process; this label is produced by a printer on the factory floor. The company also has some offices where staff carry out online sales, answer customer queries, produce monthly salary slips and develop new products.
   a Name a suitable printer for producing the labels on the factory floor. Justify your choice of printer. [2]
   b Name the equipment needed in the office to:
      i   produce wage slips.
      ii   find answers to queries from customers' emails or phone enquiries.
      iii develop new parts for use in their cars.
           Justify your choice of device in all cases. [6]

7 Five input devices (on the left), five descriptions (in the middle) and five applications (on the right) are shown in the diagram below. Draw lines to connect each input device to its correct description. Then draw lines to connect each description to its correct application.

Input device	Description	Application
Barcode reader	Device that converts sound into electric current which is then converted into digital signals	Augmented reality
Microphone	Device that reads parallel dark and light lines using a laser or LED light source	Voice control to turn lights on or off
QR reader	Device that reads paper documents and converts the hard copy image to a digital format	Automatic stock control system
pH sensor	Device that reads code in the form of a matrix of dark squares on light background	Monitoring of a chemical process
Scanner	Device that detects acidity levels of a solution; the data is in an analogue format	Passport control at an airport

[9]

8 In each of the following questions, only one of the responses is correct. Choose one of the options A–E given.

   a Which of the following output devices would an architect use to print out large plans?

A	Inkjet printer
B	Laser printer
C	Graph plotter
D	Dot matrix printer
E	3D printer

   b Which of the following output devices would you use to print 1000 high-quality black and white brochures?

A	Inkjet printer
B	Graph plotter
C	Dot matrix printer
D	Laser printer
E	Multimedia projector

   c Which one of the following can act as both an input device and an output device?

A	Multimedia projector
B	Graph plotter
C	Wireless mouse
D	Remote control
E	Touchscreen

   d Which one of the following printers would you use to produce carbon copies (multi-part) of invoices?

A	Dot matrix printer
B	Laser printer
C	Graph plotter
D	Inkjet printer
E	3D printer

   e Which one of the following output devices would you use at an information kiosk in an international airport?

A	Inkjet printer
B	Graph plotter
C	Multimedia projector
D	Loudspeaker
E	Touchscreen monitor

   [5]

3 Storage devices and media

Key objectives
The objectives of this chapter are to revise:
- storage devices
  - magnetic (hard disk drive and magnetic tape drive)
  - optical (CD, DVD and Blu-ray read/write devices)
  - solid state (solid-state drive, pen drive and flash drive)
- storage media
  - magnetic media (magnetic disks and magnetic tape)
  - optical (CD, DVD and Blu-ray discs)
  - solid state (including SD, XD and CFast cards)

Secondary storage includes all non-volatile storage devices that are not part of primary memory. The storage capacity of these devices is much larger than RAM or ROM (primary memory), but data access time is much longer. Operating systems, applications, photos, device drivers and other files/data are all stored on these secondary storage devices. There are three types of technology used by secondary storage devices:

- magnetic
- optical
- solid state

3.1 Magnetic media and magnetic storage devices

REVISED

Magnetic media rely on the property that certain materials have magnetic properties (such as iron oxide) and these properties can be used to store data (1s and 0s). Magnetic media are a type of permanent storage unless they are overwritten or deleted by the system or the user.

Two common magnetic devices are the magnetic tape drive and the hard disk drive (HDD).

3.1.1 Magnetic tape drives
Magnetic tape drives consist of reels of plastic tape coated in a magnetic oxide layer (e.g. iron oxide). The data stored, the 1s and 0s, have different magnetic signatures, which allow a read/write head to read and write data. The tape moves over the read/write head; this is basically a tiny, induced magnet that can magnetise the tape (to write data) or become 'excited' when magnetised tape passes over it (to read data).

Magnetic tapes have huge storage capacity, but data access time is very slow since the tape must fast forward or backward until the required data is found. The uses of magnetic tapes include:

- in batch processing (e.g. production of utility bills and wage slips in large numbers overnight)
- as backups of data for long-term storage/archiving (magnetic tape is very stable over a long period of time)
- for daily backups in companies that handle large amounts of data (e.g. updating customer's bank accounts).

> **Tip**
> It is important to remember that **storage medium** refers to the physical device on which the data is actually stored (e.g. a CD) and a **storage device** refers to the hardware used to read data from or write data to the medium (e.g. CD reader/writer).

3 Storage devices and media

The following table shows some of the advantages and disadvantages of magnetic tapes:

Advantages	Disadvantages
• Less expensive (per byte) than hard disk drives or solid-state drives • A very robust technology • Vast storage capacity • Very good **data transfer rate**	• Have a very slow **data access time** • Updating data requires a new tape to be produced; it is not possible to simply write over the original data – this introduces errors and is a slow process • They are affected by magnetic fields

> **Tip**
> **Data access time** is the time it takes to find data; **data transfer rate** is the time it takes to transfer data from a device to the computer (and vice versa).

3.1.2 Hard disk drives

Hard disk drives (HDDs) are one of the most common methods to store data on a computer. Data is stored on disk surfaces (called platters) that are coated in a magnetic material. The platters can be made from aluminium, glass or ceramic coated in iron oxide, and a typical disk drive has several platters. Read/write heads (containing tiny magnets) hover close to each disk surface on an air cushion to allow data to be written or read.

Actuators are used to move the read/write heads, which move back and forth across the disk surfaces as the disks spin very fast. There are two read/write heads per platter (one for each surface). Data is stored in concentric circles (called tracks); these are broken up into sectors. These sectors are mapped using a file allocation table (FAT) that shows which sectors are free and which contain data.

Magnetic disk drives suffer from **latency** (the time taken for a specific block of data on a track to rotate round to the read/write head).

The uses of HDDs include:

- to store operating systems, systems software, apps and data (such as photos and music)
- as website servers and file servers on networks used in real-time systems (such as airline bookings or booking cinema/theatre tickets).

The following table shows some of the advantages and disadvantages of HDDs:

Advantages	Disadvantages
• Very fast data transfer rates • Very large storage capacities • Tried and trusted technology, which makes them suitable for website and **cloud** servers	• Have a slow data access time and suffer from latency • Fairly easily damaged • Have many moving parts that can wear out and fail leading to data loss • They are affected by magnetic fields • They tend to be fairly noisy due to high-speed spinning disks

3.1.3 Portable hard disk drives

Portable hard disk drives work in the same way as fixed HDD devices; they have the same advantages and disadvantages. Their main use is backing up data and to allow data to be transferred between computers.

3.2 Optical media and optical storage devices

REVISED

Optical media devices use lasers to read and write data onto plastic (polycarbonate) disks. The media (disks) rely on the optical properties of certain chemical dyes and metal alloys to enable the storage of 1s and 0s. The most common types of **optical storage devices** include:

- CDs and DVDs
- Blu-ray discs.

3.2.1 CD and DVD optical disks

CDs and DVDs can be designated as 'R' (write once), 'RW' (read/write many times) and ROM' (read-only). All disks have a thin coating of alloy or light sensitive organic dye on at least one surface. Laser light alters the optical properties when writing data. As the disk spins, an optical read/write head moves to the start of the track and a narrow laser beam follows a spiral track from the centre moving outwards.

CDs and DVDs are split up into sectors and allow for direct access to data. The data is stored on the surface in **pits** (low points) and **lands** (high points) – these pits and lands are created when laser light writes data to the disk surface. Both CDs and DVDs use red lasers which read the pits and lands and convert the stored data into a binary format. The wavelength of the reflected laser light is slightly different to the original wavelength (due to the pits and lands) causing **destructive interference** – this allows the pits and lands to be read.

DVDs have **dual-layering** (two polycarbonate disks are sandwiched together), which increases their storage capacity (two recording surfaces are created).

The following table compares the uses, advantages and disadvantages of the different types of CD and DVD.

	CD/DVD 'R'	CD/DVD 'RW'	CD/DVD 'ROM'
Uses	- Home recordings of music (CD-R) and movies (DVD-R) - Transfer of data between computers	- Used to record TV programmes over and over again - Used in closed-circuit television (CCTV) because the disks can be reused - Backup for files	- Permanent storage for supply of computer games, music and software - Supplying movies on ROM format can prevent copying
Advantages	- Cheaper than RW disks - Once burned and finalised, they become ROMs	- Can go through several read and write operations - Can use different file formats each time the disk is written to - Not as wasteful as R format	- Data is permanently stored – a big advantage when used for movies, games and software (stops data being overwritten in error) - Less expensive than HDD systems
Disadvantages	- Can only record once; if an error occurs, the disk has to be discarded - Not all CD/DVD players can read CD-R and DVD-R formats	- Relatively expensive format - It is possible to accidentally overwrite data	- Data transfer rate is slower than HDD or SSD - It isn't possible to change data

3.2.2 Blu-ray discs

Blu-ray discs are an optical medium that use blue laser light. This light has a shorter wavelength than red laser light, thus increasing the storage capacity when compared to DVDs. They come with built-in secure encryption systems that help to prevent piracy and copyright infringements.

Blu-ray allows greater interactivity than DVDs, for example they allow the user to create playlists, reorder programmes stored, access websites and download subtitles/artwork. They have a much greater data transfer rate than DVDs (at least four times faster), which means they are well-suited to playback of High Definition (HD) or 4 K/8 K formats. The storage capacity is at least five times that of the equivalent DVD.

The following table compares the uses and advantages and disadvantages of Blu-ray discs.

Uses of Blu-ray discs	Advantages of Blu-ray discs	Disadvantages of Blu-ray discs
Storing high definition/4 K/8 K movies	Very large storage capacity	More expensive than DVD formats
Used as secondary storage or for backing up data	Very fast data transfer rates	Introduction of new DVDs using an HD format has eroded some of the advantages of Blu-ray
Used in some camcorders	Very good data access times	
	Have data encryption built-in for security of data	

Comparison of CDs, DVDs and Blu-ray discs

Disk type	Laser colour	Wavelength of laser light	Disk construction	Track pitch (distance between tracks)
CD	Red	780 nm	Single 1.2 mm polycarbonate layer	1.60 µm
DVD (dual-layer)	Red	650 nm	Two 0.6 mm polycarbonate layers	0.74 µm
Blu-ray (single-layer)	Blue	405 nm	Single 1.2 mm polycarbonate layer	0.30 µm
Blu-ray (dual-layer)	Blue	405 nm	Two 0.6 mm polycarbonate layers	0.30 µm

(Note: nm = 10^{-9} metres; µm = 10^{-6} metres)

(Note: Blu-ray can currently go up to six-layer technology, but this is outside the scope of this book.)

3.3 Solid-state media and solid-state storage devices

REVISED

Solid-state technology does not rely on magnetic or optical properties. They make use of the ability to control the movement of electrons across transistors and have no moving parts. By controlling electron movement, it is possible to create and read 1s and 0s in a massive grid in a very tiny space. They are often referred to as flash memories or flash drives.

Due to the technology used, solid-state devices do not suffer from latency, unlike HDDs. SSDs are also non-volatile, rewritable storage media.

3.3 Solid-state media and solid-state storage devices

3.3.1 Floating gate and control gate transistors
As they have no moving parts, solid-state devices can operate at speeds much greater than HDDs or optical disk drives. However, they still operate at speeds that are slower than RAM.

SSDs make use of floating gate transistors and control gate transistors (the transistors use CMOS and NAND technology). Solid-state memories make use of a grid; at each intersection of the grid there is a floating gate transistor and a control gate transistor. When current reaches the control gate, electrons flow to the floating gate creating a positive charge; by applying exact voltages to the transistors, a pattern of 1s and 0s can be created.

> CMOS means complementary metal oxide semi-conductor and NAND refers to a type of logic gate.

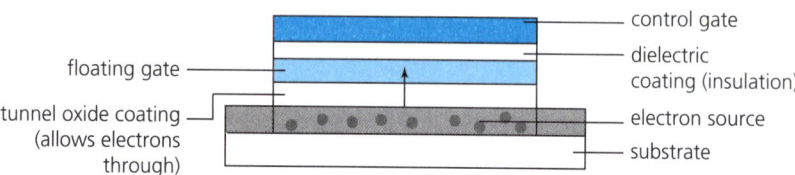

After 12 months or so, this charge can leak away, therefore solid-state devices should be used once a year (at least) to ensure they retain their memory contents.

3.3.2 Solid-state drives
Solid-state technology is used to create secondary storage devices known as **solid-state drives (SSDs)**. The following table summarises the uses, advantages and disadvantages of SSDs:

Uses of solid-state drives	Advantages of solid-state drives	Disadvantages of solid-state drives
• SSDs have largely replaced HDDs as the main type of backing storage • Used in laptops and tablets where their small size makes them very suitable as the main storage	• No moving parts – less likely to malfunction than HDDs • Much lighter in weight • Don't need to 'get up to speed' before read/write operations • Have very low power consumption and so generate much less heat than HDDs • Very thin since they only contain tiny transistors • Very fast data transfer speeds (about 100 times faster than HDDs) • Don't suffer from latency since there are no moving parts • Allow for permanent deletion of data (when writing over or deleting data on SSDs, the old data is destroyed unlike in HDDs where the data can still be recovered) – this is a very important 'end-of-life' security consideration	• **SSD endurance**/longevity is still an issue (but this situation continues to improve) • The memory chips in SSDs have a limited number of write cycles – this can lead to unrecoverable data loss • If the controller chip, memory cache or one of the NAND memory chips are damaged, it may be impossible to recover the data • They are more expensive to buy (per GB) than HDDs • Although data access is very fast, the rewriting of data can be slower than HDDs as SSDs need to delete old data first before writing the new data

3.3.3 Pen drives
Pen drives (memory sticks) are small solid-state storage devices that connect to a computer via a USB port. They are another example of a flash drive/memory. They are known as pen drives or memory sticks. The following table compares the uses and advantages and disadvantages of pen drives.

Uses of pen drives	Advantages of pen drives	Disadvantages of pen drives
• Back up files/data such as photos and music • Transport files/data between computers • A security device (e.g. containing essential files to make software work) – called a 'dongle' when used in this way • When battery-powered, SSDs can be used as **portable media (MP3) players**	• Very compact and portable storage device (e.g. can be kept on a key ring) • Very robust device (no moving parts) • Don't need additional software to work • Not affected by magnetic fields • Plug straight into a USB port • Don't need much current to operate • Allow for permanent deletion of data • Very good data transfer rates	• Longevity is still an issue (but this situation continues to improve) • It isn't possible to write-protect data; care must be taken not to overwrite data accidentally • Easy to lose due to small size • Care needed when removing device from computer (follow the correct removal procedure or data corruption or data loss can occur) • If the device internals become damaged, it may be impossible to recover lost data

3.3.4 Memory cards

Memory cards use solid-state technology. There are three common types:

- SD cards (**S**ecure **D**igital card): very small, used primarily where high capacity is needed (e.g. digital video recorders/cameras, smartphones, tablets and drones).
- XD cards (e**X**treme **D**igital card): a type of removable memory card designed for use in digital cameras.
- **C**Fast card (**C**ompact **F**ast card): a memory card used in very small devices (e.g. used as a removable memory in high-end digital cameras).

Uses of memory cards	Advantages of memory cards	Disadvantages of memory cards
• Store photos on digital cameras • In mobile phones to extend memory • In MP3 players to store music • A backing store in hand-held devices	• Very compact – can be used in small portable devices (such as a camera) • No moving parts: very durable • Makes it easy to transfer photos between devices • Relatively large memory capacities	• Expensive per GB compared to HDDs • Much lower storage than other types of portable storage device • Have a finite number of read/write cycles • Easy to lose or be stolen due to small size • Not all computers/devices have memory card readers

3.4 The future of storage devices

REVISED

Flash memory is fast becoming the most common device for storage and for transferring data between devices. However, these days, data/files are now stored on remote cloud servers. Music and movies are often **streamed** straight from the internet, thus there is no need to store the music or movies on a computer. Many televisions are now **smart televisions** and programmes can be streamed **on demand**, meaning DVD and Blu-ray players are no longer needed.

Sample questions and responses

REVISED

a) Name **three** types of media used in secondary storage devices. **[3 marks]**
b) A current secondary storage medium has enabled the development of items such as smartphones, tablets and very thin laptop computers.
  i) Name this medium.
  ii) Explain why this medium has allowed development of smartphones, tablets and thin laptop computers. **[4 marks]**

3.4 The future of storage devices

Sample high-level answer

a) magnetic (disks and tape), optical (CD/DVD/Blu-ray) and solid state.
b) i) solid-state
   ii) solid-state devices have the following features:
   - they are very thin
   - they have low power consumption and run very cool
   - they are lightweight
   - they have no moving parts and are very reliable
   - they have a very fast data transfer rate
   - data can be permanently deleted.

   All of the above features allow for smaller and smaller devices to be developed, since they don't take up much space and allow more components to be crammed into small spaces.

Sample low-level answer

a) Hard disk drive (HDD), CD/DVD writer/reader and solid-state drive (SSD).
b) i) SSD
   ii) low power consumption, big capacity and low weight.

> **Tips**
>
> In (b) four marks are awarded for naming the medium; this means no real detail is required and you can be as brief as possible. However, part (b)(ii) requires an explanation, so you need to mention the advantages and features of the technology that allowed it to be used in the development of the named devices in the question.

Teacher's comments

The first answer shows a clear understanding of the difference between medium and device and has given more than enough in part (b)(ii) to gain maximum marks.

The second answer gets no marks since they have confused medium with device in all cases – very unfortunate since they obviously knew the technologies. It highlights the importance of reading the question carefully and making sure you answer the question accurately. Part (b)(i) again names a device and not the medium. But some leeway could be exercised in part (b)(ii) since they obviously knew the question referred to solid state – two marks are possible ('big capacity' is just too vague to be worth any marks).

Exam-style questions for you to try

1. Tick (✓) whether the following devices use magnetic, optical or solid-state technology:

	Magnetic	Optical	Solid state
Blu-ray reader/writer player			
Portable hard disk drive			
Flash drive			
CFast card			
DVD-RW drive			
Pen drive			

[6]

2. a Blu-ray and DVD are two types of disk that use optical technology.
      i   Describe **three** differences between Blu-ray and DVD. [3]
      ii Give **one** application that uses Blu-ray and **one** application that uses DVD-RW. [2]
   b Hard disk drives (HDDs) and solid-state drives (SSDs) are used in many computers.
      i   Describe **three** differences between HDDs and SSDs. [3]
      ii Explain why SSDs are gradually leading to the phasing out of HDDs. [2]

3 Indicate whether the following ten statements are True or False by placing a tick (✓) in the appropriate box.

Statements	True (✓)	False (✓)
SSDs suffer from high latency due to the time it takes for disks to spin round to the read/write head		
Blu-ray discs only allow data to be read		
Platters in an HDD can be recorded on both the bottom and top surfaces		
The data transfer rate is the time it takes to locate data on an HDD		
Both DVDs and Blu-ray discs use dual-layer technology		
SSDs have a shorter working life than the equivalent HDDs		
One advantage of flash drives is that old data can be permanently deleted		
CD-RW can act as a ROM		
Solid-state drives have many complex moving parts that makes them wear out quickly		
Blu-ray discs use laser light with a shorter wavelength than DVDs		

[10]

4 Complete the following sentences by writing the correct missing term or phrase.
   a Solid-state devices use a .... and a .... at the intersection of a grid of transistors; by applying an exact .... a pattern of .... can be created. [4]
   b Blu-ray discs use .... light to read and write data; both DVDs and Blu-ray discs use .... to increase their storage capacity; .... have built-in secure encryption. [3]
   c Hard disk drives contain a number of .... which can be made from ....; each disk surface has a .... head that floats on a cushion of air; HDDs suffer from .... due to the relatively long time it takes data to be read waiting for the disk to rotate round to the read/write head. [4]

5 Explain why optical disks are slowly being phased out. In your answer, give a justification for each statement you make and indicate why they are being phased out. [4]

6 A student was looking at a laptop made in 2012 and was comparing it to one made in 2022. They noticed the 2012 laptop was much thicker and heavier than the 2022 model. They also noticed that the 2012 model had a DVD/CD player/writer in a side drawer, a touchpad and four USB connectors. However, the 2022 model had only one USB-C connector, no touchpad and no external devices, such as a DVD reader/writer.
Explain the advances in technology between the 2012 laptop and the 2022 laptop. [5]

4 Networks and the effects of using them

Key objectives

The objectives of this chapter are to revise:
- networks
  - routers
  - common network devices: network interface cards, hubs, switches, bridges
  - WiFi and Bluetooth
  - cloud computing
  - intranets, extranets and the internet
  - local area networks, wireless local area networks and wide area networks
- network issues and communication
  - security (including passwords and authentication)
  - anti-malware
  - electronic conferencing.

4.1 Networks

REVISED

4.1.1 Common network devices and terms

Network interface card
A **network interface card (NIC)** allows a device to connect to a network, such as the internet. It is usually part of the internal motherboard, but they can also be wireless (WNICs) and use an antenna to communicate with a network using microwaves (NICs can either plug into a USB port or be installed internally). Each NIC is given a unique hard-wired media access control address.

Media access control address
The **media access control (MAC) address** is a hexadecimal number that uniquely identifies a device. MAC addresses use 48 bits made up of six groups of hexadecimal digits:

NN – NN – NN	DD – DD – DD
Manufacturer's code	Device serial number

For example: 00 – 1C – B3 – 4F – 25 – FF is the MAC address of an Apple® device. MAC addresses are useful in identifying network faults since they uniquely identify each device connected to the network.

Internet Protocol address
Whenever a device connects to the internet, it is given an **Internet Protocol (IP) address** supplied by Internet Service Provider. This will change each time a user connects (website servers keep the same IP value since they don't log off the network and are always connected).

Protocols are necessary since they define the rules agreed by senders and receivers of data when communicating over the internet. There are presently two type of IP address:

- IPv4: this is based on 32 bits and is written as four groups of 8 bits (32 bits), for example: 254.25.28.77

- IPv6: since IPv4 no longer offers sufficient unique addresses on the internet as it continues to expand, IPv6 is now being adopted; this uses 128 bits written as eight groups of four hexadecimal digits, for example:

A8FB:7A88:FFF0:0FFF:3D21:2085:66FB:F0FA

Data packets

Data moved round networks is split up into data packets; each data packet travels from 'A' to 'B' independently. The data packet has a header and a trailer. The trailer indicates the end of the data packet and also contains an error-checking mechanism.

The header contains the following items:

- sender's IP address
- receiver's IP address
- sequence number (so packets can be reassembled in the correct order)
- packet size (number of bytes)
- number of packets in the whole message.

When a router receives a data packet, it checks the recipient IP address against a routing table and determines the next stage in its journey. The sequence numbers allow the data packets to be reassembled in the correct order at the destination address.

Hubs

Hubs are hardware devices usually found in local area networks (LANs). They deliver **all** data packets received by a network to **all** devices on the network. This causes unnecessary traffic on the network reducing bandwidth.

> This is not secure, as every device is receiving every data packet.

Switches

Switches are 'intelligent' hubs. They deliver each data packet to a specific device on a network (switches contain MAC addresses of all devices on a network). None of the other devices will see the data packet, thus reducing traffic and improving security.

The following table summarises the features of hubs and switches:

Switches	Hubs
• Used to exchange data packets within their own LANs • Used to connect devices in a network together • Can't exchange data with external networks	• Used to exchange data packets within their own LANs • Used to connect devices in a network together • Can't exchange data with external networks
• Switches send data packets to a specific device on the network • Security using switches is better than in hubs • Switches use MAC addresses to locate devices on the network • Switches use a look-up table to find the MAC address of the device intended to receive the data packet	• Hubs send data packets to every device connected to the network

4.1 Networks

Bridges

Bridges are used to connect a LAN to another LAN that uses the same protocol. They allow separate LANs to be joined to form a single LAN. Bridges cannot communicate with external networks.

4.1.2 Routers

Routers are used to route data packets from one network to another network using IP addresses. Routers are used to join a LAN to the internet or to other external networks:

When a data packet is received, the router inspects the IP address of the recipient and determines whether the data packet is intended for its own network or for another network; if the IP address indicates another network, the data packet is sent to the next router.

Routers use a routing table that contains information about the router's immediate network and information about routers in the immediate vicinity. This allows routers to establish how to deal with each data packet. Routers don't store MAC addresses; only IP addresses are stored so it knows where to send the data packet in the next stage of its journey. Many modern broadband routers combine the function of a router and a switch.

The following table compares the function of routers and bridges:

Router	Bridge
The main objective of a router is to connect various types of network together	The main objective of a bridge is to connect LANs together
Routers scan a device's IP address	Bridges scan a device's MAC address
Data is sent out using data packets	Data is sent out using data packets
Connected networks will use different protocols	Connects networks together that use the same protocols
A routing table is used to direct data packets to the correct device	Bridges don't make use of routing tables
A router has more than two ports	A bridge has only two ports

4.1.3 WiFi and Bluetooth

WiFi and **Bluetooth** both allow wireless communications between devices. The following table compares WiFi and Bluetooth:

WiFi	Bluetooth
• WiFi sends and receives radio waves in many frequency bands • Best suited to operating full-scale networks because it offers much faster data transfer rates, better range and better security than Bluetooth • WiFi makes use of wireless **access points (APs)** – also known as **hotspots** • Maximum effective range is 100 m • WiFi can connect many devices to a network at the same time • Uses Wireless Equivalent Privacy (WEP) and WiFi Protected Access (WPA)	• Bluetooth uses radio waves in a band of 79 frequencies (known as channels) • Used when transferring data between two or more devices in close proximity, where speed of transmission is not important (e.g. sending music to Bluetooth headphones) • When a device wants to communicate, it picks one of the 79 channels at random • If a channel is already in use, another one is chosen • Maximum effective range is 30 m • To increase security, devices constantly change channels (**spread-spectrum frequency hopping**) • Can only allow up to seven devices to be connected at once • Makes use of key matching encryption (devices are paired and a temporary key used to encrypt data). Once encrypted a long-term key replaces the temporary key and the connection is encrypted (forms a secure **wireless personal area network – WPAN**)

4.1.4 Cloud computing

Cloud storage is a method of data storage using physical remote servers. The data is frequently stored on more than one server in case maintenance/repairs need to be carried out (this is called **data redundancy**).

There are three common types of cloud storage:

- Public cloud: a storage environment where the client and cloud storage provider are different companies/entities.
- Private cloud: storage provided by dedicated servers behind a firewall; client and cloud storage provider act as a single entity.
- Hybrid cloud: a combination of public and private clouds; sensitive data is stored on a private cloud and other data is stored on a public cloud.

The following table compares the advantages and disadvantages of using cloud storage.

Advantages of using cloud storage	Disadvantages of using cloud storage
• Client files stored in the cloud can be accessed at any time, from any device, anywhere in the world, provided internet access is available • There is no need for a customer/client to carry an external storage device with them, or even use the same computer, to store and retrieve information • The cloud provides the user with remote backup of data to alleviate data loss/disaster recovery • If a customer/client has a failure of their hard disk or backup device, cloud storage will allow recovery of their data • The cloud system offers almost unlimited storage capacity (at a price!)	• Security aspects of storing data in the cloud (see below table) • If the customer/client has a slow or unstable internet connection, they could have problems accessing or downloading their data/files • Costs can be high if a large storage capacity is required; also high download/upload data transfer limits with the customer/client Internet Service Provider can be expensive • Potential failure of the cloud storage company is always possible – this poses a risk of loss of all backup data

There are issues regarding cloud security and data loss. A user needs to ask:

- What physical security exists in the building housing the servers?
- How well protected are the servers against natural disasters or power cuts?
- How secure is the data with regards to personnel who work for the cloud provider?

There have been cases of data loss through hacking (these breaches include the leaking of Facebook accounts in 2019 and Capital One bank had 80 000 banks accounts hacked in 2019)

4.1.5 Common network environments

Refer to Chapter 10, p.117 regarding extranets, intranets and the internet.

4.1.6 Network types

There are three common types of network:

- local area network
- wireless local area network
- wide area network.

Local area network

When using **local area networks (LANs)**, connected devices are usually geographically close, for example in one building. The devices are connected together using hubs or switches. One hub or switch is usually connected to a router to connect the LAN to external networks, like the internet.

4.1 Networks

The following table highlights the advantages and disadvantages of networking computers and devices (such as printers) in the form of a LAN:

Advantages of using LANs	Disadvantages of using LANs
• The sharing of resources, such as expensive peripherals (e.g. a colour laser printer) and applications software • Better communication between users of the LAN • A network administrator can control and monitor all aspects of the network (e.g. changing passwords, monitoring internet use and so on)	• *Easier* spread of viruses throughout the whole network • Queues can form for shared resources (such as a printer), which can be frustrating • Slower access to external networks, such as the internet • *Increased* security risk when compared to stand-alone computers • If the main server breaks down, in many types of network structures, the network will no longer function properly

Wireless local area networks

Wireless LANs (WLANs) are very similar to LANs, but they don't use wires and cables to connect devices together, they use WiFi. Devices, known as access points, or hotspots, are connected using wires into a network at fixed locations. Users or devices can then access the network wirelessly at these access points. WLANs use **spread-spectrum technology** (with a range of 30 m to 50 m) or **infrared** (range of less than 5 m).

The following table compares the relative advantages and disadvantages of using wired and wireless networks:

Wireless networking	Wired networking
It is easier to expand the networks and it isn't necessary to connect the devices using cables. This gives devices increased mobility provided they are within range of the wireless APs	Using cables produces a more reliable and stable network. Wireless connectivity is often subjected to interference
No cabling so there is a safety improvement and increased flexibility	Having lots of wires can lead to a number of hazards such as tripping hazards, overheating of connections (leading to a potential fire risk) and disconnection of cables during routine office cleaning
There is an increased chance of interference from external sources	Setting up cabled networks tends to be cheaper overall in spite of the need to buy and install cables
Data is less secure than with wired systems. It is easier to intercept radio waves and microwaves than cables, so it is essential to protect data transmissions by using encryption	Cabled networks lose the ability for devices to be mobile; they must be close enough to allow for cable connections
Data transmission rate is still slower than for cabled networks although it continues to improve	Data transfer rates tend to be faster and there won't be any 'dead spots'
It is possible for signals to be stopped by thick walls (e.g. in old houses) and there may be areas of variable signal strength leading to 'drop out'	

Wide area networks

Wide area networks (WANs) cover a large area geographically, for example a whole country or even larger. WANs are a number of LANs connected together by a series of routers (e.g. the network of ATMs is a WAN as is the internet).

4 Networks and the effects of using them

Due to the large geographical distances, WANs make use of the public communications infrastructure (e.g. telephone lines and satellites) but sometimes use private dedicated lines if greater security is needed. The typical distances that define the type of network are:

- WAN: 100 km to over 1000 km
- MAN: 1 km to 100 km
- LAN: 10 m to 1 km

> A MAN is a metropolitan area network; this is not in the syllabus but is included here for completeness.

Sample questions and responses

REVISED

a) Describe the differences between hubs and switches when used on a LAN. **[3 marks]**
b) Describe the differences between routers and bridges. **[3 marks]**

> **Tips**
> Both these questions are 'describe' so it is necessary to include features of hubs, switches, routers and bridges. An unbalanced answer will inevitably lose many of the available marks.

Sample high-level answer

a) First of all, there are a number of similarities between hubs and switches:
- they both allow the exchange of data within their own LANs
- neither device can communicate or exchange data with an external network
- they are both used to connect devices together to form a LAN.

The main differences can be summarised as follows:
- switches send data packets to a specific device on the network
- security using switches is better than security using hubs
- switches use MAC addresses to locate devices on the network
- switches use a look-up table to find the MAC address of the device intended to receive the data packet
- hubs send data packets to every device connected to the network.

b) The main features of routers include:
- the main objective of a router is to connect various types of network together
- routers use data packets to send out data across networks
- routers allow networks with different protocols to understand data and communications
- they use a routing table to direct data packets to the correct network and hence device.

The main features of bridges include:
- bridges connect LANs using the same protocols together
- they use MAC addresses to identify devices on the connected networks
- data is sent to devices on the connected networks and outside using data packet structures
- unlike routers, they don't use routing tables.

The above features indicate a number of similarities and differences between the four devices named in the question.

Sample low-level answer

a) Hubs and switches are used in networks to send data around the network. Hubs are used in LANs and switches are used in WLANs which is the main difference. Both use data packets to send data around networks. Switches and routers are often the same devices on a network which allows a switch to communicate outside the network.

b) Routers and bridges are used to join networks together. Bridges connect LANs together, whereas routers connect WANs together over long distances. A router is often confused with a switch.

4.1 Networks

Exam-style questions for you to try

1. a Explain what is meant by cloud computing. [3]
   b Give **three** advantages to a user of storing their data on a cloud server. [3]
   c Give **three** disadvantages to a user of storing their data on a cloud server. [3]

2. A company has offices in three cities and headquarters in a fourth city. They are going to network their operations using LANs in each office, all connected to the headquarters. The offices in each city occupy eight floors. There is a lot of data passing through the network throughout the day.
   a Describe the devices needed to have a fully working LAN in each of the four cities.
   b Describe the devices needed to allow the LANs in each city to communicate with each other; consider any external hardware that may also be needed.
   c If the LANs used wireless connectivity, what additional hardware would be needed? [8]

3. Six features of network devices are given in the following table. For each feature, tick (✓) the appropriate box to indicate whether it refers to a router, switch or hub.

Statements	Router (✓)	Switch (✓)	Hub (✓)
Device that can cause unnecessary LAN traffic and can reduce effective bandwidth			
The destination MAC address is looked up before the data packet is sent to the correct device			
Used to connect LANs to other external networks			
Uses both MAC and IP addresses to enable data packets to be sent to the correct device on another network			
All data packets are sent to all the devices on a network			
Data packets are sent only to a specific device on the same network			

[6]

4. You are the IT consultant in a large multinational company. The senior managers have asked you to write a brief note on which devices they would need to create a network of computers in the main headquarters.
   Describe which devices would be needed (the main headquarters is a building on 15 floors) to create a network on each floor and to allow the networks to communicate internally and externally. In each case, give a reason for your choice of device. [5]

5. Explain what is meant by a WAN. Give **one** example of a WAN. [3]

Teacher's comments

The first answer shows a clear understanding of the difference between hubs and switches and routers and bridges. The answer is set out in a nice, structured manner, which makes it easy to pick out the salient points. The use of bullet points is often a clear way of setting out such questions, if they are structured correctly.

The second answer is much briefer and is also a little confused. The point about sending packets of data around networks is probably worth one mark. The rest of the answer is very confused and would gain no marks. In part (b), they have made a correct point (bridges connect LANs), but then wrongly said routers join WANs together. It is possible to see what the student was trying to explain (routers are used to connect LANs together to form a WAN) and may gain a 'benefit of the doubt' mark. That makes two marks out of six for the whole question.

4.2 Network issues and communication

REVISED

4.2.1 Security issues regarding data transfer

Security of networks is covered in Chapter 8, p.96, but the next sections consider some of the ways of protecting networks against security risks.

4.2.2 Passwords

When using a network (e.g. the internet) there are a number of situations where you might need to enter a password (and very often, a user ID as well), for example accessing your email account, logging onto your online bank account or a social networking site and so on. To ensure passwords are protected, users of networks need to:

- run anti-spyware software to ensure your password isn't stolen
- change passwords on a regular basis in case they have been cracked or accidentally released
- always use strong passwords that should have:
  - upper and lower case letters
  - numerical values
  - other keyboard characters (e.g. *,!, @, & and so on)
  - at least eight characters (e.g. Sy12@#TT90kj=0 is very strong, but Pa5Sword1 is very weak).

> **Tip**
> Passwords should not be birthdays, pet names or favourite colours.

4.2.3 Other authentication methods

There are a number of authentication techniques used, other than passwords. The following table summarises some of the more commonly used authentication techniques:

> Authentication is a way to prove who you are.

Method	Description of authentication technique
Zero login and biometrics	• Allows users to log in without passwords • Relies on smart technology and the ability to recognise a user with biometrics and behavioural patterns • The system builds up a complex user profile based on biometrics (e.g. fingerprints or face recognition) and unique behaviour (e.g. where you normally use a device, how you swipe a screen etc.) – eliminating the need to key in a password • There are disadvantages, such as 'How do you know when you've logged out?', 'How secure is the system?' etc.

Magnetic stripe cards	• When used as part of a security system, magnetic stripe cards have a brown stripe on the back that contains name, unique ID, sex, date of birth, etc.
	• When swiped through a magnetic stripe card reader, this information is read and identifies a user
	• Often have a **holographic image (hologram)** embossed on the card making forgery more difficult
	• Advantages:
	  – easy system to use and not very expensive to implement
	  – cards can be remotely deactivated if lost or stolen
	  – can be multi-purpose: key cards, network access cards, vending machine cards, etc.
	• Disadvantages:
	  – less secure than biometrics (the magnetic stripe is relatively easy to copy)
	  – cards wear out with use
	  – if the card reader heads become contaminated (e.g. with dust) they fail to read the cards reliably

Smart cards	• Adding a microchip and antenna to a magnetic stripe card, they can become a smart **contactless card** (the chip can contain additional information such as a PIN, security number, history of card use, etc.) • At the entrance to a building, for example, a device reads the cards from a distance of a few centimetres • The user may also be invited to enter their PIN to see if it matches up to the one stored on the microchip

4.2 Network issues and communication

Method	Description of authentication technique

Physical tokens	• A physical token is physical, solid object, often used by banks to allow customers to access their accounts remotely. The token device contains an internal clock which is used to randomly generate an eight-digit number that changes after a few minutes
	• If a card (e.g. debit card) is inserted into the device and the user keys in their PIN, a one-time password (OTP) is generated by the physical token device
	• This OTP then needs to be typed into the bank's web page to allow the user to gain access to their account
	• Two types of physical token are:
	  – **connected physical token** – the device transmits the OTP directly to a computer using a USB port; no need to manually enter data
	  – **disconnected physical token** – user has to key in the OTP manually
	• This authentication method is very secure – the OTP only lasts for a short time and a thief would need access to the card, the PIN and a physical token recognised by the bank to gain access to the bank account

Electronic token	• There are also software tokens, installed on a computer as an app • If a user wants to log on to a website using a tablet, for example, the user opens the app and an OTP is generated • The user enters this PIN into the website as well as other authentication such as fingerprint or face recognition

4.2.4 Anti-malware software

Antivirus software is essential to protect computers on a network from attack by viruses. Antivirus software runs in the background and constantly looks for known viruses or potential viruses. All antivirus software has the following features:

- all software or files are checked before they can be run or loaded
- they use a database of known viruses as the first check (which is why antivirus software should be kept up to date since this database is constantly updated)
- they do **heuristic checking** – checking of software for types of behaviour that many viruses emulate
- if a virus, or potential virus, is detected it is first **quarantined** and then automatically deleted or the user is invited to delete it (sometimes software isn't infected in spite of the antivirus warning – this is called a **false positive**).

> **Tip**
> See Chapter 8, p.97 for more about malware

4.2.5 Electronic conferencing

This section considers video, audio and web conferencing.

Video conferencing

Video conferencing is a method that allows a conference to take place between two or more sets of people many kilometres apart. The conference occurs in real time and normally uses the internet, but some companies use a personal communications line. To carry out video conferencing, the minimum requirements are:

- a webcam and a large monitor or TV
- a microphone (placed centrally on a desk) and speakers (usually external and placed around the room)
- special software – for example, drivers to operate camera and microphone, **CODEC** to encode and decode data allowing it to be compressed and decompressed and **echo cancellation software** to allow the microphone and speakers to be synchronised).

4 Networks and the effects of using them

The following list should be followed when organising a video conference:
- it is essential to agree a time and date for the conference to take place
- the delegates in each conference room must log into the video-conference system
- the set-up needs to be checked before the meeting goes live
- webcams need to be placed in the correct position so that all the delegates in the room are within visual contact (the webcams will capture the images and then transmit them to the other delegates – they will see the images on their own large screens)
- microphones need to be placed centrally so that all of the delegates can speak – the sound is picked up by the microphones and is transmitted to the other delegates (they hear the voices through speakers in their own conference room)
- it is important for one person to be the main contact in each conference room to make sure each delegate is able to be heard; this is particularly important if more than two video conference rooms are linked up at the same time.

There are many advantages and disadvantages to using video conferencing:

Advantages	Disadvantages

• As people are in their own building, it is much easier to access important documents or bring in 'experts' in key parts of the conference – this would be difficult if they were a long way away from their office
• Can hold conferences at short notice – a conference date can be set up within a few hours as no person needs to travel very far
• Not travelling physically to meetings reduces costs:
  – reduced travel costs
  – no need for hotel accommodation or venue hire
  – reduces the cost of taking people away from their work for two or three days to travel – people are still paid their wage even though they are not in the office, so this is a large 'hidden' cost
• It may be better to use video conferencing than have delegates travel to potentially unsafe places around the world
	• Potential time lag in responses/delays when talking
	• Jerky images – usually due to poor internet/network performance or a low bandwidth
	• Can be very expensive to set up in the first place (both the hardware and software are expensive to purchase and it takes a lot of time to get set up correctly)
	• Problems with large time zone differences if the delegates live in different countries
	• Costly and time-consuming to train people to use the system correctly
	• Demotivating for staff if international travel is a 'perk' of their job
	• The whole system relies on a good network connection – if this breaks down or the signal strength is diminished, then the video conference can be almost unusable

Audio conferencing

Audio conferencing is often referred to as a **phone conference**. It requires a computer with built-in or external microphones and speakers, and a standard telephone or internet phone. The following diagram summarises the process:

1. The phone conference organiser is given two PINs by the phone company. One PIN is the organiser's personal PIN (e.g. 2151) and the second is the participant's PIN (e.g. 8422).

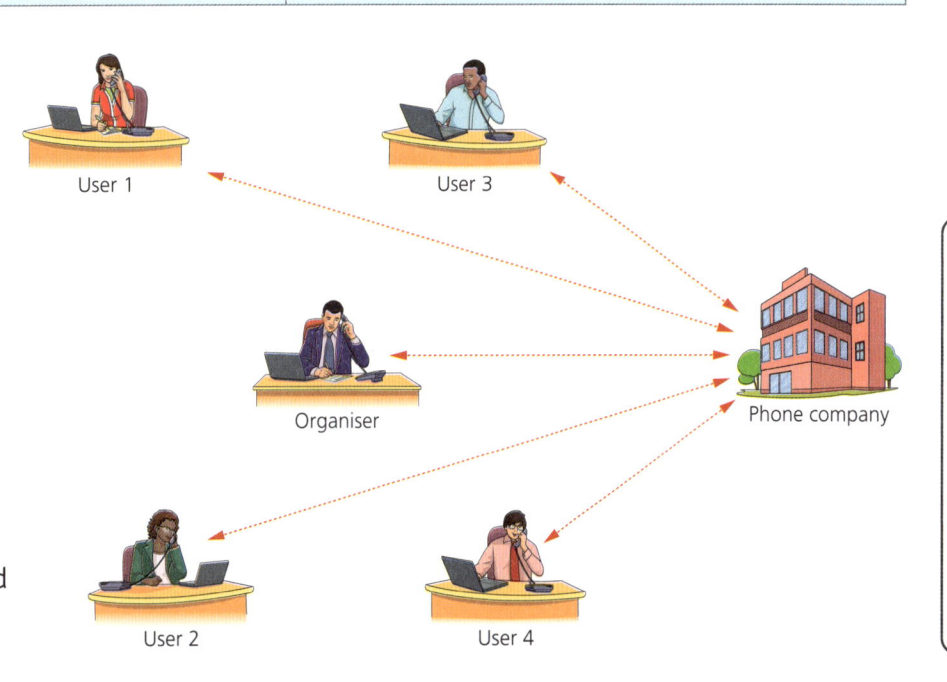

4.2 Network issues and communication

2. The organiser contacts the participants and gives them their PIN and the date and time of the phone conference.
3. When the phone conference is about to start, the organiser dials the conference phone number and, once connected, keys in their personal PIN (2151 in this case).
4. The participants then call the same conference number to join in – once they get through, they each input the PIN from the organiser (8422 in this case). Without this PIN, it will be impossible to join the phone conference.

It is possible to hold an audio conference using a computer, provided a microphone and speakers are connected. This makes use of Voice over Internet Protocol (VoIP). It is also possible to hook up an internet telephone, which usually plugs into the router or other internet device.

> For more detail about VoIP, please see *Cambridge IGCSE Information and Communication Technology Third Edition* Student's book, page 94.

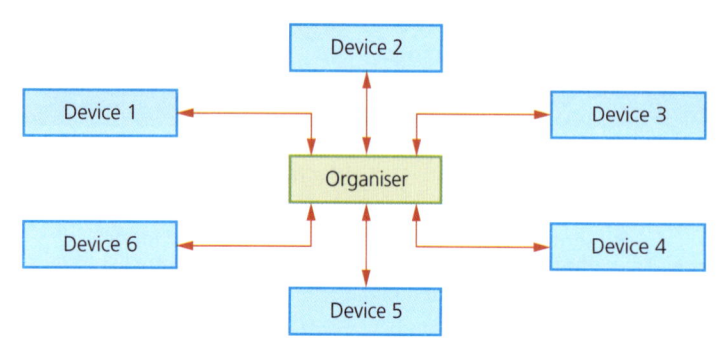

Web conferencing

Web conferencing is sometimes referred to as a **webinar** or **webcast**. Multiple computers are used in various locations to hold conferences in real time over the internet.

```
        Device 2
          ↕
Device 1 ←→ Organiser ←→ Device 3
          ↕
Device 6 ←→        ←→ Device 4
          ↕
        Device 5
```

Web conferencing allows the following types of meeting to take place:
- business meetings to discuss new ideas
- presentations
- online education or training.

The requirements are a computer and a high-speed, stable internet connection. Each user either downloads an application or logs on to a website from a link supplied in an email from the conference organiser.

Delegates can join or leave the web conference as they wish. Using the control panel on their computer, the organiser can decide on who can speak at any time. If a delegate wishes to speak, they 'raise' a flag next to their name. Delegates can post comments using instant messaging for all delegates to see at any time.

Some of the main features of web conferencing include:
- slide presentations using presentation software that can be posted on the conference website before the meeting
- drawing or writing on a 'whiteboard' using a keyboard or mouse
- transmitting images or videos using a webcam throughout the conference
- sharing documents by uploading them to the website before the conference begins
- the capability to chat verbally or by using instant messaging throughout the conference.

4 Networks and the effects of using them

Sample questions and responses

REVISED ☐

John wishes to access his account at Hodder Bank. He uses a physical token to gain access to his account.

a) Explain how John and Hodder Bank would use the physical token to allow John to have a secure link to his bank account. **[4 marks]**

b) Explain the difference between a physical token and an electronic token. **[2 marks]**

> **Tips**
> Since both parts of the question involve an explanation, it is important to make your answer as thorough as possible. In particular, part (b) needs you to include at least one difference between the two types of token.

Sample high-level answer

a) Suppose a customer has logged on to the bank's website. They get to a web page which requires some form of authentication to prove who they are. To do this, they need to use a physical token supplied by the bank. The customer inserts their debit card into the top of the token device (first authentication step) and the device either recognises the card as genuine or rejects it. The device then asks the customer to press 'IDENTIFY' and then enter their PIN (second authentication step). A one-time password is then shown on the device screen – this is usually an eight-digit code. The customer goes back to their bank web page and enters the eight-digit code. They are now given access to their account. This clearly enhances security, since a thief needs to have in their possession: the token device, a cloned card and the PIN to allow them to gain access.

b) Electronic tokens use an installed app on their device. If John wants to access his bank account, he first opens the app and it generates an OTP which John needs to type into the bank's web page. If the OTP typed in matches the one generated at the bank, then John is allowed access to his account.

Sample low-level answer

a) A physical token is a hardware device either connected to a computer through the USB port or the user has to type in a code on his device. These are a form of security and generate PINs that are stored on a computer and token device matches them up.

b) Electronic tokens use an app on a smartphone or tablet to allow the user to enter their bank account.

Teacher's comments

The first answer is well-described and has importantly mentioned connected and disconnected physical tokens. It was also good to see a diagram that helped greatly when reading their answer.

The second answer indicates some understanding but lacks any real depth. In part (a), they haven't really explained how physical tokens work. In part (b), the reference to a token app was probably worth a mark.

4.2 Network issues and communication

Exam-style questions for you to try

6 Which five computer terms are being described below?
   a A hardware device often used to access bank accounts that generates a one-time password that the user types in. The device uses an internal clock that is part of the random generation of the password.
   b A type of authentication that makes use of biometrics and a person's behavioural patterns; they remove the need to use passwords.
   c A plastic card that uses a magnetic stripe and microchip; it can be used as a security device to enter a building.
   d A method where several people in two locations, several kilometres apart, can have a meeting using visual and audio equipment over the internet or personal communications line.
   e Software that uses databases and heuristic checking to quarantine certain programs and files to check that they are safe to use. [5]
7 Describe the following three terms:
   a zero log in
   b webinar/web conference
   c antivirus software [7]

5 The effects of using IT

Key objectives
The objectives of this chapter are to revise:
- microprocessor-controlled devices
  - their positive and negative effects on various aspects of everyday life in the home
  - positive and negative effects on monitoring and controlling transport
- health issues from using a computer
  - for example, RSI, back and neck problems
  - causes of health issues and ways of preventing them.

5.1 Microprocessor-controlled devices

REVISED

5.1.1 Effects of using microprocessor-controlled devices in the home

Many common devices used in the home are fitted with microprocessors. These devices fall into two groups, labour-saving and other devices:

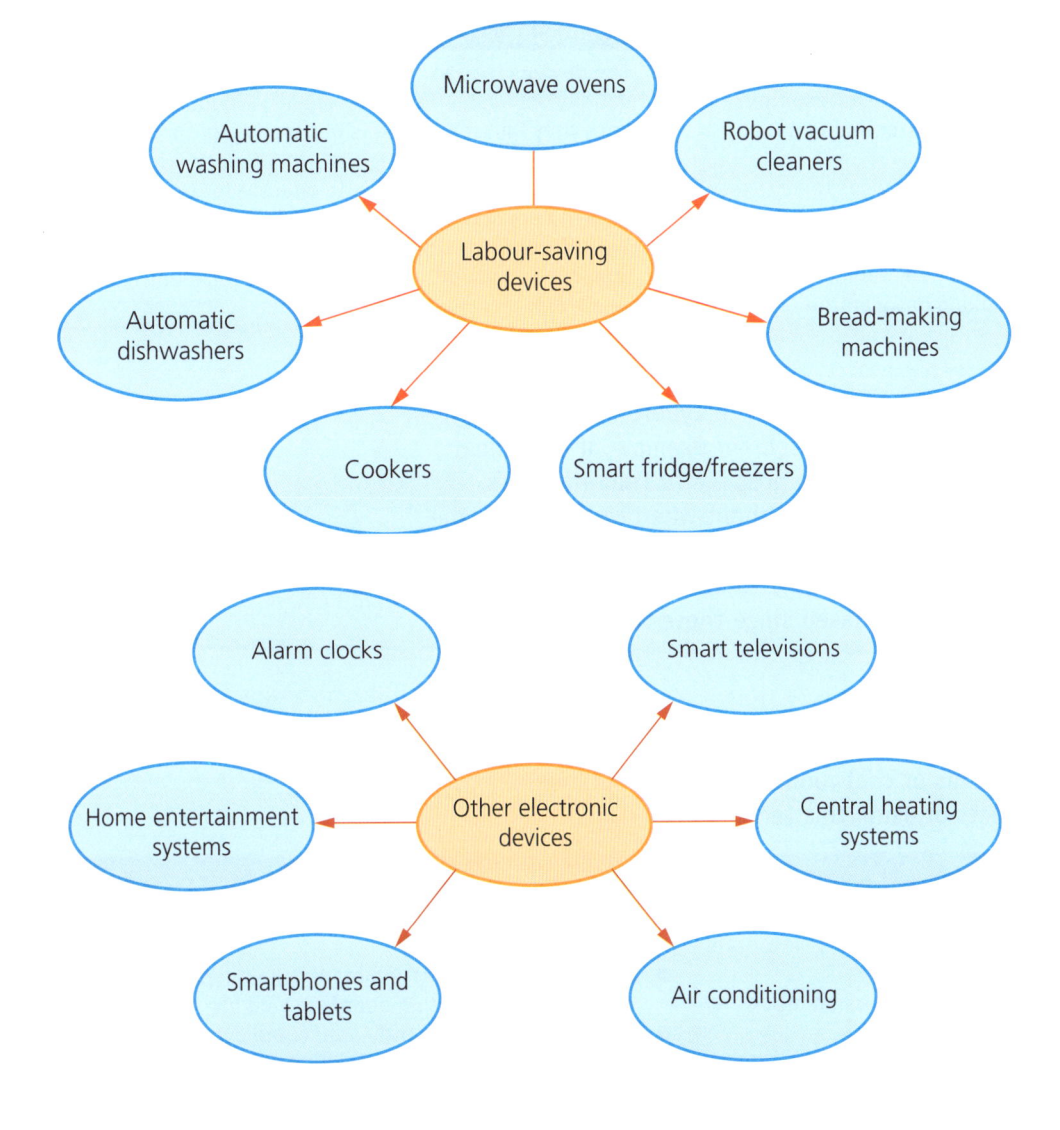

Labour-saving devices:
- Automatic washing machines
- Microwave ovens
- Robot vacuum cleaners
- Bread-making machines
- Smart fridge/freezers
- Cookers
- Automatic dishwashers

Other electronic devices:
- Alarm clocks
- Smart televisions
- Central heating systems
- Air conditioning
- Smartphones and tablets
- Home entertainment systems

5.1 Microprocessor-controlled devices

Labour-saving devices give people the free time to do other things, while other devices, such as **smart televisions**, give them a greater number of functions and make the device easier to control.

There are several advantages and disadvantages of using microprocessor-controlled labour-saving devices:

Advantages	Disadvantages
<ul><li>People do not have to do manual tasks at home</li><li>More time for leisure activities, hobbies, shopping and socialising</li><li>No need to stay home while food is cooking or clothes are being washed</li><li>It is possible to control ovens and automatic washing machines using smartphones</li><li>Automated burglar alarms give people a sense of security and well-being as they give a very sophisticated level of intruder warning</li><li>Smart fridges and freezers can lead to a healthier lifestyle (can automatically order from supermarkets using internet connections) as well as prevent food waste</li></ul>	<ul><li>Labour-saving devices can lead to unhealthy lifestyles (reliance on ready-made meals)</li><li>Tend to make people rather lazy as they depend on the devices</li><li>People can become less fit as the devices carry out many previously manual tasks</li><li>There is a potential to lose these household skills tasks; tasks carried out by people in the past are now done by the microprocessor-controlled devices</li><li>There is the risk of cybersecurity threats (this is discussed in more depth later) as with any device which contains a microprocessor and can communicate using the internet</li></ul>

The more general advantages and disadvantages of using *any* device that is microprocessor-controlled is summarised in the table below:

Advantages	Disadvantages
<ul><li>Microprocessor-controlled devices save energy because they are far more efficient – for example, they can switch themselves off after inactivity for a certain time period</li><li>It is easier 'programming' these devices to do tasks rather than turning knobs and pressing buttons manually, for example QR codes on the side of food packaging can simply be scanned and the oven automatically sets the cooking programme</li></ul>	<ul><li>The devices lead to a more wasteful society – it is usually not cost-effective to repair circuit boards once they fail; the device is generally just thrown away</li><li>They can be more complex to operate for people who are not very confident around electronic devices</li><li>Leaving some devices on stand-by (such as televisions or satellite receivers) wastes electricity</li></ul>

Data security issues

Any device fitted with a microprocessor is open to cybercriminal activity, as mentioned in the first table in this chapter. For example, if a criminal hacks into a central heating controller, it is possible to find a family's holiday dates, giving the criminal knowledge about when to break into the house. Devices that are microprocessor-controlled are also open to such criminal activity and it is therefore important to manage device passwords and install software updates when released since these will contain important security updates.

Social interactions

Devices, such as smartphones, smart TVs and tablets, allow people to communicate using VoIP, emails or chat rooms. There are a number of positive and negative aspects of using this technology:

Positive aspects	Negative aspects
<ul><li>It is easier to make new friends using chat rooms</li><li>It is easier to find people who share similar interests and concerns</li><li>Less expensive to keep in touch than using other methods (such as post, telephone)</li></ul>	<ul><li>Social isolation (people don't meet face to face as often)</li><li>Lack of social interaction may make people more anxious about meeting people in real life</li><li>People behave differently online and cyberbullying is a real issue</li></ul>

5.1.2 Monitoring and controlling transport
Microprocessors are increasingly used in transport systems:

- traffic control on smart motorways
- congestion/low emission zone monitoring in cities
- ANPR
- automatic control of traffic lights in traffic management
- air traffic control at airports
- railway signalling systems.

Smart motorways allow the monitoring and control of traffic. If there is an accident or traffic congestion, it is possible to quickly re-route the traffic. In cities and towns, traffic lights are automatically controlled to ensure traffic moves smoothly. Monitoring and control of trains and aeroplanes is very complex; the use of computers can improve overall safety and improve punctuality.

It is important to maintain high security; imagine the chaos if a cybercriminal hacked into a traffic control system and set all lights to red or green. Advantages and disadvantages of these monitoring and control systems are listed in the table below:

Advantages of monitoring/control systems	Disadvantages of monitoring/control systems
<ul><li>Smart motorways constantly adapt to traffic conditions, reducing traffic jams and minimising journey times</li><li>Transport systems are more efficient – more cars, trains and aeroplanes can use the transport network, allowing for more regular services</li><li>Traffic offences can be automatically penalised using ANPR</li><li>Stolen cars and criminals can be spotted using ANPR</li><li>Computerised control systems minimise human error, which reduces the rate of accidents</li></ul>	<ul><li>Hackers could gain access to the computerised system and cause disruption</li><li>If the computer system fails, then the whole transport system could be brought to a standstill</li><li>Poorly designed systems could compromise safety and even make the system less efficient</li><li>ANPR systems mean that innocent people's movements can easily be tracked; who has access to such data?</li><li>Criminals using false number plates could easily 'fool' such systems</li></ul>

Autonomous vehicles
Driverless (autonomous) trains have been around for many years (e.g. the underground mail train service in London), and cars and buses are now also moving towards being autonomous. These vehicles make use of sensors, cameras, actuators and microprocessors (together with very complex algorithms) to get from place to place without a human pilot/driver. Sensors and cameras allow microprocessors to be aware of their immediate surroundings. Following feedback from sensors and cameras, microprocessors send signals to actuators to control brakes, steering racks, accelerators and other systems.

Again, security is paramount since a hacker controlling the electronic system in a car, train or aeroplane could have disastrous consequences. The table on the next page summarises some advantages and disadvantages of autonomous vehicles:

5.1 Microprocessor-controlled devices

Advantages of autonomous vehicles	Disadvantages of autonomous vehicles
<ul><li>Safer because human error is removed, leading to fewer accidents</li><li>Better for the environment because vehicles will operate more efficiently</li><li>Reduced traffic congestion in cities – autonomous vehicles will be better at smoothing out traffic flow</li><li>Increased lane capacity (research shows autonomous vehicles will increase lane capacity by 100% and increase average speeds by 20%, due to better braking and acceleration responses together with optimised distance between vehicles)</li><li>Reduced travel times (for the reasons above) so less commuting time</li><li>Stress-free parking for motorists (the car will find car parking on its own and then self-park)</li></ul>	<ul><li>Very expensive system to set up in the first place (high technology requirements)</li><li>Fear of hacking into the vehicle's control system</li><li>Security and safety issues (software glitches could be catastrophic; software updates would need to be carefully controlled to avoid potential disasters)</li><li>The need to make sure the system is well-maintained at all times; cameras need to be kept clean so that they don't give false results; sensors could fail to function in heavy snowfall or blizzard conditions (radar or ultrasonic signals could be deflected by heavy snow particles)</li><li>Driver and passenger reluctance for the new technology</li><li>Using autonomous vehicles could lead to unemployment for taxi, bus, lorry and train drivers</li></ul>

Autonomous trains

Autonomous trains make use of a system called **Light Detection and Ranging (LiDaR)**. LiDaR uses lasers that build up a 3D image of their surroundings. The trains use other sensors, such as proximity sensors (on train doors) and cameras, while the position of the train is tracked using GPS technology. The table below considers advantages and disadvantages of autonomous trains:

Advantages of autonomous trains	Disadvantages of autonomous trains
<ul><li>Improves trains' punctuality</li><li>Reduced running costs (fewer staff are required)</li><li>Improved safety as human error is removed</li><li>Minimises energy consumption because there is better control of speed and minimal delays (trains stuck in stations still use energy)</li><li>Can increase the frequency of trains (automated systems allow for shorter times between trains)</li><li>It is easier to change train scheduling (e.g. more trains during busier times)</li></ul>	<ul><li>The ever-present fear of hacking into the vehicle's control system</li><li>System doesn't work well with very busy services (at the moment)</li><li>High capital costs and operational costs initially (buying the trains, expensive signalling and control equipment and the need to train staff)</li><li>Ensuring acceptable passenger behaviour particularly during busy times (e.g. jamming doors open on trains, standing too near the edge of platforms and so on)</li><li>Passenger reluctance for the new technology</li></ul>

Autonomous aeroplanes

Aeroplanes make use of numerous sensors and cameras to ensure safety and performance. By linking all this sensor information into software, it is possible to fly aeroplanes without the need for a pilot (auto-pilot has been around for many years, so this is the obvious next step to remove pilot error and improve punctuality). Actuators are used to control the throttle, flaps, tail rudder and so on. The following table summarises some of the advantages and disadvantages of using autonomous aeroplanes:

Advantages of pilotless aeroplanes	Disadvantages of pilotless aeroplanes
<ul><li>Improvement in passenger comfort (e.g. better control of the aeroplane during take-off and landing)</li><li>Reduced running costs (fewer staff are required)</li><li>Improved safety (most aeroplane crashes have been attributed to pilot-induced errors)</li><li>Improved aerodynamics at the front of the aeroplane since there would no longer be the need to include a cockpit for the pilots</li></ul>	<ul><li>Security aspects if no pilots on-board (e.g. handling terrorist attacks)</li><li>Emergency situations during the flight may be difficult to deal with</li><li>Hacking into the system (it could be possible to access flight control via the aeroplane's entertainment system, allowing a passenger to override the auto-pilot controls)</li><li>Passenger reluctance for the new technology</li><li>Software glitches (recent software issues with modern aeroplanes have highlighted that software glitches sometimes only surface a few years later causing devastating results)</li></ul>

Cambridge IGCSE Information and Communication Technology Study and Revision Guide Second Edition

5.2 Potential health problems related to prolonged use of IT equipment

REVISED

The following table summarises some of the health risks associated with using IT equipment and ways of minimising or removing the risk:

Health risk	Causes of health risk	Elimination or reduction of health risk
Back and neck strain	Sitting in front of a computer screen for long periods of time	<ul><li>Use fully adjustable chairs to give the correct posture</li><li>Use footrests to reduce posture problems</li><li>Use tiltable screens to ensure the neck is at the right angle</li></ul>
Repetitive strain injury (RSI)	Damage to fingers and wrists caused by continuous use of a keyboard or repetitive clicking of mouse buttons, for example	<ul><li>Ensure correct posture is maintained (e.g. correct angle of arms to the keyboard and mouse)</li><li>Make proper use of a wrist rest when using a mouse or keyboard</li><li>Take regular breaks (+ exercise)</li><li>Make use of ergonomic keyboards</li><li>Use voice-activated software if the user is prone to problems using a mouse or keyboard</li></ul>
Eyestrain	Staring at a computer screen for too long or by having incorrect lighting in the room (causing screen reflections)	<ul><li>If necessary, change screens to LCD if older CRT screens are still used</li><li>Take regular breaks (+ exercise)</li><li>Make use of anti-glare screens if the room lighting is incorrect (or use window blinds to cut out direct sunlight)</li><li>Users should have their eyes tested on a regular basis</li></ul>
Headaches	Incorrect lighting, screen reflections, flickering screens and so on	<ul><li>Use anti-glare screens if the room lighting is incorrect (or use window blinds to cut out reflections which cause squinting, leading to headaches)</li><li>Take regular breaks (+ exercise)</li><li>Users should have their eyes tested on a regular basis</li></ul>
Ozone irritation	Laser printers in an office (symptoms are dry skin and respiratory problems)	<ul><li>Proper ventilation should exist to lower the ozone gas levels to acceptable values</li><li>Laser printers should be housed in a designated printer room</li><li>Change to using inkjet printers if possible</li></ul>

Sample questions and responses

REVISED

a) Describe **three** advantages of using microprocessor-controlled labour-saving devices. [3 marks]

b) Describe **three** disadvantages of using microprocessors to control devices used in the home. [3 marks]

Sample high-level answer

a) They give people more time for leisure activities, hobbies, shopping and socialising. There is no longer a need to stay at home while food is cooking or to wash clothes as the devices can be programmed to do the necessary work so that people don't need to stay at home. Smart fridges and freezers can also lead to a healthier lifestyle; fresh food can be automatically ordered from the supermarket using an internet connection between device and supermarkets.

b) Microprocessor-controlled devices lead to a more wasteful society; it is no longer cost-effective to repair a device when they break down and the device is just thrown away or recycled. These devices can be more complex to operate, even setting the clock may require reference to a service manual. Many of these devices need to be left on stand-by (e.g. televisions and satellite receivers) and this is a waste of energy.

Tips

Both questions are 'describe'. The first part requires an answer giving three clear advantages of labour-saving devices – the advantages must refer to devices such as ovens, washing machines and so on, but not TVs or hi-fi, for example.

5.2 Potential health problems related to prolonged use of IT equipment

Sample low-level answer

a) Three advantages include: easier to repair (just replace a faulty circuit board), save energy and can be programmed to work remotely (e.g. recording a TV programme).

b) Three disadvantages include: more difficult to set a clock on an oven, leads to deskilling and people become very lazy.

Teacher's comments

The first student's answers clearly distinguish between labour-saving devices and other devices used in the home. They have given some description – enough for the question to be awarded three marks; the second part gives three very clear disadvantages with an explanation.

In part (a), the second student's answer fails to distinguish between labour-saving devices and other items, such as a television. The answers are too general to gain any marks. For part (b), they would probably gain two marks but the answers are a little too brief for a description. They need to explain why it leads to deskilling or makes people lazy.

Exam-style questions for you to try

1. a Name **three** health risks associated with using a computer at work. [3]
   b For **each** named risk, describe **one** way of mitigating or removing the risk. [3]
2. Many devices in the home now make use of embedded microprocessors which control the operation of the devices. They also allow for some limited programming capability, such as setting the start/end time and temperature on an oven remotely. Discuss the relative benefits and drawbacks of using microprocessor-controlled devices in the home. [6]
3. Describe the benefits and drawbacks of using autonomous cars and buses in city centres. [6]
4. a Describe the advantages of using smart signs to control the movement of traffic on main roads. [3]
   b Explain the risks associated with computer-controlled monitoring and control of traffic movement. [3]

6 ICT applications

Key objectives

The objectives of this chapter are to revise:
- communications
- modelling applications
  - financial
  - civil engineering
  - flood water management
  - traffic management
  - weather forecasting
- computer-controlled systems
- school management systems
- online booking systems
- banking applications
- computers in medicine
  - information systems
  - 3D printing
- expert systems
- computers in the retail industry
- recognition systems
  - OMR, QR codes, OCR, RFID, near-field communication and biometrics
- satellite systems
- GPS, geographic information systems and media communication.

6.1 Communication

REVISED

6.1.1 Communication media

Communication of information to the public can be done via newsletters, posters, websites, multimedia presentations, media streaming and e-publications.

Newsletters and posters

Newsletters and **posters** can easily be produced using a **word processor**. Photographs needed for either type of document can be obtained using a digital camera, finding images on the internet, finding images stored on a secondary storage device or by scanning in hard copies of photos. Spellcheckers are used to check the spelling of any text.

Newsletters are useful to get information to a target group and can be printed (and distributed) or made available online. Posters are a good way of publicising an event and can vary in size. They usually require high-quality printing and should be eye-catching and strategically placed to catch the public's attention. The following table summarises the required features for newsletters and posters to work well:

Features of newsletters	Features of posters
• They need to be well set out and easy to read • Columns should be used if there is a large amount of text and images • It is possible to use upper case letters and bold fonts to emphasise something • It is possible to use actual photos and clip art to make the newsletters and posters more interesting and informative • One drawback to remember is that newsletters may be just thrown away without even being read	• These should contain only relevant information (e.g. name of event, day of event and contact details) • Posters should be colourful and attractive in design to catch the eye • Remember that posters have a limited life (e.g. rental costs if placed on a billboard and weathering of the poster)

6.1 Communication

Websites

Websites are used to show information online rather than printed out. Fees need to be paid to the **web server** owner to allow adverts, for example, to be shown. It is also necessary to pay for the website to be developed and also for maintenance. Despite these additional costs, using websites allows advertising of products and services on a global scale. The following table summarises the advantages and disadvantages of using websites to advertise.

Advantages of using websites to advertise	Disadvantages of using websites to advertise
• Sound/video/animation can be added • Links to other websites/hyperlinks can be used • Use of hotspots • Buttons to navigate/move around the website leading to more information • Can use hit counters to see how many people have visited the website • Can be seen by a global audience • Cannot be defaced or thrown away • It is much easier to update a website (and there is no need to do a reprint and then distribute the new version)	• Websites can be hacked into and modified or viruses introduced • Risk of potential pharming • It is necessary for the potential customers to have a computer and internet connection • It is not as portable as a paper-based system (although with modern smartphones and phablets this is fast becoming untrue) • It is possible for customers to go to undesirable websites (either by accident or as a result of the pharming attack) – this can lead to distrust from customers • There is a need for the company to maintain the website once it is set up – this can be expensive • Because it is a global system, it is more difficult to target the correct audience using website advertising

Multimedia presentations

Multimedia presentations are better than, for example, static posters. This type of presentation can be set up anywhere and can make good use of sound and graphics, which are more likely to catch people's attention than a static display. There are a number of advantages and disadvantages in using multimedia presentations:

> **Tip**
> For more on presentations, see Chapter 19, p.156.

Advantages of using multimedia presentations	Disadvantages of using multimedia presentations
• Use of sound and animation/video effects which are more likely to grab the attention of the audience, and can also make the presentation easier to understand • It is possible to have interactive/hyperlinks built into the presentation. This means the presentation could access a company's website or even key files stored in the cloud (such as video footage, images, spreadsheets and so on) • Use of transition effects allows a presentation to display facts in a key or chronological order • The presentations can be interactive • They are more flexible than other types of communication media because of the links to websites and other external systems (e.g. the cloud); the presentation can be tailored to suit a particular audience	• There is a need to have special equipment, which can be expensive • Equipment failure can be a disaster when giving multimedia presentations • Wherever the presentation is given there needs to be internet access • There is a danger when using multimedia in presentations that the focus is on the medium (that is, the multimedia presentation) rather than the message or facts • It is very easy to make a bad presentation with too many animation effects and too much text or images

Media streaming

Media streaming is when users watch movies/videos or listen to music on devices connected to the internet. There is no need to download or save the files first (saving storage). Data can be transmitted and played in real time.

When streaming, a music or video file is sent out as a series of data packets, which are interpreted by the user's browser. Only internet speeds of 25 Mbits/sec or better can be used to allow for smooth streaming services. Because playback of the files is much faster than the rate at which the files are received, it is necessary to **buffer** the data packets to avoid 'freezing' (a buffer is a temporary store).

e-Publications

Most material published on paper is now available electronically online, for example:

- ebooks (digital books)
- e-magazines (digital magazines)
- e-newspapers (digital newspapers)
- e-libraries (digital libraries)

The table below summarises some of the advantages and disadvantages in offering publications online:

Advantages of e-publications	Disadvantages of e-publications
<ul><li>They can contain moving images and music/voice-overs</li><li>They are much easier to update than printed documents</li><li>They are cheaper to produce since there is no need to print out books and magazines and to distribute them</li><li>There is the potential for more advertising revenue (since the reader audience is potentially much larger)</li><li>There is no unsold stock at the end of the week/month, which wastes money and requires disposal</li><li>The books and magazines can be interactive</li></ul>	<ul><li>The need to pay for website time</li><li>The need to pay for development and maintenance</li><li>The risk of malware attacks</li><li>It can be more difficult to read since the user has to navigate between pages</li><li>Outdated software on a device may make it impossible to download the e-publication</li><li>If the user has a slow internet or poor connection, download speeds may prevent videos and sound from loading</li></ul>

6.1.2 Mobile communications

Smartphones are increasingly being used as the main form of communication. They use a cellular network of towers that give continuous smartphone coverage over large areas.

Smartphones use a **subscriber identity module (SIM) card** – this links the smartphone to the user's account, allowing them to make phone calls and access the internet on the move. Some smartphones also use e-SIM (a small chip embedded in the phone's circuitry that works like a near field communication chip and can't be removed). This allows two network providers to be used on the same phone – for example, one SIM could be for business use and the other for personal use. Since the e-SIM is writable, it is much easier to change network operators with a simple phone call.

Some of the features of smartphones include:

Feature	Description
Short messaging service (**SMS**) or **text messaging**	<ul><li>This is a quick way of communicating using a phone's virtual keyboard</li><li>The recipient of the message doesn't need to be available since the message is stored on the phone to be read whenever convenient</li><li>Uses predictive texting which speeds up typing (but can lead to some amusing errors!)</li></ul>
Phone calls	<ul><li>The most obvious use of a smartphone; their small size means they are likely to be on your person all the time</li><li>Provided there is a cellular network signal, smartphones can be used anywhere while on the move; this makes it easier to keep in contact with people</li></ul>
Voice over Internet Protocol (VoIP)	<ul><li>VoIP allows audio and visual communication over the internet</li><li>All the sender needs is a microphone and a speaker or an internet-enabled phone (a forward facing camera is also needed for video calls)</li><li>The recipient can receive calls using a smartphone, landline phone or another computer/tablet</li><li>However, sound quality can be poor at times</li><li>There are the usual security issues with internet devices</li><li>Video calling needs apps such as Skype, Facetime or Zoom</li></ul>

Feature	Description
Internet access	• Using a smartphone/tablet connected to the cellular network allows internet access on the move • Software in the phone detects the type of device connecting to the internet and the website sends out optimised web pages (the web page is modified to suit the screen size and its aspect ratio) • Smartphones automatically use WiFi if available rather than the cellular network; the WiFi connection is cheaper, consumes less battery power, utilises more bandwidth and is usually a more stable connection
Payment using mobile phones	• Refer to section 6.9
Cameras	• Smartphones and tablets have built-in cameras; this allows them to be used in a number of applications (such as reading QR codes) – refer to section 2.2

6.2 Modelling applications

REVISED

Computer **modelling** is the construction and use of a computer-based mathematical (algorithmic) representation of a real-life system. A **simulation** uses a model to study the behaviour of the system under different scenarios. It can help to predict how the system will work in unusual circumstances.

6.2.1 Computer modelling

Modelling of a real-life system has a number of advantages and disadvantages:

Advantages of using modelling	Disadvantages of using modelling
• Using computer models is less expensive than having to build the real thing (e.g. a bridge!) • On many occasions it is safer to use a computer model (some real situations are hazardous, e.g. chemical processes) • When using computer modelling it is much easier to try out various scenarios in advance • It is nearly impossible to try out some tasks in real life because of the high risk involved or the remoteness (e.g. outer space, under the sea, nuclear reactors, crash testing cars etc.) • It is often faster to use a computer model than do the real thing (some applications would take years before a result was known, e.g. climate change calculations, population growth etc.)	• A model is only as good as the programming or the data entered; the simulation will depend heavily on these two factors • Although building the real thing can be expensive, sometimes modelling is also a very costly option, and the two costs need to be compared before deciding whether or not to use modelling • People's reactions to the results of a simulation may not be positive; they may not trust the results it produces (modelling can never mimic real life and there will always be a difference between the results from modelling and reality)

Examples of modelling applications include:

- personal finances
- bridge and building design
- flood water management
- traffic management
- weather forecasting.

Personal finances

This is often done using a spreadsheet allowing 'what if?' scenarios. It makes use of the software's features to predict the outcome if various values in spreadsheet cells are changed. Refer to Chapter 20 for more information on the use of spreadsheets in financial modelling.

Bridge and building design

When an engineer or architect designs a new building or bridge, a 3D computer model is used to test the integrity of the structure. Very often a scale model is made of the final structure and a combination of computer modelling and wind tunnel tests are carried out.

A number of scenarios are considered when carrying out the simulation using models and wind tunnels; for example, when constructing a new bridge:

- How much traffic would the bridge be expected to take?
- What would be the effect of an accident (e.g. would the bridge integrity be compromised? How easy is it for the emergency services to reach the accident? and so on)?
- What are the effects of very strong winds and typical earthquake activity on the bridge structure?
- Vibration effects – every structure has a natural frequency which could cause it to sway and collapse if the frequency is reached).

Simulation studies are also carried out when designing new buildings. Again, a number of scenarios are considered:

- What are the effects of hurricane winds, extreme flooding and earthquake activity (e.g. tall buildings sway in the wind and this effect needs to be studied and minimised to prevent occupants feeling ill)?
- What are the results of disasters such as a fire (can the emergency services get to the fire before any major structural damage makes the building unstable)?
- How to efficiently move people in and out of a large building (e.g. Willis Tower (Chicago, USA) houses over 400 000 people and it is necessary to simulate that number of people leaving and entering the building (travelling between all 108 floors) – the most efficient lift usage would need to be carefully modelled).

Modelling can find out any flaws in the original designs and help to improve the final version before construction starts. Any changes during or after construction can be very expensive.

Flood water management

As the world's climate changes, flood water management becomes increasingly important. Modelling allows risk assessments to be made to identify the sources of flooding, the extent of potential flooding and any mitigation methods.

Inputs to the computer model would include:

- cross-section of rivers and sea inlets to identify bottlenecks
- bridges, weirs and other 'obstructions' in the flood area
- factors affecting the flow rate of water (e.g. tides and wind)
- boundaries (e.g. consider upstream tributary rivers)
- time of day and time of year the simulation is done
- results of previous flooding behaviour for comparison.

Flood risk management of cities is particularly important, for example Venice, London, Amsterdam and Sao Paulo are all part of the global urban flooding network. Modelling allows automated flood defence systems to be developed.

The main advantages of having an automated flood defence system are:
- sensors could be used offshore to monitor sea height and wave height (and possibly other factors, such as wind speeds); using sensors would give a much faster response to any deteriorating conditions in a bay
- using a computer system is safer, since using humans to monitor conditions could potentially put them at risk
- data collection is continuous and more accurate than manual measurements (readings can also be taken more frequently)
- because of the faster response to changing conditions, people can be warned well in advance of any flooding actually taking place
- data from the sensors could also be fed into the simulation modelling the flood area; this could lead to further improvements as more data is gathered, which means the simulation becomes closer to reality.

Traffic management

Computer modelling can be used in traffic management to see the impact of heavy traffic and accidents on the flow of traffic. Traffic management modelling is often used when setting up major roadworks to see how they affect traffic flow and when optimising traffic light times at a junction.

Data to be collected to input into a model used to simulate, for example, the traffic lights at a junction could be:

- number of vehicles passing the junction in all directions
- time of day also needs to be recorded for each vehicle being counted
- traffic at different times of day and how long it takes to clear
- other factors that affect traffic (e.g. a pedestrian crossing nearby)
- the time it takes the slowest vehicle to pass through the junction
- other factors, such as accidents, filtering and emergency vehicles.

Once the above data has been collected and is fed into the model, different scenarios can be tried out to optimise traffic light timings and to determine where to place traffic sensors in the road. The final version will receive live data and a central control box can compare actual traffic data with simulation data allowing the model to be fine-tuned.

After all the testing is done, the actual traffic light control system is installed. This works as follows:

- road sensors collect data about all vehicles travelling through the junction (in all directions)
- this data is sent to a control box
- the live data is compared to stored data from the simulation and signals are sent to the lights to change colour as necessary.

Weather forecasting

Weather forecasting can also be done by computer modelling. Data such as rainfall, air temperature, wind speed, wind direction, air pressure and humidity levels are all measured and sent to a central computer.

The central computer runs the simulation and predicts the weather forecast for the next few days (and sometimes long-range forecasts are made). After each forecast is made, the *actual* weather conditions are compared to the predicted weather allowing improvements to be made to the model.

Weather forecast simulations often show changing conditions in an animated way, for example rain, cloud, sun and wind changes are superimposed onto a map of the area under consideration.

6 ICT applications

Sample questions and responses

REVISED ☐

After running a simulation using a computer model, the city of Chicago developed a new flood management system that automatically comes into play following dangerously high rainfall.
a) Explain why a computer model is used when developing the flood management system. **[3 marks]**
b) Describe what data needs to be input into the flood management model. **[4 marks]**
c) Explain the benefits of having an automated system in place to prevent flooding. **[4 marks]**

> **Tips**
> All three parts of the question are 'describe' or 'explain', which means a set of very comprehensive answers is required for maximum marks.

Sample high-level answer

a) The number of possible scenarios is vast so it is necessary to run a computer simulation to test out all the possible scenarios. To do this manually would take many years. The simulation allows the engineers to study the flood area and to input various situations to see how any possible flood management system would work. This also allows 'unknown' situations to be modelled so that any final solution would be as robust as possible.

b) The following data would need to be input into the model:
- cross-section of rivers and sea inlets to identify bottlenecks
- bridges, weirs and other 'obstructions' in the flood area
- factors affecting the flow rate of water (e.g. tides and wind)
- boundaries (e.g. consider upstream feeder rivers)
- time of day and time of year the simulation is done
- comparison of model results with actual flood behaviour.

c) The following benefits would come from using an automatic flood management system:
- sensors could be used to monitor sea height and wave height (and possibly other factors, such as wind speeds); using sensors would give a much faster response to any deteriorating conditions in the bay
- using a computer system is safer, since using humans to monitor conditions could potentially put them at risk
- data collection is continuous and more accurate than manual measurements, and readings can also be taken more frequently
- because of the faster response to changing conditions, people can be warned well in advance of any flooding actually taking place
- data from the sensors could also be fed into the simulation modelling the flood area; this could lead to further improvements as more data is gathered, which means the simulation becomes closer to reality.

Sample low-level answer

a) A computer model would let us see the effects of flooding on Chicago. Actual data would be input so we can see on a screen how far the flooding would affect the city.
b) We would need to input the volume of water and how many days it rained to work out how much flooding would occur. The model could use this data to show the extent of the flooding.
c) It would stop the city flooding as often and improve the flood defences saving lives and reducing property damage.

Teacher's comments

The first answer is very comprehensive for all three parts. If any criticism is to be made, it is that they have probably given too much information. While this is not necessarily a bad thing, it is important to keep an eye on the clock and running out of room to write the answer is also a good clue that you have tried to write too much to gain full marks.

The second sample answers are a little too vague. One mark would probably be awarded for each of the three answers (giving 3 marks in total for the question) since they have shown some understanding of the role of models at each stage of the process.

6.3 Computer-controlled systems

Exam-style questions for you to try

1. A publishing company produces a car magazine each month, which shows new products, road tests and other motoring information. The company has decided to offer an e-magazine (digital magazine) rather than a paper-based, glossy magazine.
   Describe **three** advantages and **three** disadvantages of doing this. **[6]**

2. Here is a list of five simulations (models) and a list of five reasons why simulations (models) are carried out. By drawing arrows, match the five simulations to the **best reason** why that simulation would be done.

Simulation	Reason
1. Pilot training	A. Cost of building the real thing is too expensive
2. Environmental modelling	B. Some situations are too dangerous to human operators
3. Modelling bridge loading	C. It takes too long to get results back from the real thing
4. Modelling a nuclear reaction	D. It is almost impossible to the task for real
5. Space exploration	E. It is easier and safer to make changes to a model than change the real thing

[5]

3. A complex road junction will be modelled so that traffic lights can be installed to optimise traffic flow.
   a. Explain what data needs to be collected and how it would be used to develop and test the model
   b. Explain how the results of the model would be used in the real traffic light control system.

[8]

6.3 Computer-controlled systems

REVISED

6.3.1 Robotics in manufacturing

Robots are electro-mechanical devices designed to carry out tasks normally done by humans. They are either under computer control or have their own embedded microprocessor. Robots are used in many areas of manufacturing, such as paint spraying of car body panels, welding metals and manufacturing microchips. They can be 'trained' to do their task either by a set of programmed instructions (written by a programmer) or by using sensors to copy a human operator, with each operation then stored in memory.

6 ICT applications

The table shows a number of advantages and disadvantages of using robots in industry:

Advantages	Disadvantages
• They can work in environments harmful to human operators • They can work non-stop (24/7) • They are less expensive in the long term (although expensive to buy initially, they do not need wages) • Higher productivity (do not need holidays etc.) • Greater consistency (e.g. every car coming off a production line is identical) • They can do boring, repetitive tasks, leaving humans free to do other more skilled work (e.g. quality control or design work) • To carry out different tasks, robots are fitted with different end-effectors (attachments); for example, a spray gun, a welding gun and so on	• Robots find it difficult to do 'unusual' tasks (e.g. one-off glassware for a chemical company) • They can cause higher unemployment (replacing skilled labour) • Since robots do many of the tasks once done by humans, there is a real risk of certain skills (such as welding) being lost • Because robots are independent of the skills base, factories can be moved anywhere in the world (again causing unemployment) • The initial set-up and maintenance of robots can be expensive

6.3.2 Production control

Production line control using robots is used extensively in industry, for example bottling and canning plants. The production line will be continuous with various robots at each station given a specific task. Using robots in this way leads to:

- faster operations (the number of bottles filled is faster than a human could fill)
- much greater productivity (the production can run 24 hours a day, every day)
- greater consistency (every bottle contains exactly the correct volume of liquid)
- built-in quality control (automatic testing for foreign material such as metal filings which would result in automatic rejection from the production line)
- reduced cost to the consumer (although initial robot arms are expensive, there are far fewer staff in the factory who would need wages).

We will now look at how robots could be used in a bottling plant in full detail:

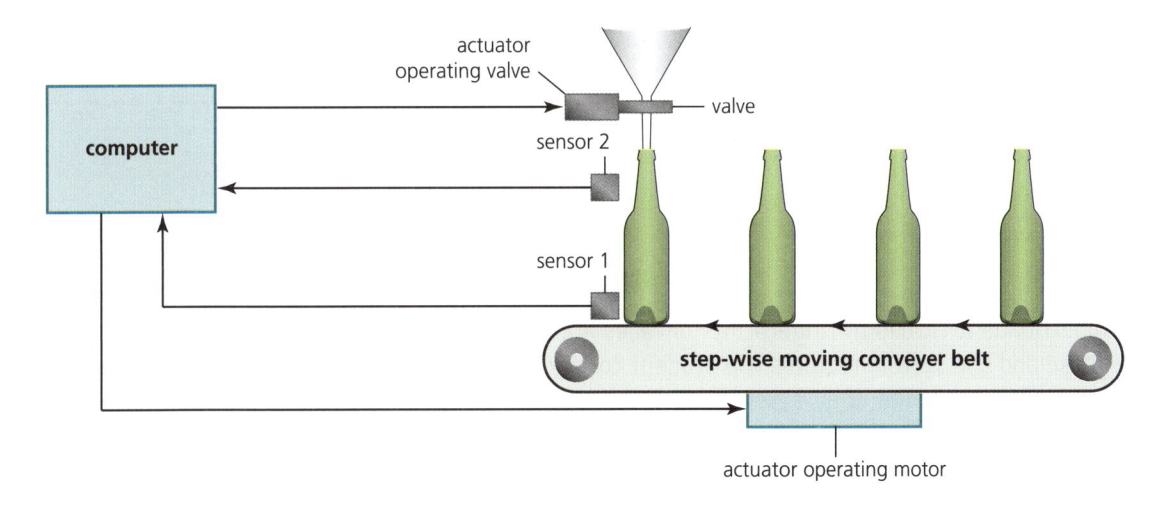

Hodder & Stoughton Limited © David Watson and Graham Brown 2022

- sensor 1 (a pressure sensor, light sensor or camera) detects the presence of a bottle; this sensor is constantly sending signals back to the computer
- when the signal from sensor 1 indicates a bottle is present, the computer sends a signal to an actuator which opens a valve allowing liquid to flow into the bottle
- sensor 2 (a level sensor) is used to detect the correct liquid height in the bottle; this sensor sends continuous signals back to the computer
- when the signal from sensor 2 indicates the bottle is full, the computer sends a signal to an actuator to close the valve
- the computer then sends another signal to a second actuator which operates a motor to move the conveyer belt to allow the next empty bottle to take its correct position
- the whole process is continuous until stopped for maintenance, errors occurring or a change in the process.

6.4 School management systems

6.4.1 Registration and attendance records of students

The traditional way to record registrations and attendance of a student is to complete a daily paper-based register; this is both time-consuming and error-prone. We will now consider two possible automatic methods that could be used to track attendance.

Method 1 – use of magnetic ID cards

- In the morning a student swipes an ID card (this contains the name of the school, student's name, student's date of birth and a unique ID number stored on a magnetic stripe).
- If the card data is read successfully then the student is registered as present on a central database.
- If the student leaves the school/college (e.g. on their lunch break), the ID card is again swiped and the database is updated as 'not present'.
- This gives a comprehensive record of the student's attendance, and is better than a paper-based register should there be an emergency (e.g. a fire), since there will be an accurate record of who is on the premises.
- This method also gives accurate attendance records for the entire school/college term.
- Additional features to improve security could be: using a chip embedded in the card so that the student needs to enter a PIN as well as present the card. This chip could also be linked to GPS so that the location of the student would also be known (but this feature could have privacy issues in some countries).

Method 2 – use of biometrics

- This second method uses fingerprint or face recognition to identify a student (biometric identification); fingerprints or faces are stored on a central database and the system requires the student to place their hand on a reader or look at a camera. Their attendance is then recorded.
- Again, if the student leaves the premises, they carry out the same process and the database is updated.
- Biometrics are unique and it would stop students 'cheating' by swiping in with a borrowed or stolen card.

There are a number of advantages and disadvantages of using biometric methods rather than using magnetic cards:

Advantages of using biometric devices	Disadvantages of using biometric devices
• Fingerprints are unique, so it would be impossible for a student to sign in pretending to be someone else (with magnetic cards, a student could give their card to a friend and ask them to sign in for them) – this gives more accurate data and improved security • Id cards could easily be lost – fingerprints cannot be lost • Id cards could be affected by magnetic fields (e.g. by being placed close to a mobile phone) which would stop them working properly • It is much easier to 'clone' (make copies of) id cards than it is to copy fingerprints (not impossible but very difficult)	• It would take a long time to collect the fingerprints for every student in the school • The equipment needed to take and read fingerprints is more expensive than magnetic stripe reading equipment • If a student cuts a finger, the fingerprint may not be identified by the system (which would prevent entry to the school) • There are 'invasion of privacy' issues and some parents may object to having the fingerprints of their children stored on a database

Student performance

Spreadsheets can be used to record results from tests and exams and analyse the results and award grades according to some criteria. The software could also produce graphs to allow student's performances to be compared (refer to Chapter 20, p.164)

School management software also exists that analyses academic achievement and behaviour (e.g. attendance) and also generates CAT scores.

> CAT standardises test results to enable each student to be measured against the same standard.

Computer-aided learning

Computer-aided learning (CAL) is used to enhance and not replace traditional classroom teaching; CAL packages allow students to use interactive software aimed at revision topics and tests. There are a number of advantages and disadvantages of using CAL:

Advantages of using CAL	Disadvantages of using CAL
• CAL is most effective when using micro-learning; this is where a topic is broken down into small modules which are easy to learn • The system allows interactive coursework to take place • Students can learn when they want to and at their own pace • It allows VR learning to be used; with VR, the student is fully immersed into the learning environment • The student can stop at any point and return later to continue where they left off • It is possible to retake tests until the student reaches the required skills level • CAL makes use of various multimedia (e.g. short video clips, animation, music and interactive learning methods) • The real goal of CAL is to stimulate student learning and not actually replace teacher-based learning; if used properly it should be an integrated part of the student's learning process • CAL can make use of multiple-choice questions (MCQs) which can be marked immediately by the computer system, giving instantaneous feedback to the student; other assessment methods can be used, such as fill in the missing words, crossword puzzles, linking correct terms to descriptions and gaming	• CAL cannot give students the experience of handling laboratory equipment, for example; experiments shown in CAL are virtual in nature • It is expensive and time-consuming to integrate CAL properly into the learning environment • Students can easily be distracted while online, for example going on to social media sites, visiting websites or even playing online games • It can lead to the isolation of a student since they are spending their time on their own in front of a computer screen; this needs to be carefully managed • CAL cannot answer unusual questions, and the student will need to seek out guidance from a teacher; in other words, CAL is not a self-contained learning system

6.5 Booking systems

6.5.1 Online booking systems

Online booking systems are used by travel agencies, theatre/music events, cinemas and sporting events. They have specific advantages and disadvantages when compared to traditional, manual booking methods:

Advantages of online booking systems	Disadvantages of online booking systems
• They prevent double-booking (which could happen in paper-based systems that didn't update the system fast enough) • The customer gets immediate feedback on the availability of seats and whether or not their booking has been successful • The customer can make bookings at any time of the day • The customer's email allows the booking company to connect 'special offers' to their email and inform them of such offers automatically • It is usually easier to browse the seating plans (particularly on flights) to choose the best seats available at the price • It is possible to reserve a seat for a period of time – this allows a customer to make up their mind before finalising the booking of the seat (this was difficult to do with the older paper-based systems) • Very often there are no printed tickets which saves postal costs and also allows impulse bookings only a few hours in advance • Online booking allows the use of modern smartphone and tablet apps technology; the customer is sent a QR code which contains all the booking information necessary (this QR code is stored on the smartphone or tablet and just needs to be scanned at, for example, the theatre or airport on arrival)	• The setting up and maintenance of online booking systems are expensive • All customers using this service need access to a computer or mobile phone and a reliable internet connection • It is often more difficult to cancel the booking and get your money back using online systems • If the server is down for maintenance or if the system breaks down, it becomes impossible to book seats by any method (a temporary paper-based system can't be used because of the risk of double-booking occurring) • If the website is not well designed, it can be difficult to make exactly the booking you want or can lead you to make mistakes. This is a particular issue with flight bookings where correcting an error can cost the customer an additional fee • Booking online does not allow you to build a personal relationship with the travel agent who might offer free upgrades or special offers that may not be available to online bookings

One example is the online booking of theatre tickets (other examples have a similar process). In this example, we have assumed that the customer has already logged on to the theatre's booking website (and the event is a music concert at a seated venue):

- The customer clicks on the performance they wish to see.
- A date and time are typed in.
- The required number of seats is also entered.
- The seating display at the venue is shown on the screen.
- The user selects their seat(s) by highlighting the actual seat(s) on the screen and then clicks CONFIRM to go to the next part of the process.
- The database is then searched to check the availability of the selected seats.

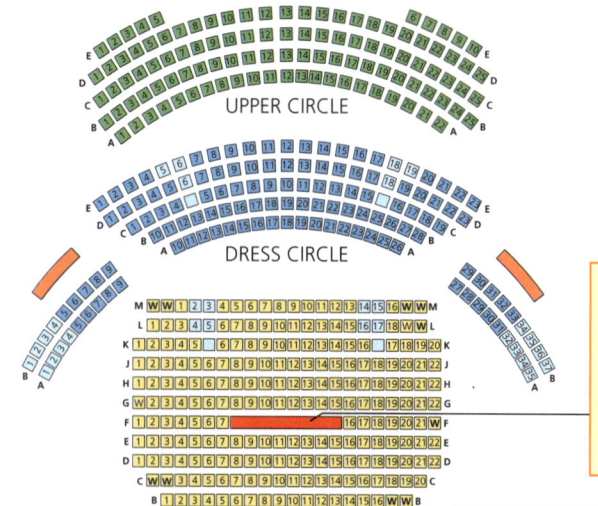

The seating display at the venue is shown on the screen

The user selects their seat(s) by highlighting the actual seats on the screen display and then clicks CONFIRM to go to the next part of the process

Please click here to confirm your seating choice

62 Cambridge IGCSE Information and Communication Technology Study and Revision Guide Second Edition

- If the seats are available, the total price is shown plus the seat numbers; this shows on another screen on the web page.
- If the customer is happy with this, they select CONFIRM on the screen.
- The seats are now temporarily set at NO LONGER AVAILABLE.
- The customer then enters their personal details or indicates that they are a returning customer (in which case the website being used will already have their details).
- Payment method is then selected and payment made.
- The theatre seats are booked in the customer's name.
- The final details are again shown on the screen.
- An email is sent that contains a QR code with all their booking details (this acts as their e-ticket); the QR code is scanned at the venue.
- The database is finally updated with the booking transaction and the seats become permanently no longer available.

6.6 Banking systems

REVISED

The use of computer technology has revolutionised how we do our banking transactions:

- Using automatic teller machines (ATMs)
- Electronic funds transfer (EFT)
- Credit/debit card transactions
- Cheque clearing
- Internet banking.

The following table summarises each of the five banking features above, including advantages and disadvantages:

Banking feature	Description	Advantages	Disadvantages
ATMs	Used by customers to withdraw or deposit cash, deposit cheques, check account balance, see a mini-statement, pay bills or do a money transfer	<ul><li>It is possible to withdraw or deposit cash at any time</li><li>It is possible to access your account anywhere in the world</li><li>It is a faster service than waiting in a queue in the bank</li><li>There is no need to visit the bank to carry out many services, such as bill paying</li></ul>	<ul><li>The number of ATMs is reducing in many areas</li><li>There is always the potential for shoulder surfing and card cloning at outside ATMs</li><li>Some banks charge for using ATMs</li><li>There is a cash withdrawal limit per day</li><li>Loss of the personal touch</li></ul>
Electronic funds transfer (EFT) and **Electronic fund transfer at point-of-sale (EFTPOS)**	EFT allows money transfer instructions to be sent directly to the bank's computer system; no actual money is transferred between accounts. It is used, for example, to pay wages into an account EFTPOS terminals are used when debit/credit cards are used to pay for services or goods; the card is read by the EFTPOS device and the transaction takes place if all checks are satisfactory	<ul><li>EFT is a very secure and very quick method of payment</li><li>It is less expensive than, for example, using cheques to pay for goods and services</li><li>Customers have the right to dispute any EFT payment for up to 60 days</li></ul>	<ul><li>Once an amount of money has been transferred, the bank can't reverse the transaction (it requires an internal procedure to take place which can take many days)</li><li>Customers must have the necessary funds available for immediate transfer (unlike cheques, for example)</li><li>It is not possible to guarantee the recipient is who they say they are (e.g. using fake ID to collect the money)</li></ul>

6.6 Banking systems

Banking feature	Description	Advantages	Disadvantages
Credit/debit cards	Small plastic cards with a magnetic strip on the back (containing account number, sort code and expiry date, for example); smart/contactless cards also have an embedded chip (this contains additional data, such as a PIN)	• Debit cards prevent debt (customers are prevented from spending more money than they have in their account) • There is usually no charge for using the cards except in certain circumstances (such as some ATMs when taking out foreign currency abroad) • They are well-suited to small payments and are a quick and convenient method of payment • Relatively easy process to be given a credit/debit card	• The funds available on cards is limited to a daily amount (which means large purchases may not be possible without informing the bank first) • They can incur very large overdraft fees if the bank allows the customer to 'go into the red' • For payments over a certain amount a PIN is required; it is easy to forget a pin and after three failed attempts the card will be cancelled
Cheques	A paper-based system that has been around for many years; cheques are slowly being phased out by banks (the cheque clearing process is described below)	• It is more convenient and safer than carrying or paying by cash • A cheque can be drawn at any time up to six months after being signed • Cheques can be post-dated • Cheques can be traced if 'lost'	• Cheques are not legal tender and can be refused as a method of payment • It can be a slow method of payment • Easier for fraudsters than credit/debit card transactions • Relatively expensive method of payment
Internet banking	This is covered fully in section 6.9.2 on p.72		

6.6.1 Chip and PIN debit/credit card payments

This system is used when a customer pays for goods or services using a keypad on an EFTPOS device.

- The customer enters their PIN using the keypad.
- The card is checked to see if it is valid (that is a check on the expiry date, is it stolen and so on).
- The PIN code is read from the chip embedded in the card and is compared to the one just entered by the customer on the keypad.
- If they match, the transaction goes to the next stage; if they don't match, the transaction is stopped and the card is declined.
- The recipient's bank now contacts the customer's bank and a check is made to see whether they have sufficient funds to cover the cost of the transaction.
- If the customer has insufficient funds, the transaction is stopped and the card is declined.
- If everything is OK at this stage, the transaction is authorised and an authentication code is generated and sent back to the EFTPOS device.
- Funds are then transferred from the customer's bank to the recipient's bank and the customer is given a printed receipt for their records.

This table shows the relative advantages and disadvantages of credit cards when compared to debit cards:

Type of card	Advantages	Disadvantages
Credit	• There is customer protection if a company stops trading or goods don't arrive • Internationally accepted method of payment • Interest-free loan if money paid back within agreed time period • Can buy items online	• Can be charged high interest rate • Annual fees often apply • Easy to end up with credit damage as sums mount up • Security risks when using credit card online (see Chapter 8)
Debit	• Money comes from customer's current account, therefore no interest charges • Safer than carrying cash • Can buy items online	• Less customer protection than credit cards if goods don't arrive or company goes out of business • No credit allowed; customers must have the funds available

6.6.2 The cheque clearing process

Suppose someone uses a bank called Hodder Bank and they pay a cheque for $50 to a company called H&S Co who bank with Smith Bank; the following procedure explains how H&S Co are credited with $50:

- The first step is called **out clearing**. The cheque is fed into a reader which takes a photograph of the cheque and built-in OCR software turns the image into an electronic record.
- Smith Bank now creates a digital record containing: money to be paid in, sort code on the cheque and account number shown on the cheque.
- *All* transactions relating to Hodder Bank during the day are added to a file (which includes the electronic record relating to this cheque) and the file is sent to a central facility (other banks will have their own separate files containing cheque transactions relating to their bank).
- The file containing cheques drawn on Hodder Bank is now processed, a 'request to pay' message for each cheque is made and a stream of 'request to pay' images (for all cheques) are sent to Hodder Bank; if the cheque hasn't been signed or fraud is suspected, then a 'no pay' message is created for each affected cheque.
- The central facility routes all 'request to pay' and 'no pay' responses to Smith Bank and the payment shown on each cheque is carried out; essentially, at this stage H&S Co are debited with $50 from the customer's Hodder Bank account.

> **Tip**
> For more on OCR, refer to Section 2.2.

Sample question and response

REVISED

Nicolae logs on to a travel agent's website. He selects flights from Bucharest to Cairo on his preferred date and time and pays for the flights.

Describe what data Nicolae will need to supply and explain how the website will ensure Nicolae has a seat reserved on his flight. **[8 marks]**

Sample high-level answer

- The customer will supply the following information regarding the flight:
  - his full name, email address and contact phone number
  - date of flight   } these are often selected by choosing
  - time of flight   } options from drop-down boxes
  - departure and destination airport
  - number of seats required
  - additional information (such as disabled passenger, dietary needs etc.),
- A seating display for the chosen flight will be shown on screen and the customer will select his seats.
- A database is searched to see if the chosen seats are still available.
- If the seats are available, the total cost plus seat numbers will be displayed (if the seats are no longer available, the customer will be taken back to the home screen and requested to make a new choice).
- If the customer is happy with the selection and price, he will confirm this.
- The customer's seats are now marked as 'temporarily unavailable' on the database to prevent double-booking.
- Payment details are then entered and the customer's bank is contacted and the transaction takes place if there are no problems.
- The customer is now sent an email to confirm his flight together with cost breakdown and any other required information.
- A QR code will be sent via email and this will act as his e-ticket.
- The travel agency database will be updated and the customer's seats for that flight will now be permanently set to unavailable.

> **Tips**
> There are 8 marks allocated to this question. This means a fairly comprehensive description needs to be given of the booking process. If it is easier, the two parts of the question could be combined to produce a single description.

Teacher's comments

The first student has given a very strong answer. They have split their answer in accordance with the original question. At least eight points have been made, together with a list of input requirements, which means the student could gain the maximum possible mark for this question.

6.6 Banking systems

> **Sample low-level answer**
>
> The customer logs onto the travel agent's website and chooses seats on a flight from Bucharest to Cairo on the day required. The travel agent will check if there are seats available and informs the customer of the result. If seats are found, the customer pays for the flight and is sent a confirmation by email. The customer is sent flight tickets as part of the confirmation email.

Teacher's comments

The second student has not really given much detail regarding the booking procedure nor have they given a list of input requirements. There is probably 1 mark for some input details (day of flight and the destination/arrival airports) and a second mark is probably given for the confirmation email.

Exam-style questions for you to try

4. A cinema manager has decided to introduce an online booking system to replace the current paper-based booking system. Give **four** advantages of using an online booking system to replace a paper-based booking system. [4]

5. Robots are being used in the mining industry to find new deposits of lithium ore.
   a. Give **three** advantages of using robots rather than humans when searching for new ore deposits. [3]
   b. Give **two** disadvantages of using robots in this scenario rather than humans. [2]

6. Describe five of the stages when clearing a bank cheque through the central clearing facility. [5]

7. a. A school uses smart cards (containing a magnetic strip and embedded chip) as a method of determining which students are on the premises at any given time. In the following table, tick (✓) the appropriate boxes to show which statements about the use of smart cards are true:

Statements	True (✓)
Smart cards prevent students signing in for each other	
It is possible to determine whether a student is on the premises in case of a fire	
It is possible to determine a student's attendance record over the whole year	
It is not possible to clone smart identity cards, making the system very secure and accurate	
Data stored on a card is the name of the school, name of the student, student's date of birth and their unique ID number	
Using a PIN only works if the identity card is fitted with an embedded microchip	

[3]

   b. Students at a school are using computer aided learning (CAL) as part of their studies. Indicate which of the following statements about CAL are true by placing a tick (✓) next to the true statements.

It is illegal to photocopy this page

66 Cambridge IGCSE Information and Communication Technology Study and Revision Guide Second Edition

Statements	True (✓)
Students can learn at their own pace	
Students must complete the whole session on a particular topic before moving on to the next topic	
CAL frees up teachers to do other things since it can replace trained teachers in the classroom	
CAL lessons can include multimedia and animations	
It is not possible for CAL to be interactive since no teachers are involved in the CAL process	
CAL allows for micro-learning where topics are broken down into manageable modules	

[3]

6.7 Computers in medicine

REVISED

6.7.1 Information systems in medicine

Computers are used to keep patient records. Databases contain information that can be shared between medical practitioners and pharmacies. They allow electronic prescriptions to be sent out for patients with regular monthly requirements, freeing up doctors' time. Typical data stored on the database could include:

- patient's medical record, unique ID number, full name, date of birth, address, email address and contact phone number
- gender and ethnicity
- current treatment and any current diagnoses together with important analytics (such as X-rays, **computed tomography (CT)** scans).

Use of 3D printers

3D printers are now used in many areas of medicine:

- Surgical and diagnostic aids:
  - using CT scans and **magnetic resonance imaging (MRI)** scans, it is possible to build up a 3D image of internal organs
  - these 3D images can be sent to a 3D printer and solid objects printed out which precisely resemble the internal organs
  - the doctor can show the patient exactly where the problem is using the solid printouts; the physical object also allows more accurate surgical planning by surgeons.
- Prosthetics:
  - 3D printers can now print out very accurate prosthetics (artificial arms, hands and legs) much more quickly and at a fraction of the cost of more traditional methods.
- Tissue engineering and artificial blood vessels:
  - 3D printers now allow printing of bio-compatible materials, cells and supporting structures
  - using **bio-inks**, artificial cells and tissue can be printed out
  - 3D printers have already been used to produce skin tissue, bone tissue, heart/artery grafts and tracheal splints
  - bio-printed tissues, such as artificial blood vessels, have also been made using 3D printers and bio-inks.

- Customised medicines:
  - 3D printers can now allow customised medicines to be made (called patient-centric medicine).
  - Sometimes referred to as **printlets**, 3D printing offers the possibility of creating personalised medicine that allows automatically controlled release of the medicine into the patient's body. Fixed-dose combinations can be created to allow optimum release of each medicine and these medicines are tailor-made for each patient.
  - 3D printers used to generate patient-centric medicines use a technology called vapour printing.
  - This technique allows tablets to be made to a very specific geometry. There is a connection between tablet geometry and medicine release into the body, which is the whole basis behind the use of 3D printers to make customised printlets.
  - The advantages of customised medicines include:
    - tailor-made medicines to suit the individual
    - better control of medicine release into the body
    - saves money (many modern medicines are very expensive)
    - better targeting of the medicine so its effects can be optimised
    - less chance of an overdose of the medicine – reducing harmful side effects.

> printlets are PRINTed tabLETS

6.8 Expert systems

REVISED

Expert systems have been developed to mimic the expertise and knowledge of an expert in a particular field. Examples include:

- prospecting for oil and minerals
- diagnostics (finding faults in a car engine or on a circuit board etc.)
- medical diagnosis
- strategy games (e.g. chess)
- tax and financial planning
- route scheduling for delivery vehicles
- identification of plants, animals and chemical compounds.

The following table summarises the advantages and disadvantages of expert systems:

Advantages of using expert systems	Disadvantages of using expert systems
- They offer the highest level of expertise and high accuracy - The results are consistent - Can store vast amounts of ideas and facts - Can make traceable logical solutions and diagnostics - It is possible for an expert system to have multiple types of expertise - Very fast response time (much quicker than a human expert) - Provide unbiased reporting and analysis of the facts - They indicate the probability of any suggested solution being correct	- Users of the expert system need considerable training in its use to ensure the system is being used correctly - The set-up and maintenance costs are very high - They tend to give very 'cold' responses, which may not be appropriate in certain medical situations - They are only as good as the information/facts entered into the system - Users sometimes make the very dangerous assumption that they are infallible

An expert system is made up of a number of components:

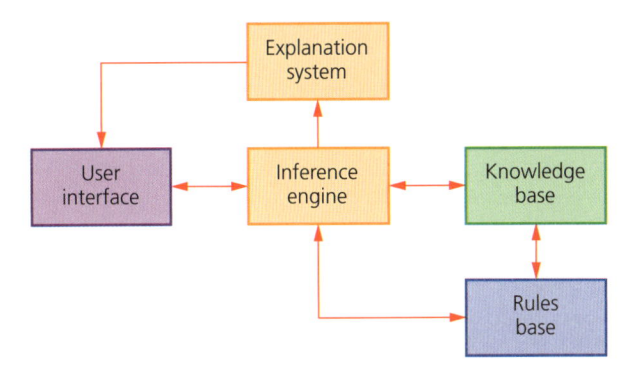

```
              ┌──────────────┐
              │ Explanation  │
              │    system    │
              └──────────────┘
                     ↑
┌──────────┐   ┌──────────┐   ┌──────────┐
│   User   │←→│ Inference │←→│ Knowledge │
│interface │   │  engine   │   │   base    │
└──────────┘   └──────────┘   └──────────┘
                   ↕                ↕
               ┌──────────┐
               │  Rules   │
               │   base   │
               └──────────┘
```

Component	Description
User interface	• This is how expert systems interact with a user • Allows interaction through dialogue boxes and command prompts • Questions are usually multi-choice or have 'yes/no' answers; questions asked are based on the answers to previous questions
Explanation system	• This informs the user of the reasoning behind the expert system's conclusions and recommendations • The expert system will supply a conclusion and any suggested action; it is important to give the percentage probability of the accuracy of its conclusions
Inference engine	• The inference engine acts like a search engine examining the knowledge base for information/data that matches the queries • Gathers information/data from the user by asking a series of questions and applying responses where necessary; each question asked is based on the responses to earlier questions • This is the problem-solving part of the expert system that makes use of inference rules in the rules base • Because the knowledge base is a collection of objects and attributes, the inference engine attempts to use information gathered from the user to find an object that matches
Knowledge base	• The knowledge base is a repository of facts and stores all the knowledge about an area of expertise obtained from various sources • It is a collection of objects (the actual item itself, such as the name of an animal) and attributes (features of the object, such as it is a mammal with four legs and lives on the land etc.)
Rules base	• A set of inference rules that are used by the inference engine to draw conclusions (the methods used closely follow human reasoning) • Follow logical thinking involving a series of 'IF' statements (e.g. IF continent = 'South America' AND language = 'Portuguese' THEN country = 'Brazil')

An expert system needs to be carefully set up using the following sequence:

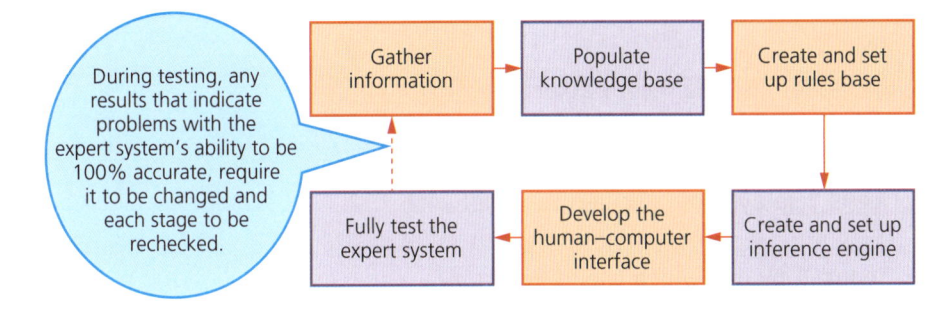

```
Gather information → Populate knowledge base → Create and set up rules base
         ↑                                                    ↓
Fully test the ← Develop the human–computer ← Create and set up
expert system      interface                    inference engine
```

During testing, any results that indicate problems with the expert system's ability to be 100% accurate, require it to be changed and each stage to be rechecked.

The following is a typical example of an expert system in a medical diagnosis:

Input screen
- First of all an interactive screen is presented to the user
- The system asks a series of questions about the patient's illness
- The user answers the questions asked (either as multiple-choice or yes/no questions)
- A series of questions are asked based on the user's responses to previous questions

Expert system
- The inference engine compares the symptoms entered with those in the knowledge base looking for matches
- The rules base is used in the matching process
- Once a match is found, the system suggests the probability of the patient's illness being identified accurately
- The expert system also suggests possible solutions and remedies to cure the patient or recommendations on what to do next
- The explanation system will give reasons for its diagnosis so that the user can determine the validity of the diagnosis or suggested treatment

Output screen
- The diagnosis can be in the form of text or it may show images of the human anatomy to indicate where the problem may be
- The user can request further information from the expert system to narrow down the possible illness and its treatment

6.9 Computers in the retail industry

REVISED

6.9.1 Retail industry

Point-of-sale terminals

Barcodes are used on many products in shops; these are read by a **barcode reader** (which uses red laser or LED to read the barcode pattern of lines). At supermarkets and other shops, POS terminals are used to read the barcodes.

A barcode is a series of light and dark lines of varying thickness. A series of numbers under the barcode is the numeric representation (allowing it to be read by a human). This number also contains a **check digit**, which is a form of **validation** to ensure the barcode was read correctly.

Barcodes are used as part of an automatic stock control system in shops:

- Each barcode is associated with a record in a stock file that contains price of item, current stock level and product description (the barcode is the primary key for the record).
- The barcode is read by a barcode reader and the record associated with this barcode is searched for in the stock file.
- Once the record is found, the information is sent back to the point-of-sale (POS) terminal and the price is displayed on a screen together with the product description.
- The stock level for the item is reduced by one which then triggers a check to see whether the stock level has now reached the reorder level.
- If the reorder level has been reached, reordering of new items is done automatically, and a flag is put on the item record to indicate a reorder has been made.

- When new items arrive, the stock level is updated and the reorder flag is removed.
- Once all items have been scanned, the total bill is calculated and the customer is given an itemised bill; payment for the basket of items is done using smart card or by electronic devices (such as a near field communication-enabled smartphone) – see below.

Electronic funds transfer at the point-of-sale terminal

When payment is made by card or electronic devices (such as a smartphone) at a POS terminal, it is known as EFTPOS. Payment can be made by:

- chip and PIN
- contactless card
- a near field communication device.

Chip and PIN card

How chip and PIN works was covered earlier, in Section 6.6.

The advantages and disadvantages of chip and PIN are shown below:

Advantages of chip and PIN	Disadvantages of chip and PIN
More secure system than magnetic stripe cards (PIN typed in must match up with PIN stored on chip)	The risk of fraud when typing in the PIN – the customer needs to be careful to ensure the PIN isn't being read by somebody else while typing it in
It's a quicker system than magnetic stripe cards and also allows for contactless payments to be made (with magnetic stripe cards, the card reader must first contact the customer's bank before any authorisation can take place)	Some countries still don't accept chip and PIN cards

Contactless cards

These were discussed in detail in Section 2.2, p.14, together with their advantages and disadvantages.

Near field communication devices

The technology behind **near field communication (NFC)** can be found later in Section 6.10. When using NFC payment at a POS terminal, the following sequence of events takes place:

- The NFC-enabled electronic device (e.g. a smartphone) is held close to the NFC reader (the terminal).
- When NFC (contactless) payment is initiated, the NFC terminal and electronic payment device pass encrypted data between each other to enable a secure payment to be made.
- When the NFC device is a smartphone, **tokenisation** is used to improve security.

Tokenisation and smartphones

Tokenisation is used when setting up a mobile wallet. The card details (after a photo of the card is taken by the smartphone) are sent by the smartphone wallet company to the bank that issued the card. The bank replaces the card details with a series of randomly generated numbers, called **tokens**, which they send back to the smartphone manufacturer who then programs the random numbers into the user's smartphone. These random numbers are then used in all transactions involving the smartphone. The numbers change for every transaction.

6.9 Computers in the retail industry

6.9.2 Internet shopping and banking

Online shopping and **internet banking** allow a customer to carry out banking and shopping using a home computing device.

There are many advantages and disadvantages to using online shopping and banking, as shown in this table:

Advantages to online shopping and banking	Disadvantages of online shopping and banking
• There is no longer a need to travel into town centres, reducing costs (money for fuel, bus fares etc.) and wastage of time; it also helps to reduce town centre congestion and pollution • Users now have access to a worldwide market and can look for products that are cheaper. This is obviously less expensive and less time-consuming than having to shop around by the more conventional methods; they will also have access to a much wider choice of goods • Elderly people and people with disabilities can now access any shop or bank without the need to leave home, which is of great benefit to them • Shopping and banking can be done at any time on any day of the week (i.e. 24/7); this is particularly helpful to people who work during the day as the shops/banks would normally be closed when they finished work • People can spend more time doing other things – going shopping at the supermarket probably took up a lot of time; by doing this online (e.g. setting up repeat items) people are now free to do more leisure activities • Many people find it less embarrassing to ask for a bank loan using the internet rather than enduring a face-to-face discussion with bank staff • There are often long queues at banks or checkouts at shops, so internet banking saves time • The shops and banks save money by not having as many staff working for them (reduced wage bill) or hiring high street premises (reduction in rental costs) – these savings are often passed on to the customer in the form of lower interest rates, cheaper goods or higher rates of interest for savers	• There is the possibility of isolation and lack of socialisation if people stay at home to do all their shopping and banking • There are possible health risks associated with online shopping or banking because of lack of exercise; if people physically go shopping then they are getting some exercise • Security issues are a major concern (e.g. hacking, stealing credit card details, etc.) as are viruses and other malware (e.g. phishing, pharming and so on) • Accidentally using fraudulent bank or shopping websites is always a risk and this is linked to security issues • It is necessary to have a computer and to pay for the internet to be able to do online shopping and banking • Unlike high street shopping, it is only possible to see a picture of the goods (which might not portray the exact colour of a dress for instance), nor can you try something on to see if it fits before buying it; you also have to wait several days for the goods to arrive and returning goods is expensive • High street shops and banks are closing because of the increase in online shopping and banking and this is leading to 'ghost towns' forming • It is easier to make errors with online banking and transfer money to the wrong account

Effects on companies due to the spread of online shopping and banking

As well as customers, companies and other organisations have also been affected by the growth of information and communication technology (ICT) and online shopping. Some of the effects are listed below:

- Companies can save costs since fewer staff need to be paid and it isn't necessary to have as many shops and banks in high streets to deal with potential customers.
- Because the internet is global, the potential customer base increases.
- There will be some increased costs because of the need to retrain staff and the need to employ more staff in despatch departments.
- There are also costs due to the setting up and maintaining of websites to enable online shopping and banking.
- Since there is very little or no customer–employee interaction, this could lead to a drop in customer loyalty which could lead to loss of customers (this could also be brought about by the lack of personal service associated with online shopping and banking).
- Robberies are less likely due to having fewer high street banks.
- Banks also need to employ fewer security staff which has a cost benefit.

6.10 Recognition systems

Recognition systems include: OMR, barcode readers, QR code readers, OCR, RFIDS and biometric recognition systems. Most of these devices were discussed in Section 2.2, page 14. The following section covers applications that use these recognition systems.

6.10.1 Optical mark recognition to read multiple-choice question papers

OMR can be used to automatically read forms marked in specific places, for example:

> The area filled in by pen or pencil is called a lozenge

A template is created to map out X–Y coordinates of each lozenge or other type of mark. The coordinates of the lozenges of the 'correct answers' are stored on this template. The OMR sheet is then placed on a reader and the position of each filled-in lozenge (or other marks) is read. The position of the filled-in lozenges are compared to the corresponding coordinates of the 'correct answers' on the template; if the coordinates match up, then the answer is marked as correct.

Advantages of OMR devices	Disadvantages of OMR devices
• It is a very fast way of inputting the results of a survey etc. – the documents are fed in automatically and there is no user input • Since there is no typing, they are more accurate than keying in the data • They are more accurate than OCR methods	• The forms need to be carefully designed to make sure the marks/shading are correctly positioned to gather accurate information • There can be problems if they have not been filled in correctly and sometimes have to be manually checked before being read – this is both time-consuming and expensive • Often only work with black pen or pencil • They are limited to the questions on the paper; it isn't possible to get expansion to answers in a questionnaire, for example

6.10.2 Optical character recognition

OCR is another method used in recognition systems. It is used in automated number plate recognition (see below) and in the cheque clearing process (see Section 6.6.2). For more on OCR refer to Section 2.2.

6.10.3 Automated number plate recognition system

Automated number plate recognition (ANPR) is used to read number plates on vehicles, for example in a car park controlling entry and exit. The sequence of events could be:

- As the car approaches the car park entrance, a sensor detects the presence of the car and sends this signal to a central computer, which then instructs a camera to capture an image of the front of the car.
- An algorithm is used to locate and isolate the number plate from the image; the brightness/contrast of the number plate is then adjusted. Each character on the number plate is segmented and using OCR software converted into a string of electronic text.
- The electronic text is then stored on a database (together with the date and time of entry) and the barrier to the car park is raised. The driver is also issued with a ticket showing time of entry.
- When the motorist returns, they insert their ticket into a payment machine and pay the amount due.

- The motorist then drives up to the exit barrier and the ANPR system again reads the number plate on the car and checks the database for the number plate and whether payment has been made.
- If everything is OK, the barrier is raised.

ANPR has a number of advantages and disadvantages:

Advantages of ANPR	Disadvantages of ANPR
- Can be used to automatically monitor average speed of vehicles over a stretch of road; this can be used in smart traffic management systems (see Section 6.2) - No need to employ car park security guards, which saves money - Much faster system than having to check a ticket at the exit; car parks can issue tickets on entry, but this ticket is simply used for payment purposes by the motorist before leaving the car park and isn't used at the exit since payment will now be linked to the number plate on the car - Can be used to automatically control the entry and exit to a car park or private roads - Can be used as a security system, preventing illegal parking and preventing unauthorised access to private car parks - Used to analyse driver behaviour (e.g. route choice and destinations) to help in transport planning - Used in inner-city congestion charging systems; it is possible to automatically charge a motorist if they enter a congestion zone, but it also allows in permitted vehicles without charge (e.g. emergency vehicles, buses and electric zero-emission vehicles)	- A lack of manned security car park surveillance could lead to vandalism (and other crimes) since nobody is checking on a regular basis; CCTV is often used, but not till 'after the event' - Invasion of privacy issues due to the recording of driver's number plates - Damaged or very dirty number plates won't be recognised by the system - Number plate cloning; the ANPR system only recognises the number plate and not the car, so it is possible for a car to be fitted with a cloned number plate thus bypassing car park security, for example

6.10.4 Radio frequency identification devices

Radio frequency identification devices (RFIDs) were covered in Section 2.2. Here we will look at four uses of RFID:

- Tracking of stock:
  - This can be the tracking of stock in a shop or livestock tracking on a farm.
  - RFID tags are made up of a microchip and antenna and can be *passive* (uses energy from the RFID reader) or *active* (has its own power source).
  - Livestock tracking is used to keep track of every animal on a farm and it also allows the farmer to keep medical data about each animal. Because of the distances involve, active tags would be used in this application.
  - Retail tracking could be used in the same way as a barcode in a shop, but could also be used in distribution centres to locate items being shipped to customers; RFID tags also allow a parcel to be tracked by a customer so they can determine when it might arrive.
- Passports
  - A microchip and antenna are now embedded into passports, using passive tags.
  - When a passport is presented to an RFID scanner, a device reads data on the passport chip (the data is encrypted).
  - Data stored on the chip includes a photo, fingerprint scan and other personal data.
- Use of RFID in vehicles
  - Can allow or deny access to vehicles in a private car park.
  - Lorries and vans can use RFID tags at weigh stations.
  - Tags can be used on toll roads to automatically raise barriers.
  - RFID tags can be used in car production to automatically track progress through the assembly process.

6 ICT applications

- Contactless credit/debit cards
  - Also refer to Sections 6.6 and 2.1.
  - Contactless cards use passive RFID tags which allow contactless payment at a checkout.

Near field communication

- NFC is a subset of RFID technology.
- NFC can be used by smartphones to make payments and it can also be used in car key fobs (when the driver approaches his vehicle, the NFC device 'talks' to the car and the doors are automatically unlocked).
- There are three distinct modes of operation with NFC:

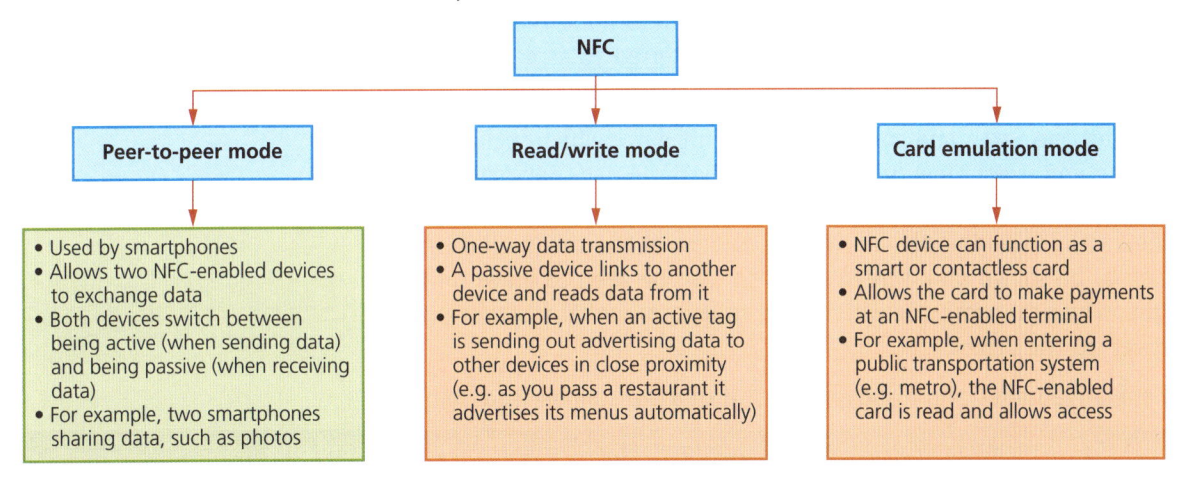

```
                              NFC
          ┌────────────────────┼────────────────────┐
  Peer-to-peer mode      Read/write mode       Card emulation mode
```

Peer-to-peer mode
- Used by smartphones
- Allows two NFC-enabled devices to exchange data
- Both devices switch between being active (when sending data) and being passive (when receiving data)
- For example, two smartphones sharing data, such as photos

Read/write mode
- One-way data transmission
- A passive device links to another device and reads data from it
- For example, when an active tag is sending out advertising data to other devices in close proximity (e.g. as you pass a restaurant it advertises its menus automatically)

Card emulation mode
- NFC device can function as a smart or contactless card
- Allows the card to make payments at an NFC-enabled terminal
- For example, when entering a public transportation system (e.g. metro), the NFC-enabled card is read and allows access

Biometric recognition systems

Biometrics used as a recognition system includes:

- face recognition
- iris and retina recognition
- fingerprint and thumbprint recognition
- hand recognition
- voice recognition.

Face recognition, retina recognition, iris recognition, and finger and thumb recognition systems will be covered in depth in Chapter 8. Hand recognition (gesture control) and voice recognition systems were covered in Chapter 1. For completeness, we will consider one additional example here, iris recognition:

- A digital camera is utilised, which uses both visible and near infrared light to take a sharp photograph of a person's iris.
- The method produces a unique pattern of a person's iris by locating and taking an image of:
  - the centre of the pupil
  - the edge of the pupil
  - the edge of the iris
  - the eyelids and eyelashes.

The system works with contact lenses and glasses and it even works with people who are blind. It is used as a method for uniquely identifying a person and, because of the speed of verification (less than five seconds), is used a security system in the following areas:

- immigration control (in some countries)
- in the UK, the TSB Bank have introduced this in some branches as a security feature.

Hodder & Stoughton Limited © David Watson and Graham Brown 2022

75

6.11 Satellite systems

REVISED

6.11.1 Satellites

Satellite systems include:

- GPS – sometimes called *satnav*
- geographic information systems
- media communication systems (satellite TV and mobile phone networks).

Global positioning systems and satellite navigation

The **Global Positioning System (GPS)** is used to determine the exact location of a car, ship or aeroplane. It is often referred to as **satellite navigation** (satnav) when used in vehicles such as cars and lorries.

Satellites orbit the Earth and constantly transmit data, which includes their position and exact time (using atomic clocks). A car's GPS/satnav reads signals from at least three satellites to determine the position of the car on the Earth. In-built maps allow the position of the car in relation to the map to be shown on a screen – the car can be seen to move on the map so the driver can work out which road to use, or verbal instructions can be given to the driver.

Some of the advantages and disadvantages of GPS are summarised below:

Advantages of GPS	Disadvantages of GPS
• The driver does not have to consult paper maps, so it is far safer • It removes errors (can warn drivers about one-way streets, street closures etc.) • The system can warn the driver about the location of speed cameras (again aiding safety) • The system can estimate the time of arrival • It is also possible to program in the fastest route, routes to avoid towns etc. • The system can also give useful information such as location of petrol stations	• If the maps are not kept up to date, they can give incorrect instructions • Unless the system is sophisticated, road closures, due to accidents or roadworks, can cause problems • Loss of satellite signals can cause problems • If an incorrect start point or end point is keyed in, the system will give incorrect information

Geographic information systems

A **geographic information system (GIS)** is a system that allows a user to map, model, query and analyse large amounts of data according to a location. GIS allows the following:

- combining information into easily understood maps
- performing complex analytical calculations and then presenting the results as a map, table or graphics
- can be used by many groups, such as geographers, scientists and engineers, to see data in different ways.

Examples of GISs use include:

- emergency services to send the closest emergency personnel to a location
- biologists and environmentalists to protect animal life and plants in endangered areas
- carrying out crime mapping in regions
- management of agricultural crops

6 ICT applications

- public health issues (used in 2020 to 2022 during the Covid-19 pandemic to show how the virus spread in certain regions, and the data was combined, for example, with different age groups and population density, to create a unique insight into its spread)
- mapping of wildfire outbreaks (used in 2019 in Australia to map the spread of fires, and combined the maps with wind speed, wind direction and so on).

Advantages of GIS	Disadvantages of GIS
<ul><li>Allows the exploring of both geographical and thematic data in a way which shows them how interconnected they are</li><li>Allows the handling and exploration of huge amounts of data (massive number crunching)</li><li>Allows data to be integrated from a wide range of very different sources (which appear at first to be totally unconnected)</li></ul>	<ul><li>The learning curve on GIS software can be very long</li><li>GIS software is very expensive</li><li>GIS requires enormous amounts of data to be input (thus increasing the chances of errors)</li><li>It is difficult to make GIS programs which are both fast and user-friendly; GIS requires very complex command language interfaces to work properly</li></ul>

Media communication systems

Satellites allow communication around the globe. Signals (converted to analogue if necessary) are beamed from a satellite dish on the ground to a satellite orbiting the Earth. Once data reaches the satellite, it is boosted (and usually the frequency is also changed) and then sent back to the Earth and is picked up by satellite dishes. This allows signals to be sent around the whole globe using a network of satellites as seen here:

Advantages of communication satellites	Disadvantages of communication satellites
<ul><li>Good global coverage (covers the majority of the Earth's surface)</li><li>Much cheaper (and faster) than laying cables around the world</li><li>Has a very high bandwidth</li><li>Relatively easy to expand the network (there are numerous companies now manufacturing satellites for various uses)</li><li>Security in satellite transmission is very good because the data is coded and the receiver requires decoding equipment to read the data</li><li>During emergency situations, it is relatively easy to move stations on the ground from one place to another; satellites can also change their orbits if necessary using the built-in boosters</li></ul>	<ul><li>There is a time delay in receipt of the signals (can be a problem in voice communications where even 0.5 seconds delay can be noticeable as the sound and video appear out of synchronisation) or there may appear to be an 'echo' on the sound</li><li>The signals received can be affected by bad weather (e.g. heavy rain or hailstones), obstructions (such as tree branches) and whether the satellite dish has been correctly orientated</li><li>Sunspot activity can affect the performance of a satellite</li><li>Satellites need to be monitored and controlled on a regular basis to ensure they remain in the correct orbit</li></ul>

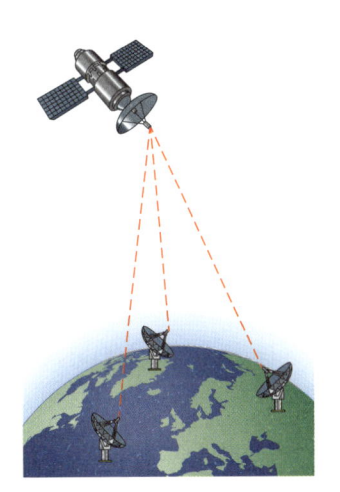

Sample question and response

Explain how an expert system could be used in the search for new mineral deposits. **[6 marks]**

> **Tips**
>
> You are asked to explain, so it is necessary to include notes on how an expert system would be used, what results you would expect and how the results would be used. Do not give generic responses; your answer should refer back to the scenario given in the question.

6.11 Satellite systems

Sample high-level answer

An interactive user screen will appear and questions about the geological profile would be asked. The user would answer these questions by typing in known geological data; the next questions from the system would take responses from previous questions into consideration. The inference engine searches the knowledge base and uses the inference rules found in the rules base to look for matches from previous geological studies. The expert system would use logic and knowledge of geological data to suggest a probability of what minerals would be expected to be found based on the data input. An explanation system would inform the users of how the expert system arrived at its conclusions and the percentage accuracy of its results. Finally maps would be output showing mineral densities in the area under study; these would be on screen and also printed out.

Sample low-level answer

A user types in the results of rock samples and the system will look for rock sample data in its knowledge base. It will look for rocks already found and see if there are any matches. If there are any matches in the knowledge base, then the user would be told how good the chances would be of finding minerals in the region. The results would be shown on screen.

Teacher's comments

The first answer is fairly comprehensive and is probably worth between 4 and 6 marks depending on how much detail is expected. The answer given does cover all three parts of the question and also refers to the scenario. It might have been a good idea to include a diagram of an expert system which could be referred to throughout the description.

The second answer shows little real understanding of expert systems. But they would gain 1 mark for the comments about input data and the idea of matching up with data on the knowledge base. Probably 2 marks would be a reasonable estimate here.

Exam-style questions for you to try

8 The managers of a company are concerned about illegal parking in their car park. Drivers are parking their cars in the private car park and then walking to the local sports match. There have been a few instances of damage to employees' cars. A decision has been made to install a number plate recognition system and barrier so they can control cars entering and leaving the car park. Anyone visiting the company will need to register their car's number plate with the receptionist prior to their visit.
  a Explain how this system could check that a car approaching the barrier had been registered with the receptionist beforehand. [4]
  b After a visitor parks their car, they have to report to the receptionist. They are then given a badge which contains an RFID tag. The chip in this tag is read to allow the visitor access to certain floors in the building. Prior to this electronic system, badges contained a barcode. Discuss the advantages and disadvantages of using RFID chips rather than barcodes on visitors' badges. [6]

c The company would like to offer visitors access to their facilities such as the restaurant, coffee shop and gift shop. Before arriving at the company, visitors are sent a QR code which they can download to their smartphone.
Describe how the visitor could use this QR code to find out more about the company. [3]

9 Use words or phrases from the following list to complete the paragraph below. The words or phrases may be used once, more than once or not at all.

- binary numbers
- biometric data
- built-in camera
- change
- debit card
- face ID
- randomly generated
- random numbers
- remains the same
- smartphone
- tokenisation
- tokens
- touch ID
- transaction
- wallet

.... is used when setting up a smartphone ....
The details from the debit card are photographed using the smartphone .... The image is changed to electronic data and sent by the smartphone.................. company to the bank that issued the debit card.
The bank replaces the .... details by a series of .... numbers, called ...., which they send back to the.................. manufacturer who then program these .... into the user's smartphone. Every time a .... now takes place, these tokens .... to improve security. [6]

10 a Eight statements about expert systems are made in the following table, but only some of the statements are correct. Put a tick (✓) next to the statements you think are correct.

Statements	Correct (✓)
They contain a knowledge base made up of attributes and objects	
They are part of the 3D printing process	
They refer to inference rules in a rules base	
They make use of near field communication technology	
Each question asked is based on the response to a previous question	
They can be used in tax and financial planning	
They make use of a tokenisation system	
They are examples of a search engine	

[4]

b Describe briefly how an expert system could be set up to identify any species of plant. [3]
c Describe how an expert system could be used to diagnose a fault in a television set. [3]
11 a Explain what is meant by near field communication. [2]
b Explain the **three** distinct modes of operation used by NFC devices. [3]

6.11 Satellite systems

12 Six statements are shown on the left and 12 computer terms are shown on the right. By drawing arrows, connect each description to the correct computer term.

Description	Term
1. A system used to read multiple-choice question papers by recognising the position of filled-in lozenges	A. Rules base
	B. Geographic information system
2. Debit card details are sent by a mobile wallet company to the bank issuing the debit card; the card details are replaced by random numbers that are then used when the smartphone is used to make transactions	C. Radio frequency identification
	D. Near field communication
3. A subset of RFID in which devices have to be in close proximity to each other to receive and send signals	E. Tokens
	F. Optical mark recognition
4. A computer system used to determine the exact location of a vehicle using a number of satellites surrounding the Earth; each satellite transmits its position and the exact time	G. Inference engine
	H. Knowledge base
5. A type of database that uses objects and attributes to store information that can be accessed by other parts of an expert system	I. Simulation
	J. Global positioning system
6. A computer system that combines maps with data; they are very complex systems used by emergency services and to monitor, for example, the spread of a disease throughout a country	K. Tokenisation
	L. Optical character recognition

[6]

7 The systems life cycle

Key objectives

The objectives of this chapter are to revise:
- analysis stage
  - methods of analysing the current system
  - identifying the inputs, outputs and processing in the current system
  - hardware and software requirements for the new system
- design stage
  - file structures, input and output formats
  - validation routines
  - use of data capture forms
  - screen and report layouts
- development and testing stage
  - test strategies and test plans
  - use of test data (including live data)
- implementation stage
  - direct changeover
  - parallel running
  - pilot running
  - phased implementation
- documentation stage
  - technical documentation
  - user documentation
- evaluation stage
  - evaluation of new solution
  - compare solution to original system.

7.1 Analysis stage

REVISED

When an organisation decides to upgrade their existing ICT system, they need to undertake systems analysis, using a **systems analyst**. The reasons for upgrading could include:

- existing computer equipment is now obsolete and no longer supported
- changes to laws requiring an overhaul of the software and hardware
- better, more efficient hardware becoming readily available
- the company needs to expand its operations.

The **system life cycle** can be summarised as follows:

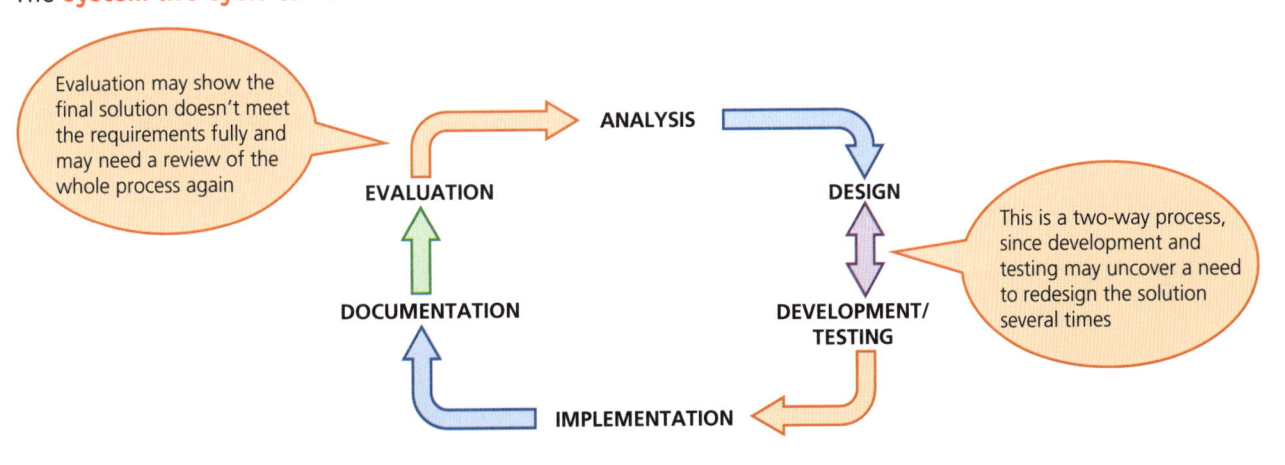

Evaluation may show the final solution doesn't meet the requirements fully and may need a review of the whole process again

ANALYSIS → DESIGN → DEVELOPMENT/TESTING → IMPLEMENTATION → DOCUMENTATION → EVALUATION → (back to ANALYSIS)

This is a two-way process, since development and testing may uncover a need to redesign the solution several times

7.1 Analysis stage

7.1.1 Analyse current system
The first stage in the process is the analysis of the current system. This involves:

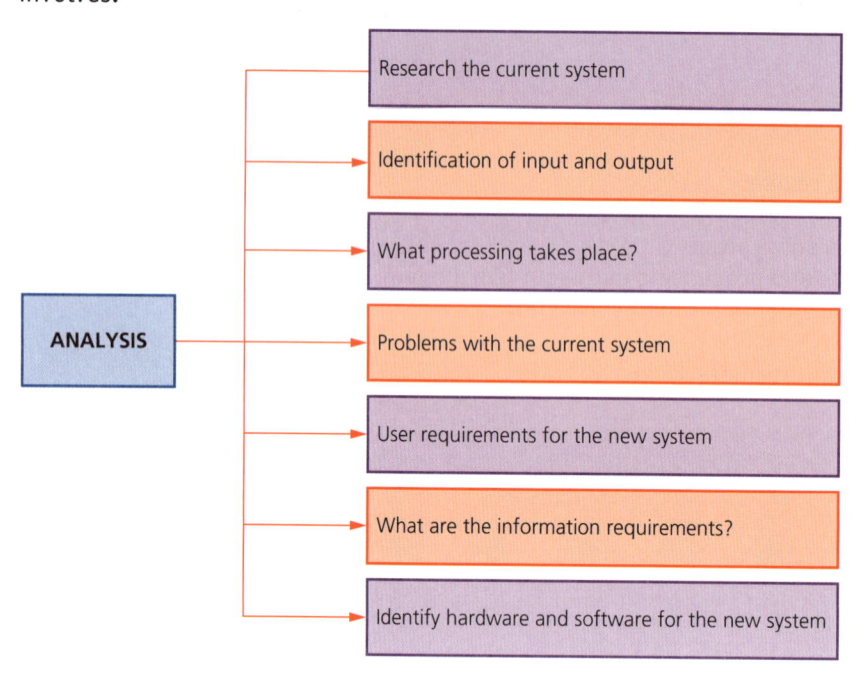

ANALYSIS
- Research the current system
- Identification of input and output
- What processing takes place?
- Problems with the current system
- User requirements for the new system
- What are the information requirements?
- Identify hardware and software for the new system

There are four methods used to research current systems: **observation**, **interviews**, **questionnaires** and examination of the current system (including any documentation). There are several advantages and disadvantages of all four systems; these are summarised in the following table:

Name of research method	Description of research method	Advantages of research method	Disadvantages of research method
Observation	Involves watching personnel using the existing system to find out exactly how it works	• The analyst obtains reliable data • The analyst gets a better overall view of the system than when using other methods • Relatively inexpensive method – only involves the analyst • All inputs and outputs of the current system are seen	• People are generally uncomfortable being watched and may work in a different way (the Hawthorne effect) • If workers perform tasks that are not standard procedures, they may not do this while being watched
Interviews	Involves a one-to-one question-and-answer session between the analyst and the employee/customer. It is a good method if the analyst wants to probe deeply into one specific aspect of the existing system	• It gives the opportunity to motivate the interviewee into giving open and honest answers to the analyst's questions • The method allows the analyst to probe for more feedback from the interviewee (questions can be extended) • It is possible to modify questions as the interview proceeds and ask questions specific to the interviewee • Analyst can watch body language and facial expressions	• It can be a time-consuming exercise • It is relatively expensive (team of interviewers and analyst needed) • The interviewee can't remain anonymous and may hide information or not be honest with their answers • Interviewee may give answers they think the interviewer wants to hear • Interviewees may not be available at times to suit the analyst

Cambridge IGCSE Information and Communication Technology Study and Revision Guide Second Edition

Name of research method	Description of research method	Advantages of research method	Disadvantages of research method
Questionnaires	Involves distributing questionnaires to the workforce, clients or system users to find out their views of the existing system and how some of the key tasks are carried out	• The questions can be answered fairly quickly • Relatively inexpensive method (only need to produce questionnaires) • Individuals can remain anonymous (may give more truthful answers) • Allows for a quick analysis of the data • Interviewees can fill in questionnaire in their own time • Allows a greater number of people to take part	• The number of returned questionnaires can be low; it's not always a popular method • The questions are rigid because they are generic; it isn't possible to ask follow-up questions • No immediate way to clarify a vague answer; it isn't possible to expand their answers • Users tend to exaggerate their responses as they are anonymous • Since anonymous, the interviewees may not take it seriously
Looking at the existing system (including paperwork)	Allows the analyst to see how the files are kept (including paper filing), look at operating instructions and training manuals, check the accounts etc. The analyst can get some idea of the scale of the problem, memory size requirements, type of input/output devices needed etc.	• Information can be obtained that isn't possible by any of the other methods • The analyst can see for themselves how the paper system operates	• It can be a very time-consuming exercise • Relatively expensive because the analyst's time is needed

7.1.2 Record and analyse information about the current system

Data flow diagrams (DFDs) are often used to analyse inputs, outputs and processing carried out by the current system under review. DFDs can uncover:

- what inputs take place in the current system
- what outputs are produced
- what processing is done and what the storage requirements are
- any known problems with the current system
- user and information requirements.

User requirements will inform clients of the systems analyst's view on what needs to be done and describes what the analyst thinks the client does with the current system. Information requirements will form a **requirements specification** (i.e. how a new system will be developed and implemented, including timescales).

7.1.3 System specification

The DFD and other information gathering processes allow the analysis team to identify and justify what hardware and software is needed to run the new system. The following needs to be considered:

- identification and justification regarding which input and output devices will be needed in the new system
- identification and justification of new software, for example:
  ○ which operating system is needed

- which applications software is needed:
  - 'off-the-shelf' (it already exists and has been fully tested and is well known, but it may not fully meet the requirements of the new system – much quicker since no development time, much cheaper and also has considerable global support)
  - bespoke (i.e. written specifically for the company; this is time-consuming and very expensive to develop but will fully meet the company requirements)
- storage requirements – type of storage and capacity.

7.2 Design stage

REVISED

After analysis, the design stage considers:

- data structures
- input formats (including data capture)
- output formats (screen layouts and reports)
- validation routines.

7.2.1 Design

File structures and data structures

File structures and data structures need to be considered. Files consist of **records** and records are made up of **fields**; each record is uniquely identified by a **primary key field**.

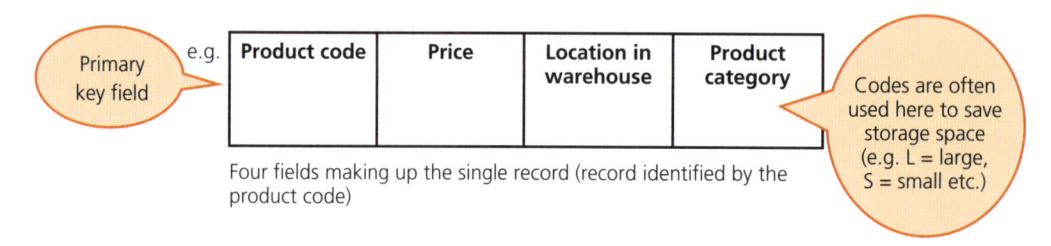

e.g. Primary key field → | Product code | Price | Location in warehouse | Product category |

Codes are often used here to save storage space (e.g. L = large, S = small etc.)

Four fields making up the single record (record identified by the product code)

Each field needs to be defined by field name, field length, data type and whether it is a primary key. Data types can be categorised as follows:

Data type	Description	Examples
Alphanumeric	This type of data can store alpha characters (letters or text) and numeric data (numbers)	A345FF or 07432011122
Character	This is just a single letter	X or d
Text	This can be a string of letters or numbers or other symbols	example_of_text_string
Boolean	This data type stores data in a Yes/No or True/False format (logical options)	Y or N
Numeric	This data type is used to store numeric data (this doesn't include telephone numbers, for example, since these have to be stored as alphanumeric); there are several different types of numeric data:	
	integer (whole numbers)	234 or – 1245
	decimal/real (non-integer values)	25.54 or – 150.22
	currency (allows inclusion of currency symbols)	$24.55 or €123.50
	date/time (allows dates and time to be stored)	14/05/2020 or 12:45

It is now possible to define the file structure completely, for example:

Field name	Field length	Data type
product_code	30	text
year_of_manufacture	4	numeric: integer
product_description	40	text
price_$	6	numeric: currency
department	1	character/text

> product_code is used as a primary key in this record.

7.2.2 Validation routines

When data is input into a computer it needs to be validated – a process where data entered is checked by the computer against a set of criteria. **Validation** does not check whether data is correct or accurate; it only checks if it is reasonable within a given set of criteria. There are a number of validation checks to consider:

> **Tip**
> See more about validation checks in Chapter 15, p.138.

Validation check	Description	Examples
Range	Checks the data input lies between an acceptable upper value and an acceptable lower value	To see if an entered temperature, which should lie in the range 10 to 50, is not <10 or >50
Type/character	Checks the data entered is of the correct type (i.e. letter or number only)	A person's name shouldn't contain numbers, but their height should be numeric only
Length	Checks the data input contains only the required number of characters	If a password contains eight characters, then an input with seven characters or nine characters should produce an error message
Format	Checks the data input is in the correct format	If the date has to be entered as dd/mm/yyyy, then the input must be in that format and cannot be, for example, 08/31/2021
Presence	Checks that data has been entered into a field and it hasn't been left empty	When using an online form, a person's telephone number may be a 'required field'; if no date is entered, this should give rise to an error message
Check digit	This is an extra digit added to a number which has been calculated from the other digits	Check digits can identify three types of error: 1 if two digits have been transposed during input; for example, 13597 instead of 13579 2 an incorrect digit has been entered; for example, 13559 instead of 13579 3 a digit has been missed out or extra digit added; for example, 1359 or 135799 instead of 13579 (In all cases, the check digit would be changed if an error had been made)

7.2.3 Input formats (data capture forms)

Data capture forms are often used to put new data into a computer system. These forms need to be designed very carefully to ensure they collect the correct information and are easy to fill in and error-free. They can be paper-based or computer-based; the following examples shows two data capture forms – the first is paper-based and the second is on-screen computer-based.

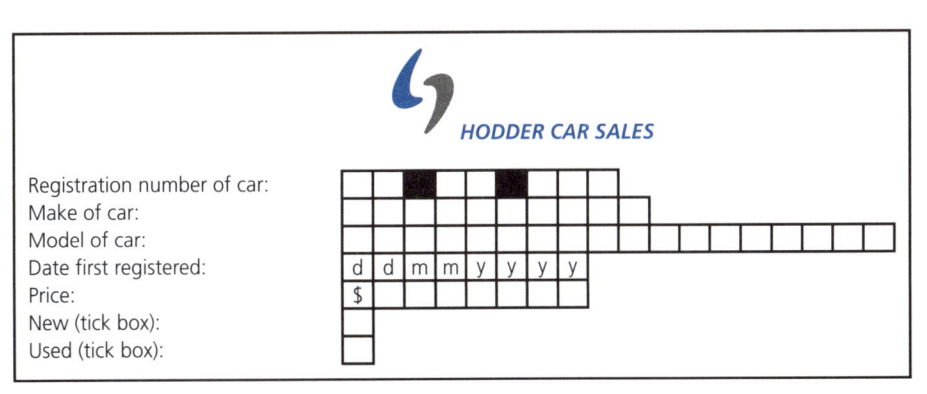

The paper-based form contains boxes to enter characters and tick boxes where possible. Using a computer's ability access considerable amounts of data, this form could be improved as follows when used as an on-screen data capture form:

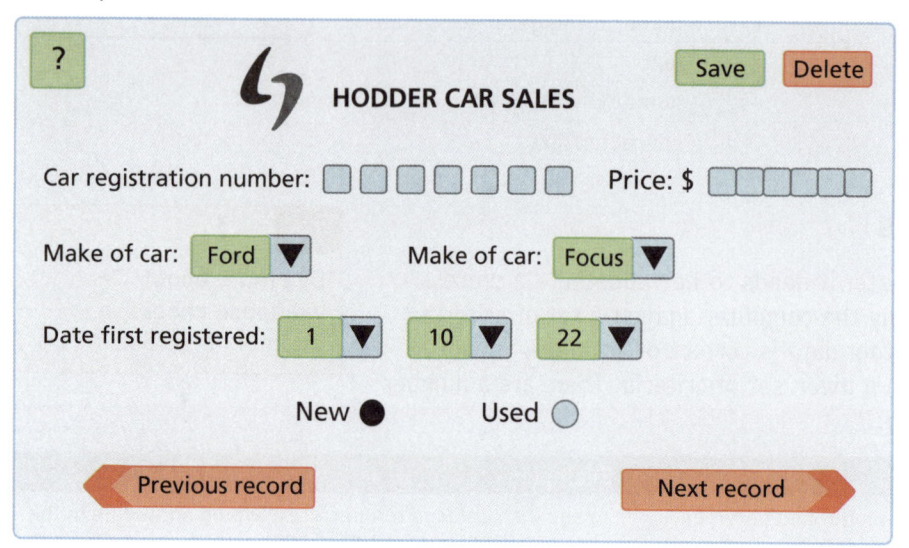

[Form image: HODDER CAR SALES data entry form with fields for Car registration number, Price, Make of car (Ford), Make of car (Focus), Date first registered (1, 10, 22), New/Used radio buttons, and Previous record / Next record navigation buttons, plus Save, Delete and Help (?) buttons.]

Note the use of drop-down boxes where there are limited possibilities (e.g. car make and model and dates) and the use of the use of radio buttons (e.g. for new/used car). Each field will have some validation check associated with it so data can be checked as it is entered, for example presence checks to make sure data has been entered, type checks to ensure numeric data is used in the price field and so on – obviously drop-down boxes only need a presence check. Also notice the navigation buttons and help button.

7.2.4 Output formats – screen layouts and report layouts

The design of screen or paper outputs showing the results of processing need to:

- be correctly sized to show all output fields
- give clear instructions
- utilise the whole screen or page
- use clear fonts and colours.

> **Tip**
> Report layout controls the content and format of a printed or on-screen report (e.g. text styles, margins, paragraph alignment, images, use of columns and so on).

7.3 Development and testing stage

REVISED

7.3.1 Testing

Testing of the final system is very important to ensure it operates in a stable manner for many years. It is necessary to test the final file structures to ensure they are robust, and all validation and verification methods used must be fully tested to ensure they work and trap data entry errors. Testing needs to ensure the input interfaces work and are easy to use (the input hardware needs to be taken into consideration at this stage).

Test designs

Since test designs cover how a system works, it is necessary to ensure the following aspects can be achieved:

- testing the data structures
- testing the file structures
- testing the input methods
- testing the output formats
- testing the validation rules.

The following table describes the different test designs.

Test design	Description
Data structures	Tests that all data is in a correct format or has been stored in the correct way (e.g. whether tables hold data correctly)
File structures	Tests that the file structures function correctly (i.e. data is stored in the correct format and can be correctly retrieved when required)
Input formats	Tests that all data can be entered into the system correctly (e.g. if a date is to be entered, the input format permits the date to be entered correctly)
Output formats	Tests that screen outputs and reports are all in the correct format (e.g. the output results are clear, complete and correctly match the input data)
Validation routines	Determines what data is needed to test to see if all the validation rules work (e.g. the system correctly rejects unreasonable data being input)

Test strategies

Test strategies need to be carefully considered:

- Many programs/software are designed in **modular** form (i.e. designed and tested in smaller parts, called modules).
- Each separate module needs to be fully tested and then tested again once all the modules are joined together.
- The results of testing may indicate a need to change file structures, input interface, validation routines and verification routines and then fully test everything again.

Test plans

Once a test strategy has been decided, it then becomes necessary to formulate a test plan per module; the plan should include:

- all the tests that need to be carried out
- what data needs to be used
- type of test data (normal, extreme and abnormal)
- use of live data
- the expected outcomes
- a check on whether the outcomes match the expected results.

Normal, extreme, abnormal and live data

All test data falls into four categories:

- **Normal**: this is data that is acceptable/valid and has an expected (known) outcome; for example, the month of a year can be **any** whole number in the range 1 to 12.

- **Extreme**: this is data at the **limits** of acceptability/validity; for example, the month can be either of the two end values, that is 1 *or* 12.
- **Abnormal**: this is data **outside the limits** of acceptability/validity and should be rejected or cause an error message; for example, none of the following values are allowed as inputs for the month:
  - any value <1 (e.g. 0, −1, −15 etc.)
  - any value >12 (e.g. 32, 45 etc.)
  - letters or other non-numeric data (e.g. July etc.)
  - non-integer values (e.g. 3.5, 10.75 etc.).
- **Live**: after the system has been fully tested, it is tested with live data, with known outcomes. Live data refers to actual real-life data used in the old system. This data has actual known outcomes so it is used in the new system to ensure it gives the same results as the system it is replacing. This could result in a need to rewrite the validation and verification routines, for example.

7.4 Implementation stage

REVISED

7.4.1 System implementation

Once a system is fully tested and is working correctly, it needs to be implemented at the same time as full training of staff. Implementation occurs in two stages:

- transfer of data from the existing system to the new system
- changeover fully to the new system.

Changeover

Changeover can occur in one of four ways. These are summarised in the following table, together with the relative advantages and disadvantages of all four methods. When deciding the best method of changeover, all the factors in the following table need to be considered:

Implementation method	Design of implementation method	Advantages and disadvantages of the implementation method
Direct changeover	The old system is stopped overnight; the new system is introduced immediately	• can be disastrous if the new system fails because the old system is no longer available • benefits are immediate • reduced costs (only one system is used; there is no need to pay for two sets of staff) • malfunction less likely because the new system will have been fully tested
Parallel running	The old and new systems are run side by side for a time before the new system takes over altogether	• if the new system fails, the old system is still available as a backup • staff could be gradually trained • more expensive than direct changeover because extra staff are needed to run both systems together • more time-consuming than direct changeover because data needs to be entered into two systems
Pilot running	The new system is introduced into one branch/office of the company and its performance is assessed before being introduced elsewhere in the company	• if the new system fails, only one part is affected; the remainder is unaffected • staff could be trained in one area only – much faster and less costly than parallel running • also less costly than parallel running because only one part of the system is being used in the pilot

Implementation method	Design of implementation method	Advantages and disadvantages of the implementation method
Phased implementation	Only part of the new system is introduced and only when it is proven that it works satisfactorily is the next part introduced, and so on, until the old system is fully replaced	• if the latest part fails, it is only necessary to go back in the system to the point of failure – failure isn't disastrous • more expensive than direct changeover because it is necessary to evaluate each part before moving to the next part • very time-consuming – each part needs to be fully evaluated before making any further changes to the system • possible to ensure the system works properly before expanding

7.5 Documentation stage

REVISED

A large amount of documentation needs to accompany any new system. The documentation must consider the people who may need to modify or develop the system in the future (**technical documentation**) and the enduser (**user documentation**).

Both types of documentation contain the following:

- purpose of the system/software and any limitations
- input formats/screen layouts
- output formats/print layouts
- hardware and software requirements
- sample runs (with results from test data)
- meaning of any error messages.

The following table shows the different features in technical and user documentation:

Technical documentation	User documentation
• Program listing/coding and file structures • Programming language used • Program flowcharts/algorithms • System flowcharts • Minimum memory requirements • Known 'bugs' in the system • List of variables used (and their meaning/description) • Validation rules	• How to load/install/run the software • How to save files • How to do a search • How to sort data • How to do printouts • How to add, delete or amend records • Troubleshooting guide/help lines/frequently asked questions (FAQs) • How to log in/log out • Tutorials and glossary of terms

7.6 Evaluation stage

REVISED

Once a system is up and running, it needs to be fully evaluated and any necessary maintenance carried out. Evaluation involves:

- comparing the final solution with the task requirements
- identifying any limitations of the system
- identifying any improvements that need to be made to the system
- evaluating responses from user feedback through interviews and questionnaires
- observing the system to see if it operates better than the old system.

The results of the evaluation could lead to the updating of the hardware and software. This could be due to feedback from end users, better hardware becoming available, company changes or changed to legislation requiring software updates.

7.6 Evaluation stage

Sample questions and responses

> REVISED

a) Describe what is meant by the evaluation stage in the systems life cycle. **[3 marks]**
b) Give **two** reasons why hardware may need to be updated ten years after it was first introduced to run a company. **[2 marks]**
c) Give **two** reasons why software may need to be updated by a company after a number of years in use. **[2 marks]**

Tips

Part (a) is a 'describe' question, which means it needs an explanation of what is meant by evaluation, giving examples where possible. Parts (b) and (c) only require a short sentence for each reason.

Sample high-level answer

a) When a system is finally implemented (and has completely replaced the old system), it becomes necessary to evaluate how well it has worked. It is imperative that new systems meet the original task specification and only minor 'teething problems' occur. Evaluation involves checking the new system for inherent limitations, how it compares to the old system and opinions of end users. Getting feedback could be from interviews or from questionnaires. Evaluation of all this information could lead to modifications to hardware and software.

b) Two reasons could be:
- new hardware becomes available or old hardware no longer supported
- the company may change how it operates and new input/output devices or storage may be needed.

c) Two reasons could be:
- negative feedback from end users
- changes in legislation (e.g. tax).

Sample low-level answer

a) Evaluation means to check how well something works. Is it better than the old system? Was it worth spending all that money? Both managers and systems analyst need to look at the new system in operation and see how well it is working.

b) Two reasons could be: new or upgraded hardware comes on the market and feedback from workers indicating the hardware needs improving.

c) Two reasons could be: feedback from workers indicating the software needs improving and the company changes how it operates.

Teacher's comments

The first answer has given a good description of the evaluation stage and has given some ways evaluation can be done and what results from the evaluation. Parts (b) and (c) give four distinct reasons why hardware and software may need changing.

The second answer would gain one mark for the first two sentences in part (a). But in the rest of the answer they didn't say how the managers or systems analyst could find out how well or how badly the new system worked – so no additional marks would be awarded. In parts (b) and (c), the candidate has given the same basic answer twice in reference to feedback; this could only be given credit once. The first reason in part (b) is also a valid point for a second mark; but the second reason in part (c) is just too vague since they haven't really said what might change. Overall, three marks.

7 The systems life cycle

Exam-style questions for you to try

1. Some scientists are gathering daily temperatures at a weather station in Greece as part of their climate change studies. The data is entered manually using a keyboard. The scientists need to check that the software processing their data is working correctly. Part of the task is to ensure that the validation checks are working correctly.
   a. Explain what is meant by:
      i. normal data
      ii. extreme data
      iii. abnormal data. [3]
   b. Give suitable examples of each type of data described in part (a), with reference to the scenario described in the question stem. [3]

2. In the following table, six data entry scenarios are given. By ticking (✓) the appropriate column, indicate the best method of validation to check the data entered in each scenario. More than one validation method may work for each scenario.

Input scenario	Length check	Presence check	Range check	Format check	Type check
Input a post code/zip code, such as LA21 4NN, in the correct layout					
Entering a number that must be greater than 0, but not greater than 100					
In an online form, a mandatory field, email address, must not be left empty					
Check that a telephone number must contain exactly 11 characters					
Input data that can only be numeric and no other characters are permitted					
A date must be entered as DDMMYY, for example 11 10 23 or 3 6 21					

[6]

3. a. Put the following stages of the systems life cycle in their correct order:
      Analysis   Design   Development and testing   Documentation   Evaluation   Implementation [2]
   b. A systems analyst can research the current system using interviews, questionnaires and observation. For **each** method, give **one** advantage and **one** disadvantage. [6]
   c. An airport is replacing its old air traffic control system with a new state-of-the-art system. Which method of implementation of the new system would you recommend? Explain your answer including reasons why you chose your implementation method and ruled out the other two. [3]

4. A database is being designed to store information about used mobile phones sold by a company. The following information about each phone needs to be stored:
   - date phone refurbished (dd/mm/yyyy)

- refurbished price ($)
- is the phone unused or used
- type of phone (Apple, Samsung, Nokia or Motorola)
- condition (excellent, good or poor)
- brief description of the phone.

Design an on-screen data capture form to allow all of the mobile phone information to be easily input. The database has been set up with the appropriate data structure for each field. No field can be left blank. In your design consider ease of use and how the user could move between mobile phone records as required. **[4]**

5 In the table below, by using a tick (✓) indicate whether each component is found in user documentation only, in technical documentation only or in both types of documentation.

Description of component	Technical documentation (✓)	User documentation (✓)	In both types of documentation (✓)
How to save files on the system			
The meaning of error messages			
Programming language used			
How to do a printout			
List of variables used			
Software requirements			
Screen and report layouts			
FAQs			
Known limitations of the system			
Minimum memory requirements			

[5]

6 Which five computer terms are being described below?

Statement	Computer term
A type of online validation check to make sure a mandatory field hasn't been left blank	
Check that data entered is reasonable and meets the given criteria	
Data with known outcomes used in a previous system; used to check if a new system works in the real world	
Information supplied that includes, for example, program coding, flowcharts, limitations of a system, test results and a list of variables used in the coding	
Method of researching a current system that has the drawback known as the Hawthorne effect (i.e. where people behave differently when being watched)	

[5]

8 Safety and security

Key objectives

The objectives of this chapter are to revise:
- physical safety issues
- e-safety issues:
  - data protection acts
  - personal and sensitive data
  - e-safety when using the internet
- data security:
  - threats to data
  - protection of data.

8.1 Physical safety

REVISED

Physical safety is different to health risks (see Chapter 5). Health safety is how to stop people becoming ill, or being affected by daily contact with computers, while physical safety is concerned with the dangers that could lead to serious injuries or even loss of life. The following table summarises some of these physical safety risks:

Safety risk	Cause of safety risk	Prevention measures
Electrocution	<ul><li>Spilling liquids/drinks on electric equipment</li><li>Exposed wires/damaged insulation</li><li>Unsafe electrical equipment</li><li>Unsafe electrics (e.g. wall sockets) in the office</li></ul>	<ul><li>No drinks in the computer room</li><li>Check all wires regularly and renew wires if there is any sign of damaged insulation</li><li>Ensure all equipment is checked by a qualified electrician regularly</li><li>Use RCBs (residual current breakers) to prevent electrocution</li></ul>
Fire hazard	<ul><li>Overloaded wall sockets (several items plugged into one wall socket)</li><li>Overheating of computer equipment (due to poor heat dissipation)</li><li>Exposed wires causing a short circuit</li></ul>	<ul><li>Increase the number of wall sockets and do not use too many extension blocks</li><li>Do not cover the cooling vents on computer equipment</li><li>Clean out dust accumulation in computers to prevent overheating</li><li>Fully test all equipment regularly</li><li>Ensure the room has good ventilation</li><li>Use low-voltage equipment wherever possible</li><li>Have a number of fully tested carbon dioxide/dry powder fire extinguishers</li></ul>
Tripping hazard	<ul><li>Trailing wires on the floor</li><li>Damaged carpets and other flooring</li></ul>	<ul><li>Use cable ducts to make the wires safe</li><li>Cover exposed wires and hide wires under desks away from general thoroughfare</li><li>Use wireless connectivity wherever possible – no need for trailing cables</li></ul>
Personal injury	<ul><li>Heavy equipment unstable or falling from desks</li><li>Desks collapsing under weight/desks not designed to take the weight</li></ul>	<ul><li>Use desks strong enough to take the weight of the computer equipment</li><li>Use large desks and tables so that hardware is not too close to the edge where it could fall off</li></ul>

8.2 e-Safety

REVISED

8.2.1 Data protection

Most countries have a **data protection act (DPA)** that is designed to protect people's data from being sold or vulnerable to cyberattacks. While these acts are different in each country, they all have the same common principles:

1 Data must be fairly and lawfully processed.
2 Data can only be processed for the stated purpose.
3 Data must be adequate, relevant and not excessive.
4 Data must be accurate.
5 Data must not be kept longer than necessary.
6 Data must be processed in accordance with the data subject's rights.
7 Data must be kept secure.
8 Data must not be transferred to another country unless they also have adequate protection.

There are also guidelines to stop data being obtained unlawfully:

- do not leave printed data lying around on a desk
- always lock filing cabinets
- log off from a computer when it is not attended
- always use passwords and user IDs that are difficult to crack and change them regularly.

8.2.2 Personal and sensitive data

Personal data refers to data that can be used to identify a person directly from the data itself or in conjunction with other data. The following diagram lists data items regarded as being personal:

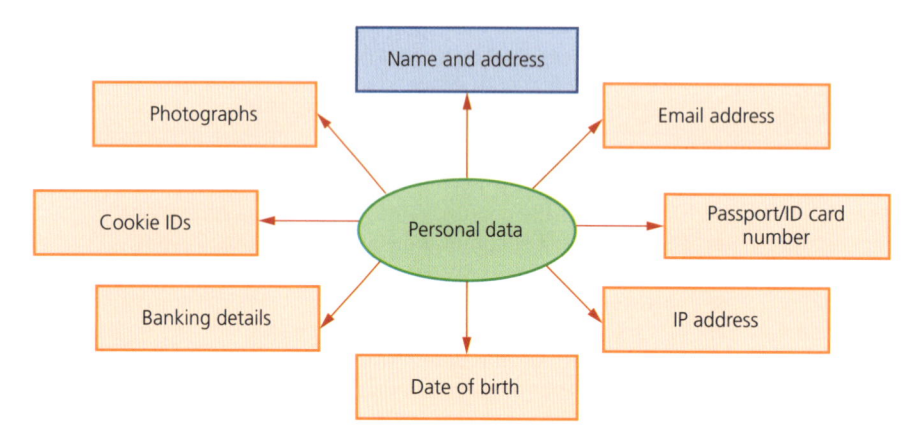

Personal data:
- Name and address
- Photographs
- Email address
- Cookie IDs
- Passport/ID card number
- Banking details
- IP address
- Date of birth

> **Tip**
>
> Personal and sensitive data are kept safe by companies adhering to a DPA in the countries where they operate. Such data should not be allowed outside the company and the DPA prevents misuse and appropriation of data by using passwords/user IDs and anti-spyware software.

Some personal data is extremely sensitive and disclosure could lead to personal harm (e.g. blackmail or refusal to give somebody a job). Extra care needs to be taken of sensitive personal data.

8 Safety and security

The following diagram lists data items regarded as being sensitive data:

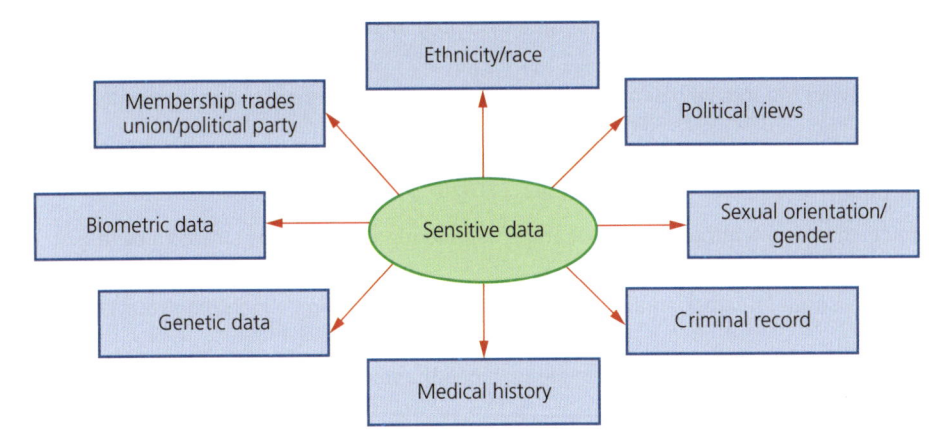

```
                    Ethnicity/race
Membership trades
union/political party              Political views

Biometric data    Sensitive data   Sexual orientation/
                                   gender

Genetic data                       Criminal record

                   Medical history
```

8.2.3 e-Safety

e-Safety refers to benefits, risks and responsibilities when using ICT, for example when using the internet, sending and receiving emails and messages, using social media or being involved in online gaming.

The following table summarises some e-safety advice when using ICT for different tasks.

Tasks	Advice when using task
Using the internet	Only use websites that are safe, trusted and recommended by teachers or parents
	Only use websites that offer secure, encrypted connections
	Always use the highest level of security when using search engines and only use search engines that allow access to age-appropriate websites
	Be very careful when downloading information from the internet
	Always log out at the end of a session
	When using a browser, ensure https appears in the browser address and make sure that cookies are deleted at the end of the website session
Sending/ receiving emails and messages	Avoid using 'cc' or 'to' boxes when sending multiple emails or messages (see Chapter 10)
	Only open emails and attachments from known sources
	Only reply to an email if you know the person who sent it (or the organisation, if you are 100% certain it is genuine)
	Ensure your Internet Service Provider has effective email filters
	Check email addresses or website addresses refer to a genuine company
	Remember the unsubscribe link itself may be unsecure
	Avoid clicking on hyperlinks in emails – they could be a phishing scam
	Manually type in email addresses and website addresses
	Never send somebody you do not know a photograph of yourself
	Never send any information to anyone you do not know that could identify you when replying to an email or message
Using social media	Do not publicly post or give out password information to people you do not know
	Do not send photos to people you don't know
	Do not post photos with you wearing a school uniform
	Always make sure privacy settings are 'on' when posting photos
	None of the photos posted should link you to your address or school/college or place of work
	Do not forward messages/emails that use inappropriate language – block or report anybody who acts suspiciously or uses inappropriate language
	Be careful in chat rooms or when sending instant messages (always use public chat rooms, use a nickname and never agree to meet somebody from social media on your own)

8.3 Security of data

Tasks	Advice when using task
Using online gaming	There is an inherent danger from predators (people who prey on others' weaknesses) when online gaming
	Beware of cyberbullying (people who send out messages of an intimidating and threatening nature)
	Be careful when using webcams (use a neutral background setting on your computer rather than your real background)
	Be careful of voice-masking technology – this can be used to mask somebody's real voice (e.g. it makes them sound younger and so on)
	Do not reveal any personal information about you or others while gaming – including your real name
	Beware of cyberattacks, such as viruses or phishing, since these can be sent via online gaming links
	Beware of violence in the game itself that can lead to violent behaviour in reality; remember it's just a game and not real life

8.3 Security of data

REVISED

8.3.1 Data threats

There are a number of security risks to data held on a computer (or other devices with an internet connection) or to data being transferred around a network. The risks are shown in this table:

Security risk	Description of security risk	Possible effect of security risk	Ways of removing or mitigating the risk
Hacking	The act of gaining illegal/unauthorised access to a computer system	• Can lead to ID theft or misuse of personal data • Data can be deleted, changed or corrupted	• Use firewalls • Use strong passwords • Make use of anti-hacking software • Use of IDs as well as passwords
Phishing	Creator sends legitimate-looking emails to a user. As soon as the recipient clicks on a link in the email, the user's browser is redirected to a fake website where the cybercriminal can gain personal data	• Email creator can gain personal data, such as bank account numbers • Can lead to online fraud or identity theft	• Many Internet Service Providers and browsers can filter out potential phishing scams • Users should be cautious when opening emails and attachments • Don't click on any attachment that ends in: .exe, .bat, .php etc.
Smishing	Short for 'SMS phishing'. Uses the SMS system on mobile phones to send out fake text messages (e.g. 'We were unable to deliver your parcel today. Please pay $4.99 for redelivery.')	• User may click on a uniform resource locator in the fake message or call a number sent in the message • User could then be tricked into revealing personal information • More dangerous than phishing since most people think mobile phones don't have the same level of security threats as computers	• Users need to be careful when opening any links in an instant message or calling numbers embedded in the message

8 Safety and security

Security risk	Description of security risk	Possible effect of security risk	Ways of removing or mitigating the risk
Vishing	'Voicemail phishing'; a form of phishing where the cybercriminal uses a voicemail message to trick the user into calling a number (e.g. pretending to be the anti-fraud department at a bank)	• Once the user calls the number, they will be tricked into supplying private details (e.g. pretending to be from the bank and tricking customers to move money to another account)	• Never call any number in a voicemail message unless you know who left it and then delete the message
Pharming	Malicious code installed on a user's computer or on a web server. The code redirects a user's browser to a fake website without the user's knowledge (the user takes no action to initiate the scam, unlike phishing)	• Creator of the malicious code can gain personal data such as credit/debit card details when the user is redirected to the fake website • Pharming can lead to fraud or identity theft	• Some anti-spyware can identify pharming scams and warn users or delete the spyware • User should be alert and look out for clues that they have been redirected • User should look out for https and/or the green padlock in the browser address window

Viruses and malware

Malware is one of the biggest risks to the integrity and security of data. The most common examples are shown in the table below:

Malware risk	Description of malware risk and ways of mitigating the risk
Viruses	• Programs that can copy themselves with the intention of deleting or corrupting files/data on a computer • Often cause a computer to malfunction (e.g. crash or become unresponsive) • Need an active host program on the target computer • The risk can be reduced by using antivirus software, which must be regularly updated • Do not to open/click on links in emails unless you're 100% certain they are genuine emails
Worms	• A type of stand-alone virus that can also replicate and does not need an active host program to be opened to cause damage – they remain inside applications, which allows them to spread throughout a network without any user action • They replicate without targeting any specific files • Worms arrive as a message attachment and only one user on a network needs to open the worm-infested email to infect the whole network • They can be located and removed using antivirus software
Trojan horse	• A malicious program disguised as legitimate-looking software (e.g. a virus checker) but contains embedded malicious coding; it replaces all or part of the legitimate software with the intent of damaging a computer system • Requires some action by the end user; it often generates as pop-up messages informing the user that their computer has been infected with a virus and that they need to take immediate remedial action (such as downloading the fake antivirus software) • Once installed on a user's computer, Trojan horses will give the cybercriminal access to personal information on the computer; very often spyware and ransomware are installed on a computer via a Trojan horse • As they rely on user activity, firewalls and other security systems are often useless since the user has effectively overruled them by initiating the download

8.3 Security of data

Malware risk	Description of malware risk and ways of mitigating the risk
Keylogging	- A form of spyware that gathers information by monitoring a user's keyboard activity - The keystrokes are stored in a small file that is automatically emailed back to the cybercriminal responsible for the spyware - They are primarily designed to monitor and capture web browsing activity - Keyloggers can be detected and removed by antivirus software - Banks, for example, try to overcome this problem by using only parts of a password and changing the required characters every time a user logs on (thus the cybercriminal never gets the whole password); sometimes drop-down boxes are used to avoid keyboard activity – but some spyware now carry out screen recording that picks up screen images and sends them back to the cybercriminal
Adware	- Malware that can flood an end user's computer with unwanted adverts - They highlight weaknesses in a user's security and can be hard to remove since most anti-malware software doesn't recognise adware as harmful - However, although they may be nothing more than a big nuisance, they can hijack a browser and create their own default internet searches
Ransomware	- Programs that encrypt data on a user's computer - Cybercriminals then request a sum of money to send the user the decryption key to unlock their data - When ransomware is executed, it encrypts the files immediately or waits to determine how much the ransomware victim can afford - They can be mitigated against by avoiding phishing emails - It is almost impossible to reverse the damage done if the ransom isn't paid; the best solution is to keep regular backups of data thus avoiding the need to pay a ransom to decrypt affected data

Card fraud

Card fraud is the illegal use of credit/debit cards. It can be initiated by shoulder surfing, card cloning or keylogging software:

Card fraud risk	Description of fraud
Shoulder surfing	- A form of data theft where criminals steal personal information from a victim while they are using an ATM or using a hand-held POS or paying by smartphone - Shoulder surfing is done by somebody watching the user entering their pin, listening to card details being given over the phone or using digital cameras placed strategically to gather information
Card cloning	- Copying the data on the magnetic stripe of a credit/debit card, using a skimmer - Smart cards that use a microchip were introduced to combat card cloning; however, using a shimmer allows the microchip to be read as well as the magnetic stripe - Although the chip itself can't be cloned, its contents can be read; the data from the chip and magnetic stripe are written to a magnetic stripe on a fake card – this allows online purchases to be made with the fake card
Keylogging	- Keylogging software can detect keyboard strokes and send back data, such as card number and security code, to the cybercriminal (see earlier notes on keylogging software)

8.3.2 Protection of data

Authentication is used to verify that data comes from a trusted source (i.e. to prove the identity of the data source). Together with **encryption**, this makes data very secure when transferred across the internet. There are a number of authentication techniques to restrict access to authorised personnel.

8 Safety and security

The most common ways to protect data and to provide secure access to areas include:

- biometrics
- digital certificates
- Secure Sockets Layer
- encryption
- firewalls
- two-factor authentication
- user ID and password.

Biometrics

Biometrics depends on certain unique characteristics of humans. The following table summarises biometric authentication techniques:

Biometric technique	Comments	Benefits	Drawbacks
Fingerprint scans	• Fingerprints are unique unlike, for example, magnetic cards, and can't be cloned • This makes it impossible to sign in as somebody else	• Very high accuracy • One of the most developed biometric techniques • Very easy to use • Relatively small storage requirements for the biometric data created	• For some people it is very intrusive, since it is still related to criminal identification • Scans can make mistakes if the skin is dirty or damaged (e.g. cuts to the finger)
Signature recognition	• An example of behavioural biometrics used to identify a person • The signature is read by an optical scanner or camera or in real time when signing your name on a tablet that reads the pressure, slant of letters, and so on to identify the signee	• Non-intrusive • Requires very little time to verify (about five seconds) • Relatively low-cost technology	• If individuals do not sign their names in a consistent manner, there may be problems with signature verification • High error rate of 1 in 50
Retina scans	• Maps the unique pattern of a person's retina using low power infrared light • The technique is used in high-level government and military establishments	• Very high accuracy • There is no known way to replicate a person's retina pattern	• It is very intrusive • It can be relatively slow to verify retina scan with stored scans • Very expensive to install and set up
Iris recognition	• The iris is illuminated with infrared light which picks up the unique patterns on a person's iris (picks out furrows, rings, striations and so on)	• Very high accuracy • Verification time is generally less than 5 seconds	• Very intrusive • Uses a lot of memory for the data to be stored • Very expensive to install and set up
Face recognition	• Uses features of the face, such as distance between the eyes, width of the nose, length of jaw line, shape of eyebrows and so on	• Non-intrusive method • Relatively inexpensive technology	• Affected by changes in lighting, the person's hair, their age and if the person is wearing spectacles

Hodder & Stoughton Limited © David Watson and Graham Brown 2022

8.3 Security of data

Biometric technique	Comments	Benefits	Drawbacks
Voice recognition	• Looks at the wave pattern of a person's voice; this is unique to each person • Requires the user to say a keyword into a microphone and the voice pattern is matched to voice patterns stored on a database – if a match is found, entry is allowed	• Non-intrusive method • Verification takes less than 5 seconds • Relatively inexpensive technology	• A person's voice can be easily recorded and used for unauthorised access • Low accuracy • An illness, such as a cold, can change a person's voice, making absolute identification difficult or impossible

Digital certificates

A **digital certificate** is a pair of files stored on a user's computer – these are used to ensure the security of data sent over the internet. Each pair of files is made up of a public key (known to everyone) and a private key (known to a single computer user only). Digital certificates essentially confirm the ID of a web server.

Digital certificates are used when sending an email. When the message is received, the recipient can verify it comes from a known/trusted source by viewing the public key information, which is usually part of the attachment. A digital certificate has six parts:

- the sender's email address
- the name of the digital certificate owner
- a serial number
- expiry date (the date range during which the certificate is valid)
- public key (which is used for encrypting the messages and for digital signatures)
- digital signature of certificate authority (CAs) – an example of this is VeriSign.

Secure Sockets Layer

Secure Sockets Layer (SSL) is a protocol that allows data to be sent and received securely over the internet. When a user logs onto a website, SSL encrypts the data using a public key.

SSL certificates are small data files that digitally bind an encryption key to an organisation's details. A user knows if SSL is being applied when they see https in the browser address bar or a small green padlock: 🔒
The following diagram shows what happens when a user wants to access a secure website and receive and send data to it:

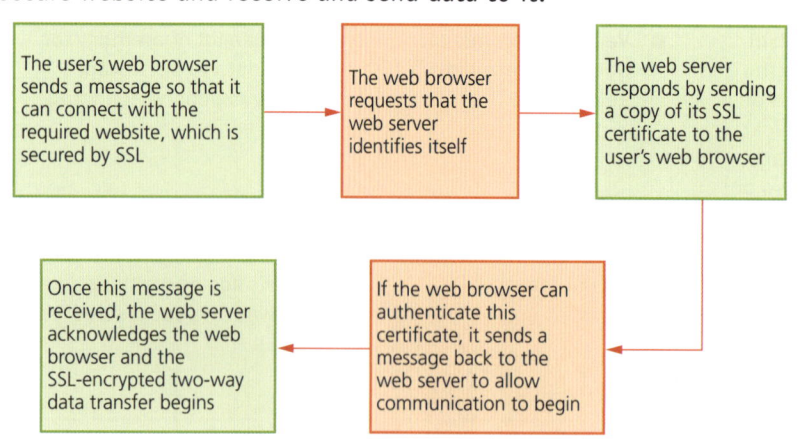

```
The user's web browser        The web browser           The web server
sends a message so that it    requests that the         responds by sending
can connect with the      →   web server            →   a copy of its SSL
required website, which is    identifies itself         certificate to the
secured by SSL                                          user's web browser
                                                              ↓
Once this message is          If the web browser can
received, the web server      authenticate this
acknowledges the web      ←   certificate, it sends a
browser and the               message back to the
SSL-encrypted two-way         web server to allow
data transfer begins          communication to begin
```

100 Cambridge IGCSE Information and Communication Technology Study and Revision Guide Second Edition

8 Safety and security

SSL is used in the following areas:

- online banking and all online financial transactions
- online shopping/commerce
- when sending software out to a restricted list of users
- sending and receiving emails
- using cloud storage facilities
- intranets and extranets (as well as the internet)
- VoIP when carrying out video chatting and/or audio chatting over the internet
- instant messaging
- when making use of a social networking site.

Encryption

Encryption is used to protect data from being read if intercepted by a third party or hacked. It uses a secret key that has the capability of altering characters in a message, making it unreadable without this secret key to decrypt it again. The secret key is called an **encryption key**. To decrypt (decipher) the message a **decryption key** is used.

When a message undergoes encryption, it is then known as **cypher script** (or cypher text) and the original message is known as **plain text**. The following diagram shows how these two are linked together.

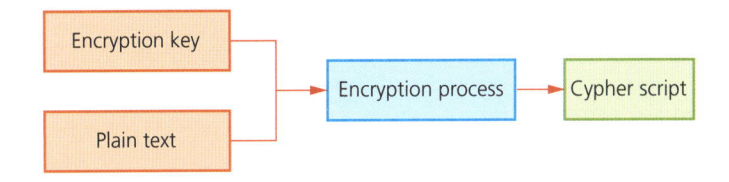

```
Encryption key ┐
               ├─→ Encryption process ─→ Cypher script
Plain text     ┘
```

Here is an example of the encryption and decryption process:

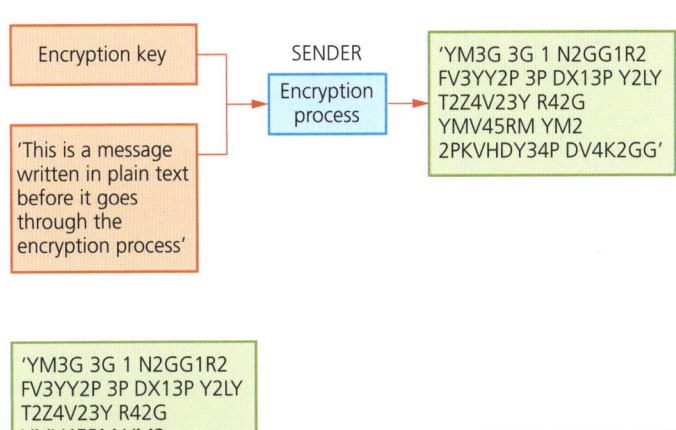

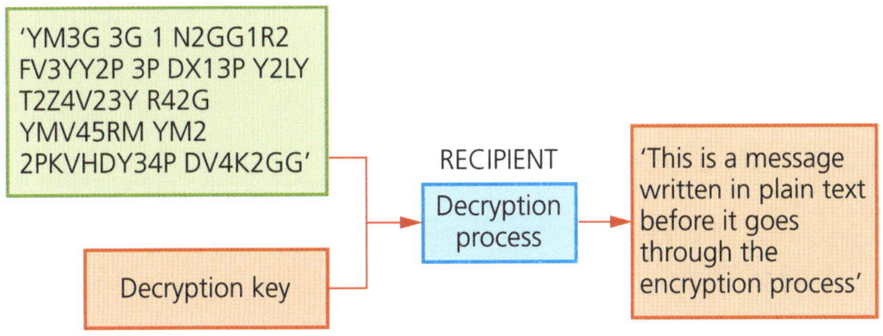

```
Encryption key ┐       SENDER
               ├─→ Encryption    ─→ 'YM3G 3G 1 N2GG1R2
'This is a message │    process        FV3YY2P 3P DX13P Y2LY
written in plain text ┘                T2Z4V23Y R42G
before it goes                         YMV45RM YM2
through the                            2PKVHDY34P DV4K2GG'
encryption process'
```

```
'YM3G 3G 1 N2GG1R2
FV3YY2P 3P DX13P Y2LY
T2Z4V23Y R42G         ┐      RECIPIENT
YMV45RM YM2           ├─→ Decryption ─→ 'This is a message
2PKVHDY34P DV4K2GG'   │    process       written in plain text
                      │                  before it goes
Decryption key ───────┘                  through the
                                         encryption process'
```

Hodder & Stoughton Limited © David Watson and Graham Brown 2022

101

8.3 Security of data

Due to the many online risks (such as phishing or hacking), encryption is very important in the protection of data. It doesn't stop a hacker intercepting the data or deleting it, but it does stop them making any sense of it.

The encryption of emails at all stages is very important; when the email is sent via an Internet Service Provider, the connection used and the email itself need to be encrypted (this includes any backup emails and the Internet Service Provider server itself). Data stored on cloud servers also needs to be encrypted; this is best done by encrypting data before sending it to the cloud server so that if the server is compromised, a user's data is still secure.

Firewalls

A **firewall** sits between the user's computer and the internet/external connection. Firewalls can be hardware or software. When the firewall is a hardware interface between computer and internet, it is known as a **gateway**.

Firewalls carry out the following tasks:

- examine the 'traffic' between the user's computer (or internal network) and a public network (e.g. the internet)
- check whether incoming or outgoing data meets a given set of criteria
- block the 'traffic' and give the user (or network manager) a warning that there may be a security issue if the data fails the criteria
- log all incoming and outgoing 'traffic' to allow later interrogation by the user (or network manager)
- prevent access to certain undesirable sites using set criteria; the firewall can keep a list of all undesirable IP addresses
- help to prevent viruses or hackers entering the user's computer (or internal network)
- warn the user if some software on their system is trying to access an external data source (e.g. automatic software upgrade); the user is given the option of allowing it to go ahead or request that such access is denied.

Two-factor authentication

Two-factor authentication makes use of physical and electronic tokens. It is a type of authentication for logging onto a secure website. Users are only allowed access after successfully presenting at least two pieces of evidence to prove who they are: usually a password and user ID at stage 1 of the log on and then an additional eight-digit one-time password (OTP) or PIN is sent to a mobile phone linked to the user. Once this eight-digit PIN is entered (stage 2), the user is allowed access to the website.

Physical and electronic tokens were covered in detail in Section 4.2.3, p.40

User IDs and passwords

Passwords are used to restrict access to data or systems. They should be hard to break and changed frequently. Passwords can also take the form of biometrics. In addition to protecting access levels to computer systems, passwords are frequently used when accessing the internet, for example:

- when accessing email accounts
- when carrying out online banking or shopping
- when accessing social networking sites.

8 Safety and security

It is important that passwords are protected. Some ways of doing this are:

- regularly changing passwords in case they have come into the possession of another user illegally or accidentally
- running anti-spyware software to make sure that passwords are not being sent back to the person/organisation that put the spyware on the computer
- not using your favourite colour, name of a pet or favourite rock group; passwords are grouped as either strong (hard to break or guess) or weak (relatively easy to break or guess)
- making a password strong but also easy to remember.

Strong passwords should contain at least one numerical value, a capital letter and one other keyboard character (such as @, *, & etc.). An example of a strong password would be: Sy12@#TT90kj=0. An example of a very weak password would be: GREEN.

When the password is typed in, it often shows on the screen as ******** to prevent anybody from seeing what the user has typed in. If the user's password doesn't match up with the username, then access will be denied.

Many systems ask for the password to be typed in twice as a verification check. To help protect the system, users are only allowed to type in their password a finite number of times – usually three times is the maximum number of tries allowed before the system locks the user out. After that, the user will be unable to log on until they have reset their password.

When using an online company, if a user forgets their password or they need to reset it, they will be sent an email which contains a link to a web page where they can reset their password. This is done as an added precaution in case an unauthorised person has tried to change the user's password.

Sample questions and responses

REVISED

a) Discuss e-safety issues and how to stay safe when using a social networking site. **[5 marks]**
b) Data can be classified as personal or sensitive. Give **two** examples of each type of data. **[4 marks]**

Sample high-level answer

a) Do not publicly post personal information or photos for people you don't know; this can lead to identity theft. Always make sure your privacy settings are on or set so that only your 'friends' are able to see your posts and photos. None of your photos should show a link to where you live, work or go to school or college (e.g. don't show a car number plate, street name or a photo of you wearing a school uniform). Only make friends with people well known to you or your friends; this will avoid stalking by social network predators. When using chat rooms on social networks be careful with the language you use and only use public chat rooms; never agree to meet somebody you don't really know on your own and beware of cyberbullying.
b) Personal data: name and address AND banking details (such as account number). Sensitive data: ethnicity or race AND medical history.

Tips

The first part of the question is a discussion. It is necessary to consider the main issues regarding e-safety within the scenario given. It will also require a reason why any issue quoted is indeed a risk. The second part simply requires short answers giving examples of both types of data.

8.3 Security of data

Sample low-level answer

a) When using 'Facebook' only talk with friends and be careful with the language you use. Your photos should be hidden except to friends. When opening a social networking site, make sure the green padlock is in the browser window. Don't give out confidential information and don't give out your email address or phone numbers.

b) Since personal data and sensitive data are the same, examples are: your name, your email address, your date of birth and sex.

Teacher's comments

The first answer has given a very thorough response to part (a) with reasons given to back up the safeguards described. In part (b), the student has given four correct answers and has clearly distinguished between personal and sensitive data.

The second answer is much briefer in part (a). They have mentioned only talking to friends and keep photos hidden but no mention of how this could be done by privacy settings. The answer to part (a) is probably worth only two marks since they show some idea about keeping certain data safe. In part (b), they have made the error of claiming personal data and sensitive data are just the same. This means a maximum of two marks could be awarded for part (b).

Exam-style questions for you to try

1 There are a number of health issues and safety issues associated with using IT equipment in the office. The diagram below shows seven health and safety issues. By drawing seven arrows indicate whether the issue is safety-related or health-related. **[7]**

   Health

   A. Continuous use of keyboard or repeated clicking of mouse

   B. Tripping over loose wires and cables on the floor

   C. Overheating of equipment or overloaded wall sockets causing a fire

   D. Eyestrain caused by looking at a monitor in poor room lighting

   E. Breathing in of ozone gas and toner particles from a laser printer

   Safety

   F. Exposed wires leading to the risk of electric shock

   G. Back injury from incorrect posture when using a computer

2 Explain each of the following terms and give an example of where each might be used.
   a shimming and skimming
   b fingerprint scans
   c encryption
   d Secure Sockets Layer
   e vishing **[10]**

3 Complete the following paragraph using the words or phrases from the following list. Each word or phrase may be used once, more than once or not at all.

authentication	hacking	Secure Sockets Layer
biometrics	malware	sensitive data
certification	pharming	smishing
cypher text/script	phishing	two-factor authentication
encrypted	privacy settings	user ID
e-safety	protocols	vishing

.... refers to the risks and responsibilities when using the internet. Data, such as ethnicity or sexual orientation, are examples of .... When using the internet, users need to be aware of ...., which is the illegal access to a computer without permission, and to the risk of .... such as viruses and Trojan horses. Mobile phones are prone to .... where fake text messages are sent to users. To prevent messages being understood by hackers, they are .... to produce .... refers to methods such as biometrics to prove who you are. One way of proving who you are is the use of .... where a one-time password or PIN is produced. [5]

4 a Describe **four** of the tasks carried out by a typical firewall. [4]
   b Explain the term 'gateway' as part of the data protection system. [1]

5 a Explain what is meant by the data protection act. [2]
   b Name **three** of the principles that underpin any data protection act. [3]
   c One of the reasons behind a data protection act is to protect personal and sensitive data from being abused by third parties. Name **two** examples of personal data and **two** examples of sensitive data. [4]

6 The diagram below shows what happens when a user wants to access a secure website to receive and send data. Complete the diagram by writing the letters **A**, **B**, **C**, **D** or **E**, where each letter refers to the following five statements:
A: If a web browser can authenticate this certificate, it sends a message back to the web server to allow communications.
B: User's web browser sends a message so that it can connect with the required website that is secured by SSL.
C: Web server responds by sending a copy of its SSL certificate to the user's web browser.
D: Once this message is received, the web server acknowledges the web browser and the SSL-encrypted two-way data transfer begins.
E: Web browser requests that the web server identifies itself.

[5]

7 Ten descriptions are given in the table below. In the right-hand column write the ICT term that is being described.

Description of term	Term being described
Malicious programs disguised as legitimate software; they replace all or part of the legitimate software	
Device used in an ATM slot to copy the magnetic stripe on a debit/credit card enabling it to be cloned	
The act of gaining unauthorised and illegal access to a computer system without permission	
Type of stand-alone malware that can replicate itself; it doesn't need an active host to infect other computers	
Programs that encrypt the data on a user's computer; a decryption key is sent to the user once they pay some money	
Sending out legitimate-looking emails to target users; as soon as the recipient clicks on a link, the browser is sent to a fake website	
Makes use of voicemail messages to trick mobile phone users into calling a number where a criminal will try to gather personal information	
Gathering of information, such as PINs, by observing somebody at an ATM; may involve use of mini-cameras or mirrors	
Software that floods a user's computer with unwanted advertising; usually in the form of pop-ups	
Program code that replicates itself with the intention of deleting or corrupting data; needs an active host program to work	

[10]

9 Audience

Key objectives

The objectives of this chapter are to revise:
- audience appreciation
- software copyright.

9.1 Audience appreciation

REVISED

When planning and creating IT solution or products, it is important to consider the audience who will use or take part in the solution or use the product.

9.1.1 Giving a presentation to an audience

Once a new IT product or solution has been developed, a presentation to users of the new system needs to be planned. There are many factors that need to be considered when preparing the presentation. The first factor to consider is the audience: the age of the participants, and their experience, expectations and knowledge.

Other factors to consider include:

- language used
- the need for multimedia
- the length of the presentation
- the need for audience participation (an interactive approach)
- the examples used to illustrate certain points.

Let us look at each of these in turn.

Various methods are used to gather information about audience requirements (for example in presentations or developing new software). These methods are covered in the section on analysis (research methods) in Section 7.1.1 of this book and the *Cambridge IGCSE Information and Communication Technology Third Edition* Student's book, page 219.

9.1.2 Audience characteristics (when developing new ICT solutions)

Suppose we are developing a new ICT product (solution). This could be a new website, a new computer game, a database or a new virtual reality system. We need to carefully consider the audience we are aiming our product at, including:

- audience characteristics
- the needs of our audience
- why we need to consider the needs of our audience.

9.1 Audience appreciation

- No vulgarity or use of inappropriate language since this can easily offend people
- The use of technical terms should be reserved for an experienced or technical audience

→ Language used

- Use of sound, video and animation will always catch the attention of the audience …
- … But it is important not to overdo it in case the message gets hidden because of too many distractions in the presentation
- A young audience is more likely to respond to loud music and embedded video clips
- Complicated descriptions are often better explained using graphs and/or animations

→ Multimedia used

- Long presentations will only work if they are interesting and engage the audience
- A very young audience would quickly get bored and start to become restless

→ Length of presentation

- Asking questions or getting the audience to 'try' things is always a good strategy …
- … But always be aware that not everyone wants to take part

→ Interactive presentation

- When using examples to illustrate ideas, remember to be understanding (e.g. don't refer to meat products if the audience is vegetarian)

→ Examples used

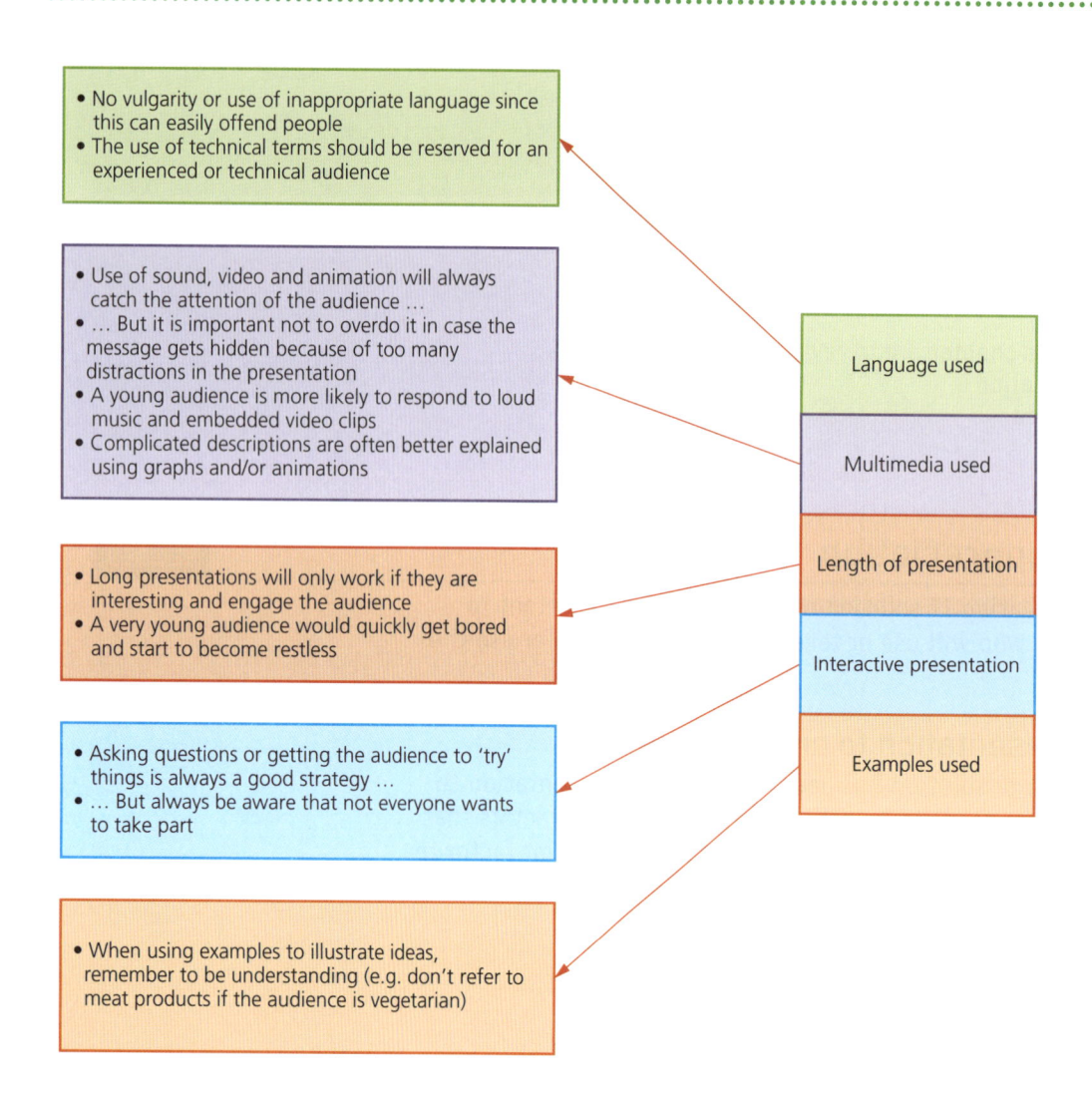

Audience characteristics

We will use the development of a new website as our example of product development. First of all, who will be using our new website? Let us first consider the characteristics of our target audience when using the new website:

- age range
- income levels
- interests
- do we need to consider disabilities?

Age range →
- Very young children need to have animations, bright colours, large font size and sound
- Older users will be more interested in actual content; therefore a simple attractive colour scheme which is easy to navigate is very important

Income →
- Suppose our website is selling cars.
- It is essential to carefully consider the target audience income levels; this will clearly dictate which model ranges are advertised on the website.

Needs of the audience

Depending on who the new ICT product is aimed at, it is necessary to understand their specific needs to ensure the final product is fit for purpose. Again, let us consider the development of our new website as the ICT example. In this section, we will consider the needs of three different age groups using the final website:

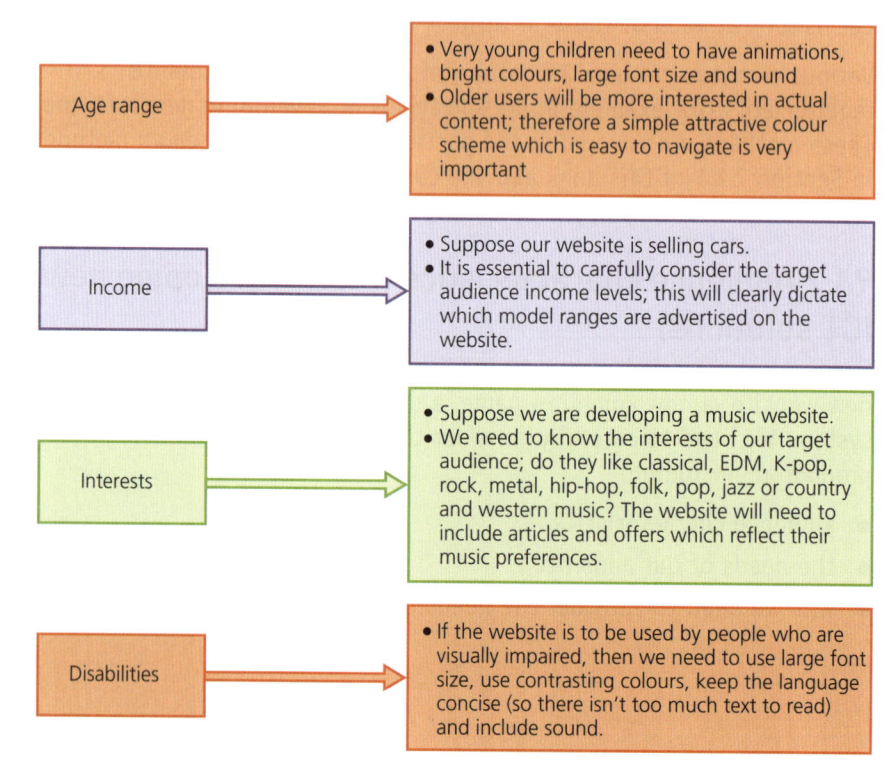

Interests →
- Suppose we are developing a music website.
- We need to know the interests of our target audience; do they like classical, EDM, K-pop, rock, metal, hip-hop, folk, pop, jazz or country and western music? The website will need to include articles and offers which reflect their music preferences.

Disabilities →
- If the website is to be used by people who are visually impaired, then we need to use large font size, use contrasting colours, keep the language concise (so there isn't too much text to read) and include sound.

Cambridge IGCSE Information and Communication Technology Study and Revision Guide Second Edition

9 Audience

Why we need to consider the needs of our audience

The above section considered the needs of three groups of people. Why is it important that we respectfully consider these needs?

- Complex language can be a real turn-off to children or people who have English as their second language; the text needs to be easy to read for these reasons.
- It is necessary to hold the attention of the users, otherwise they will give up using the website.
- Good, attractive screen designs will attract users to the website.
- If the audience is made up of older people, or people with disabilities who have visual impairments, then it is important to make sure the website has clear-to-read fonts.
- Keeping interfaces clear and easy to use attracts people; lots of typing can be very frustrating, as badly designed websites can be where the user seems to go 'round in a big circle'.

Young children
- Bright, cheerful colours
- Animation and sound
- More pictures than text (less writing)
- Large font and simple short words
- Include games where possible
- Must be an easy-to-use interface (for example, touching characters or voice interface)

Adults and older children
- Attractive display
- The content must be interesting
- Require a good mixture of text and images
- Careful to use appropriate language level
- Use bullet points to make the content easier to read

Older people
- Contrasting colours (makes it easier to distinguish words)
- Larger font size (in case of reading difficulty)
- Easy-to-use interface (touchscreen)
- Make the display consistent from page to page
- Do not use too much technical language as they may be less familiar with this

9.2 Copyright

REVISED

9.2.1 Software copyright and piracy

Software is protected by **copyright** laws. If software is supplied on CD/DVD or from an online source (such as an app store), there are certain rules about copying all or part of the software, as shown here:

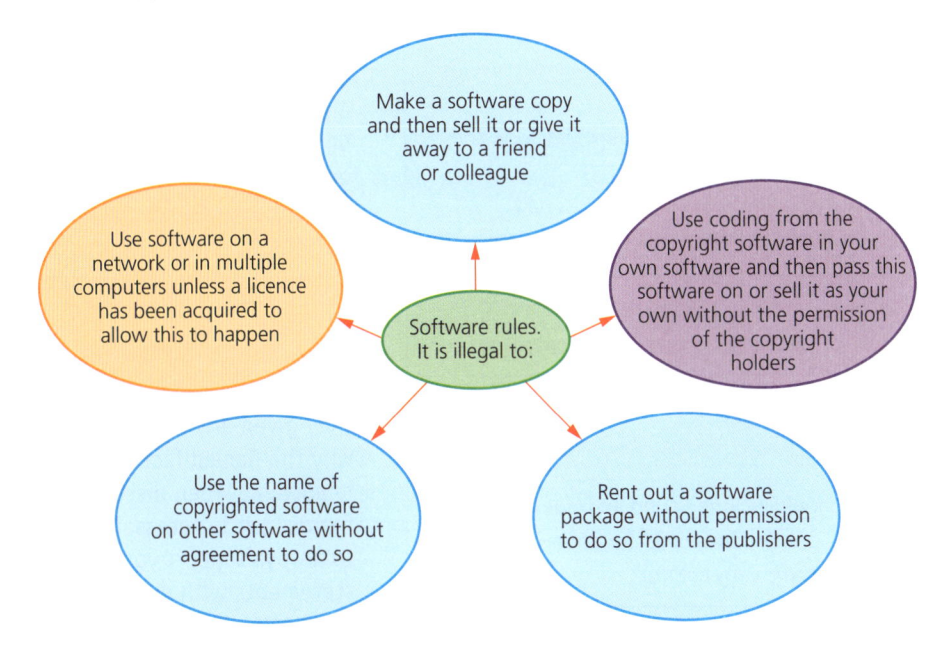

Software rules. It is illegal to:
- Make a software copy and then sell it or give it away to a friend or colleague
- Use coding from the copyright software in your own software and then pass this software on or sell it as your own without the permission of the copyright holders
- Rent out a software package without permission to do so from the publishers
- Use the name of copyrighted software on other software without agreement to do so
- Use software on a network or in multiple computers unless a licence has been acquired to allow this to happen

Hodder & Stoughton Limited © David Watson and Graham Brown 2022

9.2 Copyright

Software **piracy** is illegal and companies take many steps to protect their products. The installer will be asked to agree to certain conditions or to methods that require the original software to be present for it to work:

- When software is being installed, the user will be asked to key in a unique reference number or **product key** (a string of letters and numbers) that was supplied with the original copy of the software (for example: 4a3c 0efa 65ab a81e).
- The user will be asked to click 'OK'/'I AGREE' or put a cross in a box to agree to the licence agreement before the software installs.
- The original software packaging often comes with a sticker informing the purchaser that it is illegal to make copies of the software; the label is often in the form of a **hologram** indicating that it is a genuine copy.
- Some software will only run if the CD-ROM, DVD-ROM or memory stick is actually in the drive; this stops illegal multiple use and network use of the software.
- Some software will only run if a dongle is plugged into one of the USB ports.

> **Tip**
>
> A dongle is a small memory stick device, usually plugged into one of the computer's USB ports. It is used to protect software (e.g. it may contain important files and the software will only run if the dongle is plugged into the computer).

Sample question and response

REVISED

A company are introducing a new mobile phone and need to give a presentation to phone network companies and to the general public. When designing this presentation, a number of factors need to be taken into consideration. Discuss five key factors that need be considered when preparing the presentation to a group of different people.

[5 marks]

> **Tips**
>
> Since this question requires a discussion, it is necessary to name the different features that need consideration and give reasons why these factors need to be taken into account.

Sample high-level answer

The designers need to consider five things:
- The language used: inappropriate language should not be used and care needs to be taken not to make the presentation too technical.
- Using multimedia: good use of sound, video and animation helps to describe new features of the mobile phone in an entertaining and easy-to-understand manner.
- Length of presentation: the presentation mustn't be too long otherwise the audience will 'switch off' and start to lose interest.
- Interaction: audience participation always helps when describing a new product; however, presenters must be aware that not everyone likes to be interactive.
- Examples: examples of the new features of the mobile phone should be demonstrated either by a short video or by animation in the presentation.

Sample low-level answer

Presentations should not be too long and should include sound and video wherever possible. Use of nice, bright colours and big text can be helpful for those at the back. Handing out presentation notes can also be very helpful.

Teacher's comments

The first answer gives five very clear factors to consider when preparing a presentation. More importantly, they have given good reasons for why the five chosen factors need to be considered.

The second answer is a little too brief with only two or three factors mentioned. Neither have they given any reasons why the named factors are important. When discussing features, it is necessary to always support your statements with examples of why you have mentioned them. It is probably worth only one mark for an overall response.

Exam-style questions for you to try

1 A team are developing a new online computer game. They are giving a presentation to a number of magazines and games' critics to launch their new product.
   a Using examples, describe what needs to be taken into consideration when developing the presentation. Give a reason for each example chosen. [4]
   b The games software is to be supplied on DVD or offered at online app stores. The developers are concerned about software piracy. Describe ways the software can be protected from piracy. [4]

2 Which terms about preventing software piracy are being described below?
   a A unique reference number (usually a string of letters and numbers) supplied with the software proving it is original.
   b A sticker placed on the CD/DVD which can change its image as it is rotated; the image produced in certain orientations is proof the software is genuine.
   c A small memory stick containing important files which must be inserted in the computer to enable the software to run correctly.
   d Rules protecting the copying of software illegally. [4]

3 A railway station in Bucharest, Romania, is designing a new information system to be used by tourists to the city. Management want to introduce a number of automated information kiosks that will be distributed throughout the railway station. It is expected that tourists using the system will be between the ages of 18 and 80 years old.
It is also expected that Romanian, French and English will be the most common languages used by the tourists. The kiosks must also be user-friendly to people with a range of disabilities.
   a Describe the various audience characteristics that need to be considered when developing the new kiosk. [4]
   b Describe the needs of each age group and explain why it is important to consider these audience needs. [4]
   c Describe how the managers at the railway station could determine the different characteristics of all the customers using the information kiosks. [4]

4 Software is protected by a number of copyright rules. Describe **four** of the rules that protect software from being illegally copied and distributed. [4]

10 Communication

Key objectives

The objectives of this chapter are to revise:
- communication via emails:
  - uses and constraints, making copies, security, netiquette
  - language used
  - attachments
  - spam
- effective use of the internet:
  - differences between the World Wide Web and the internet
  - intranets
  - extranets
  - blogs and wikis
  - social networking sites
  - forums
- ISPs
- search engines
- internet protocols and risks.

10.1 Communication using emails

REVISED

10.1.1 Characteristics, uses and constraints

Emails are one of the most common ways people use to communicate with each other. To maintain safety a number of rules need to be considered.

Legislation

Many countries have laws to protect people against misuse of emails:

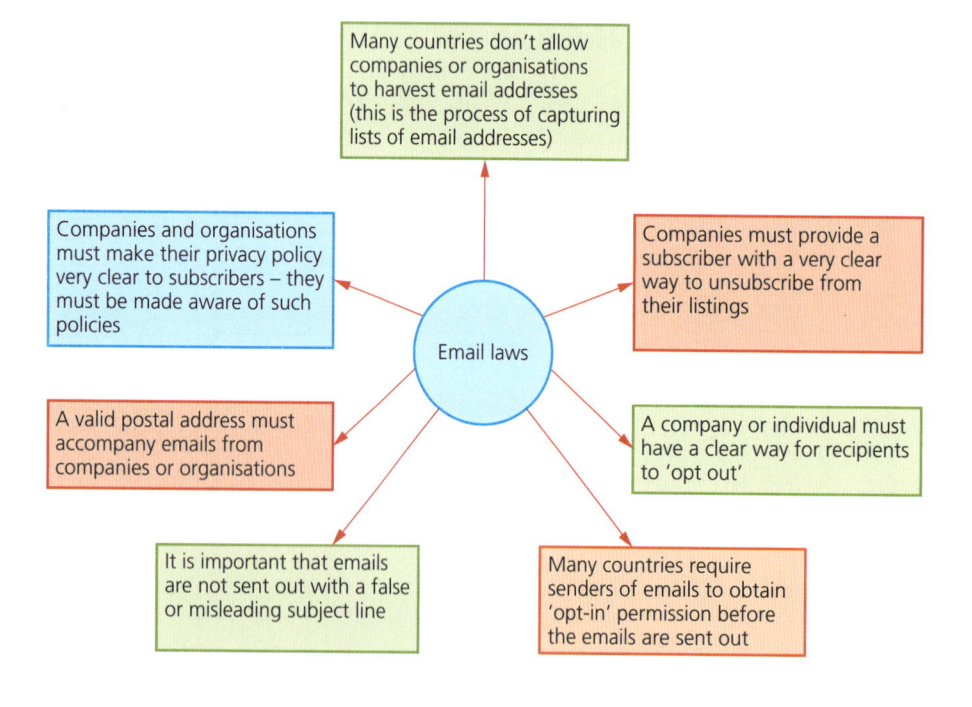

Email laws:

- Many countries don't allow companies or organisations to harvest email addresses (this is the process of capturing lists of email addresses)
- Companies and organisations must make their privacy policy very clear to subscribers – they must be made aware of such policies
- Companies must provide a subscriber with a very clear way to unsubscribe from their listings
- A valid postal address must accompany emails from companies or organisations
- A company or individual must have a clear way for recipients to 'opt out'
- It is important that emails are not sent out with a false or misleading subject line
- Many countries require senders of emails to obtain 'opt-in' permission before the emails are sent out

Cambridge IGCSE Information and Communication Technology Study and Revision Guide Second Edition

Language used
The language used in emails should follow an agreed practice:
- no obscene language or images should be used
- no racist, exploitative or violent messages should be sent
- illegal material or messages should not be sent.

Employer guidelines
Companies must set guidelines that all employees should follow when sending out emails and they need to enforce these rules or face potential legal action. The rules and guidelines should cover:
- emails must be related to the company's business and sent out using specified, registered devices and employees' individual accounts
- the content and style of emails should be specified (this is often done using templates stored on the user devices)
- confidentiality should be clear as should the security of emails used and stored on the system
- protection using anti-malware must be used at all times; data traffic to and from company devices should always pass through a firewall
- regular training should take place to ensure all employees are aware of the rules, confidentiality and security of emails.

Copyright and security of emails
Emails, as with any electronic material, are subject to copyright laws. This includes attachments, so it may break copyright laws if any attachments are forwarded or printed; the user needs to check first if it is legal to do this.

When sending emails as a company employee, email addresses should contain the company name (e.g. A.N.User@company_name.com). Attachments and emails sent out should contain a statement regarding copyright protection.

Security and password protection
Emails should be protected by strong, regularly changed, passwords. Email address boxes should contain spam filters and antivirus software should be run at all times. Emails can be subject to passive and active attacks:
- **Passive attack**: a security breach in which the system is not harmed but messages, settings or data (such as password data sent in an email) are read by an unauthorised third party.
- **Active attack**: a security breach that involves changing or harming a system (e.g. malware that deletes files or phishing attacks).

> **Tip**
> See Chapter 8, p.102 for more information about password security.

Netiquette
Netiquette (Inter**NET** et**IQUETTE**) refers to the need to respect other users' views and display common courtesy when posting views in online discussion groups or when sending out emails. The rules of etiquette include:
- remember that posts are public in most cases and can be read by anyone
- do not be abusive – do not threaten people
- do not send spam – do not repeatedly send somebody the same information
- be clear and succinct with your message – do not 'waffle'
- always check your spelling and grammar – give a good impression

10.1 Communication using emails

- respect other people's privacy and do not discuss or publish information that might embarrass others
- forgive people's mistakes – you do not have to respond to an error
- do not use CAPITAL LETTERS to highlight comments – this is seen as 'shouting' in emails, text messages or online forums
- do not plagiarise – always acknowledge quotes used in any messages you write
- do not use too many emoticons as they might annoy your readers.

Email groups
Emails are often grouped together for the following reasons:

- It is easier to send out multiple emails if all the email addresses are grouped together under a single name.
- Marketing purposes – where companies send out the same emails to target groups according to age, hobbies, favourite music and so on.
- 'Spammers' use email grouping to target many users at the same time.
- When setting up meetings, grouping people together makes sure everyone gets the same information, meeting invitations and so on.

Email operations
There are a number of options regarding email recipients:

- To, Carbon Copy (Cc)
- Blind Carbon Copy (Bcc)
- Forward.

Forwarding is the sending of an email to another recipient not in the original recipient list. Care is needed in case the original email contains malware or personal information.

The difference between Cc and Bcc is that Bcc address details are invisible to everyone receiving the email apart from the Bcc recipient; all those in the Cc list can be seen by all recipients. Bcc is often used for security reasons as all email recipients are grouped together under a single name and this name is used in the Bcc field.

Email attachments should be treated with caution as they could contain malicious content.

10.1.2 Characteristics and effects of spam
Any unsolicited email is regarded as **spam**. Software, known as 'spambots', is used to collect email addresses from the internet and build up spam mailing lists (emails can be gathered from websites, forums, chat rooms, social networking sites and so on). Spambots are easy to write since all email addresses have a very distinct format. Spam can affect any device – computer, tablet or phone. Although spam can appear harmless, it can cause the following issues:

- use up people's time and is annoying
- use up valuable bandwidth on the internet, slowing it down
- contain viruses and other malware
- clog up a user's inbox.

> **Tip**
> Look back at Chapter 8 for ways to prevent spam.

10 Communication

Sample questions and responses

REVISED

a) What is meant by the term 'netiquette' when referring to emails? Why are rules of netiquette required? **[3 marks]**
b) Name **three** rules of netiquette. **[3 marks]**

Sample high-level answer

a) Netiquette is short for internet etiquette and is required to ensure emails display common courtesy and non-inflammatory language is used. Since a user can't see a person's facial expression, see their body language or hear their voice, it is necessary to make emails very clear and be careful what is written so you are not misunderstood.
b)
- don't use abusive or obscene language
- remember posts may be public and could be read by anyone
- respect users' privacy and do not discuss or publish personal or private information without strict permission.

Tips

Although part (a) contains two questions, they can be joined together and tackled as one question. Ensure the answer refers to emails and is not a generic response. Since it only asks for three rules in part (b), it will be sufficient to make a single statement for each example. The answers to part (b) can be generic.

Sample low-level answer

a) Netiquette is used to ensure we don't offend people on the internet by using emails which contain bad language or bullying. This is needed to protect people online.
b)
- make sure emails are accurate
- make sure emails are sent to the correct people
- make sure emails are in English.

Teacher's comments

The first student has given a good explanation of why netiquette is important. They have also given three different and distinct examples of the rules of netiquette. You would expect this answer to gain 5 or 6 marks in total.

The second student has only explained why netiquette is needed and not what is meant by netiquette; only 1 mark would be expected in part (a). In the second part, the rules given are very vague and are not really adequate to gain any marks at all.

Exam-style questions for you to try

1 Indicate which of the following statements are true or false by putting a tick (✓) in the appropriate box.

Statement	True (✓)	False (✓)
Only those in the Cc box of an email can see the name of all of the intended email recipients		
Email addresses are often grouped together for the purposes of marketing		
The use of too many emoticons in an email can often annoy the recipients		
Passive attacks on emails involve the changing or harming of the recipient's system		
Emails (and their attachments) are not subject to the copyright laws		

[5]

2 Describe what is meant by each of the following ICT terms:
   a spam
   b spambot
   c passive attack
   d active attack
   e email **[5]**

3 a Give **three** reasons why emails are often sent under a group name rather than sending them as individual emails. [3]
   b Some emails are regarded as spam. It is important to filter out these spam emails. Give **three** reasons why spam emails are regarded as a risk to the internet. [3]
   c Employees of a company will need to send out emails to colleagues and to customers. The company need to set guidelines when sending and replying to emails. Describe **three** examples of guidelines the company should supply to their employees. [4]

10.2 Effective use of the internet

REVISED

10.2.1 Characteristics, uses, advantages and disadvantages of the internet

Internet means **INTER**connected **NET**work because it is a physical infrastructure that allows networks and individual devices to connect to each other. In contrast, the **World Wide Web (WWW)** is only a part of the internet, which users can access using a (web) browser. The World Wide Web is a massive collection of web pages based on the http protocol.

The following table summarises the differences between the World Wide Web (WWW) and the internet:

WWW	Internet
A collection of multimedia web pages and other information on websites	Users can send and receive emails
Uses http(s) protocols to send Hypertext Markup Language (HTML) documents	Allows online chatting (via text, audio and video)
Uniform resource locators are used to specify the location of web pages	Makes use of transmission protocols (TCP) and internet protocols (IP)
Web resources are accessed by web browsers	It is a worldwide collection of interconnected networks and devices
WWW uses the internet to access information from web servers	

Intranets and extranets

An **intranet** is a computer network based on internet technology but designed to meet the internal needs for sharing information within a single organisation or company. Intranets sit behind a **firewall**.

Some of the advantages of intranets include:

- more secure than the internet since there are no external links to other networks, making it easier to avoid virus attacks and make it more difficult for hackers
- better bandwidth since the data traffic is much less.

10 Communication

The differences between the internet and an intranet are shown in the table below:

The internet	An intranet
The term internet comes from the phrase **INTER**national **NET**work	The term intranet comes from the phrase **INT**ernal Restricted **A**ccess **NET**work
The internet covers topics of global or general interest	An intranet is used to give local information relevant to the company or organisation
Possible to block certain websites with the internet but it is more difficult	Possible to block out certain websites using the intranet
The internet can be accessed from anywhere in the world provided the user has an Internet Service Provider account	An intranet requires user id and password entry and can only be accessed from agreed points/computers
Protection against hackers and viruses is more difficult with internet access since it is more open on an international scale	An intranet is behind a firewall, which gives some protection against hackers, viruses and so on
Information used on the internet is stored on thousands of servers and computers internationally which can be accessible to anyone; thus any data available on the internet cannot be regarded as secure	Information used in intranets is usually stored on local servers, which makes it more secure from outside users

Extranets allow intranets to be extended outside the organisation or company. This allows trading partners to have controlled access to intranet data. Extranets can link to an intranet through:

- mobile phones (a number of safeguards permit only certain users to have access)
- a **virtual private network (VPN)** – this uses the internet and makes use of secret keys to encrypt all communications between the extranet user and the intranet.

Blogs, wikis, social networking sites and forums

	Description	Features
Blogs	**Web logs (blogs)** are personal internet journals where the writer (blogger) will type in their observations on a topic, for example a review about the latest movie release and perhaps links to some relevant websites Blogs tend to range from minor projects (such as the performance of a rock star) through to important social issues. However, the comments made on blogs are not immune from the law; bloggers can still be prosecuted for writing offensive material Similar to blogs, **microblogs** are most often used on social networking sites to make short, frequent posts. The posts can be done using instant messaging, emails or use other social networking vehicles (such as tweets). Social networking sites use microblogs to allow members to update their personal profiles, for example	- Updated on a regular basis by the author - Usually organised in reverse chronological order (most recent to least recent entry) - Normally public – anyone can read them - Entries normally come from a single author - Other internet users can't change blogs – they can only read them
Wikis	**Wikis** are web applications or websites that allow users to create and edit their web pages using any web browser. They have often been described as 'web pages with an <edit> button'. A wiki supports hyperlinks and uses a very simple syntax (known as wiki markup) to create pages	- Anyone can edit, delete or modify the content - Many authors can be involved in a wiki - It is possible to organise a page any way the author(s) wish(es) - Shows/keeps track of all entries (stores a document history) - Can be easily edited using a web browser - Allows large documents to be seen by many people – it is easier than emailing several people

Hodder & Stoughton Limited © David Watson and Graham Brown 2022

10.2 Effective use of the internet

	Description	Features

Social networking sites	Social networking sites enable people to share photos, videos and music, hobbies, favourite eating places and so on. They build online communities of users who share the same interests and activities. The members do this by creating public profiles and thus form 'relationships' with other users. The dangers of such sites were covered earlier in Chapter 8	• Each member is provided with free web space
		• Members can:
		  – Build their own private and public profiles
		  – Upload content such as text messages, photos and videos
		  – 'Write on each other's wall'
		  – Use free instant messaging and video chatting
		  – Email other members within the community
		  – Create pages where they can post photos, articles and so on
		  – Invite people to become friends
		• Members have control over who can access their private or personal data

Moderated forums are online discussion groups or forums under the control of an administrator who determines what is allowed to be posted. This gives greater protection from spam and from inappropriate material being posted. An **unmoderated forum** is 'owned' by no one and therefore isn't policed. Essentially the internet is an unmoderated forum relying on voluntary co-operation between users.

10.2.2 Internet functionality

An **Internet Service Provider (ISP)** is a company that provides users with access to the internet for a monthly fee. The ISP company has equipment and telecommunication lines that are required to allow internet access.

Web browsers are software that allow a user to display a web page on their screen. They interpret or translate HTML from websites. Most (web) browsers have the following features:

- A home page.
- The ability to store a user's favourite website/pages – bookmarking.
- They keep a history of the websites visited by the user – user history.
- They provide the ability to go backwards and forwards through websites.
- They have **hyperlinks** that allow users to **navigate** between web pages; these hyperlinks are shown as **blue_underlined_text** or use a small picture, such as a pointed finger, under a phrase or image. By clicking on these hyperlinks the user is sent to another website or web page.

Web browsers use **uniform resource locators (URLs)** to access websites, retrieve files and so on. URLs are represented by a set of four numbers, for example 109.108.158.1 (that is, http://109.108.158.1). However, this is not very user friendly, and an alphanumeric format is usually used instead:

    protocol://website address/path/filename

where:

- protocol is usually either http or https
- website address:
  - domain host (www)
  - domain name (name of website)
  - domain type (.com, .org, .co, .net, .gov)
  - sometimes a country code (.uk, .us, .de, .in, .mu, .cn)

- path, which is a web page (if omitted then root directory of website)
- filename is the item on the web page.

for example, https://www.hoddereducation.co.uk/cambridge-igcse-it

If a website or web page cannot be found, the user will get an error message. HTTP Error 404.0 means not found; HTTP Error 404.1 means website not found and so on.

10.2.3 Search engines

Search engines are software that help a user to find websites using keywords or phrases. They use complex **bots** (or **web crawlers**) that look at web page titles, contents and keywords that match up with the search criteria.

The successful websites are displayed with the 'most relevant' on page 1 – each identified web page is called a **hit**. There are three key stages in the process of search engines categorising websites:

- Crawling: use of web crawlers (bots) that scour the internet on a daily basis searching for new websites.
- Indexing: this is the categorising of the contents of web pages using keywords.
- Ranking: websites are ranked according to keyword density, speed and links, thus allowing the most relevant search results to be displayed first.

> **Tip**
> These key stages are useful extra information to help you understand how search engines work. However, they go beyond the syllabus.

By being more precise with the search criteria, the number of hits will be reduced; for example, 'ICT text books' gives 75 million hits, 'ICT text books + Hodder + IGCSE' reduces the number of hits to 200 000 and so on.

> Such values constantly change due to the way search engines, such as Google, carry out their searches.

There are a number of advantages and a number of disadvantages in using search engines to find information:

Advantages of using search engines	Disadvantages of using search engines
- Information on the internet tends to be up to date as it is quicker and easier to amend web pages, for example, than to reprint books - The amount of information on the internet is vast, almost limitless - Using a search engine to find information is fast and easy - Most people can look for information in the comfort of their own home – there is no need to travel to a library to find the required book or books - Information on the internet is essentially free of charge - Pages on the internet can have multimedia elements (e.g. videos, animations, cartoons and music/voice-overs) that make learning more interesting and often make it easier to understand the topics	- The internet is not regulated – anything can be posted on a web page. Information may be biased or totally incorrect (books, on the other hand, usually undergo some form of review before being published) - There is always the risk of accessing inappropriate websites when using search engines; these can take many forms and can be very distressing to certain people - It is very easy to be distracted when searching on the internet – for example by computer games or social networking sites - If the user lacks the necessary experience or expertise when using search engines, there is the risk of 'information overload' - There is a huge risk of plagiarism because it is very easy to copy material from the internet (more likely to occur than when using books) - Research skills can be lost when using the internet as search engines do all the work for you

Internet searches are not always the fastest way to find information; there is a need to narrow down the search criteria for search engines to work well. Search engine website ranking may not be the same as the user's request – how search engines rank websites is kept a secret.

10.2 Effective use of the internet

10.2.4 How to evaluate information found on websites
There are six criteria to consider when evaluating information found on the internet:
1 Is it possible to verify the legitimacy of who wrote the posted material; does the material come from a legitimate source?
2 Is there a way to check if the information is factually correct; can it be verified from another source?
3 Is the information objective? Is there any evidence of bias (e.g. does the article contain any advertising or links to organisations that hint at any bias in the way the articles are written)?
4 Is the information dated? When was it last reviewed and who reviewed it?
5 Does the article cover all aspects of the topic and are all arguments fully supported either by information or by external references?
6 Does the website look legitimate? Do all the links work?

10.2.5 Internet protocols
There are a number of internet **protocols** that require consideration:

Protocol	Description of the protocol
Hypertext Transfer Protocol (http)	• A set of rules used when transferring website data across the internet • http tells the browser that http rules are being used • If additional security is being used, then the protocol is called https
File Transfer Protocol (FTP)	• A network protocol used when transferring files between computers across the internet • It specifically refers to files being transferred
Secure Sockets Layer (SSL)	• A protocol that allows data to be sent and received securely over the internet • When SSL is used, the http protocol shows as https (also a green padlock shows in the browser window) • SSL is used in the following applications: 　– online banking, finance and shopping 　– sending out software to a restricted user list 　– sending and receiving emails 　– using cloud storage 　– intranets and extranets 　– when using VoIP, instant messaging and social networking sites

10.2.6 SSL certificates

When a user logs onto a website, SSL encrypts the data – only the user's computer and the web server are able to make sense of what is being transmitted. As mentioned earlier, a user will know if SSL is being applied when they see https or the small padlock 🔒 in the status bar at the top of the screen.

> **Tip**
> SSL and SSL certificates are covered in more detail in Chapter 8, p.100.

The address window in the browser when https protocol is being applied, rather than just http protocol, is quite different:

using https: 🔒 secure | https://www.xxxx.org/documents

using http: ⓘ http://www.yyyy.co.uk/documents

10 Communication

The following bullet points show what happens when a user wants to access a secure website and receive and send data to it:

- The user's browser sends a message so that it can connect with the required website which is secured by SSL.
- The browser then requests that the web server identifies itself.
- The web server responds by sending a copy of its SSL certificate to the user's browser.
- If the browser can authenticate this certificate, it sends a message back to the web server to allow communication to begin.
- Once this message is received, the web server acknowledges the web browser, and the SSL-encrypted two-way data transfer begins.

> An **SSL certificate** is a form of digital certificate which is used to authenticate a website. This means any communication or data exchange between browser and website is secure provided this certificate can be authenticated.

10.2.7 Internet risks

In this section we will consider the arguments for and the arguments against policing the internet:

Arguments for policing the internet	Arguments against policing the internet
• It would prevent illegal material being posted on websites (e.g. racist comments, pornography, terrorist activities and so on) • Some form of control would stop incorrect information being published on websites • It is much easier to discover information which can have serious consequences (e.g. how to be a hacker and so on); although this can be found in books, it is much easier for a novice to find the required information using a search engine • Some form of control would prevent children and other vulnerable groups being subjected to undesirable websites, including criminal material	• Material published on websites is already available from other sources • It would be very expensive to 'police' all websites and users would have to pay for this somehow • It would be difficult to enforce rules and regulations on a global scale • It can be argued that policing would go against freedom of information/speech • Many topics and comments posted on websites are illegal and laws already exist to deal with the offenders • Who is to decide what is illegal or offensive? Many things are only offensive to certain people but not necessarily to the majority

Additional precautions include parental, educational and IP control filters put in place to prevent certain websites being accessed by children under a certain age. It is also possible to prevent unnamed devices from accessing certain websites through the user's ISP provider.

Sample question and response

REVISED

Explain the differences between the internet and the World Wide Web (WWW). **[5 marks]**

> **Tips**
>
> For a strong answer, it is necessary to give at least three or four differences between the internet and WWW. Make sure your answers are not simply opposites (e.g. do not write: 'the internet makes use of transmission protocols (TCP) and internet protocols (IP)' and then make the following statement about the World Wide Web: 'WWW does not use TCP and IP protocols' since this would only count as one point).

10.2 Effective use of the internet

> **Sample high-level answer**
>
> Internet features:
> - users can send and receive emails
> - allows online chatting via text, audio and video
> - makes use of the following protocols: TCP and IP
> - it is a worldwide collection of interconnected networks and devices.
>
> World Wide Web features:
> - it is a collection of multimedia web pages and other information on websites
> - uses http(s) protocols to send HTML documents
> - URLs are used to specify the location of web pages
> - web resources are accessed by web browsers
> - it uses the internet to access information from web servers.

> **Sample low-level answer**
>
> There is very little difference between the two. We use the internet to send and receive emails but when we want to access a website, we have to use 'WWW' in the browser window; this means the two terms are interchangeable. The internet isn't really a physical object, whereas the World Wide Web consists of web servers and other computer equipment.

Teacher's comments

> The first student has given a very good list of differences between the two terms. Four or five differences are given, which means they have a very good chance of gaining full marks.
>
> The second student has made the classic mistake of thinking the internet and WWW are different names for the same thing. They would probably gain one mark for the second sentence and last sentence when put together.

> **Exam-style questions for you to try**
>
> 4 a Explain the differences between an intranet and the internet. [3]
>   b It is possible to access an intranet using a feature known as an extranet. Describe **two** ways an intranet can be accessed externally using the extranet feature. [3]
>   c Internet users make use of browsers. Explain the main features of a browser. [3]
> 5 a Explain each of the following internet terms giving at least **one** feature in each case:
>   i   blog
>   ii wiki
>   iii social networking site
>   iv moderated forum [4]
>   b Explain the difference between a blog and a microblog. [1]
>   c Describe the differences between a moderated forum and an unmoderated forum. [2]

Cambridge IGCSE Information and Communication Technology Study and Revision Guide Second Edition

6 Many people have suggested that the internet should be policed to stop users posting offensive comments on, for example, social networking sites.
Give arguments in favour of policing the internet and arguments against policing the internet. Draw a conclusion at the end of your discussion. [7]

7 Six descriptions are shown on the left and six computer terms on the right.
Draw lines to connect each description to its correct term.

Description	Term
1. Discussion website consisting of discrete diary-style entries; displayed in reverse chronological order	A. Netiquette
2. Collection of articles that multiple users can add to or edit; users can use a web browser to edit or create the website	B. Extranet
3. Code of good practice that should be followed when using the internet or writing emails	C. Blog
4. Software application for accessing information on the World Wide Web; retrieves and translates html embedded in a web page	D. Wiki
5. Type of intranet that can be partially accessed by authorised outside users	E. Search engine
6. Software that does a systematic trawl of websites to find websites based on given criteria	F. Web browser

[5]

11 File management

Key objectives

The objectives of this chapter are to revise:
- saving your work
- generic file types
- reduction of file sizes for storage or transmission
- file compression.

11.1 Manage files effectively

REVISED

11.1.1 Save files in a planned hierarchical directory/folder structure

Work should always be saved using a planned folder structure using folders and sub-folders. Filenames should show a progression of work using **version control**. Use an 'old versions' folder to reduce the number of files in a working folder. Make backups of your work and archive files/folders to save storage space for work that is not used regularly but still needs to be kept.

11.1.2 Save, export and print files in a variety of formats

You can save your work in different file formats using File and Save As in many packages and using File and Export in others, particularly to export a file into Portable Document Format (.pdf) or into a compressed file format.

11.1.3 File formats

Generic file types

Common generic text file formats:

Extension	Name	Notes
.csv	Comma Separated Values	It takes data in the form of tables (that could be used with a spreadsheet or database) and saves it as text, with no formatting, separating data items with commas
.txt	TeXT	A text file that is not formatted and can be opened in any word processor
.rtf	Rich Text Format	This is a text file type that saves a limited amount of formatting with the text

Common generic image file formats:

Extension	Name	Notes
.gif	Graphics Interchange Format	Stores still or moving images and is widely used in web pages
.jpg or .jpeg	Joint Photographic Expert Group	Stores still images and is widely used in web pages
.pdf	Portable Document Format	A document which has been converted into an image format. It allows documents to be seen as an image so they can be read on most computers. The pages look like a printed document but can contain hyperlinks, buttons, video, audio and so on. Can be protected from editing
.png	Portable Network Graphics	Was created to replace Graphics Interchange Format and is now the most used lossless image compression format used on the internet

11 File management

Common generic video file format:

Extension	Name	Notes
.mp4	Moving Pictures experts group layer 4	A multimedia container used for storing video files, still images, audio files, subtitles and so on. It is often used to transfer video files on the internet

Common generic audio file format:

Extension	Name	Notes
.mp3	Moving Pictures experts group layer 3	A compressed file format with high-quality yet relatively small file sizes, which makes it suitable for use on the internet

Common generic website authoring file formats:

Extension	Name	Notes
.css	Cascading Style Sheet	This is a stylesheet which is attached to one or more web pages to define the formatting of the page
.htm or .html	HyperText Markup Language	This is a text-based language used to create markup that a web browser will use to display information in a web page

Common generic compressed file formats:

Extension	Name	Notes
.rar	Roshal ARchive	This is a container which can hold several files, each with different file types, in a compressed format. It is used to reduce the number of bytes needed to save a file, either to save storage space or to reduce transmission time. This was designed for the *Microsoft Windows*® Operating System
.zip	Zip file	This is a container which can hold several files, each with different file types, in a compressed format. It is used to reduce the number of bytes needed to save a file, either to save storage space or to reduce transmission time

Common errors

REVISED

Error	Why it is wrong
Backup and archive are the same thing	Backups are used to quickly recover a file when (current) data is accidentally overwritten, deleted or corrupted. It is often used to quickly recover an overwritten file or corrupted database. Archive files store version(s) of a file that need to be used very rarely and are usually held on other media stored in a different building/location
A file saved as a .pdf is a generic text file	A pdf file is a generic image file as the original document has been changed into an image of the document

Sample questions and responses

REVISED

a) Name **three** examples of generic image file formats and for each identify the file extension. **[3 marks]**
b) Compare and contrast these three file formats. **[6 marks]**

Sample answers
a) ○ Joint Photographic Expert Group (.jpg)
   ○ Portable Network Graphics (.png)
   ○ Moving Pictures experts group layer 4 (.mp4).
b) PNG and JPEG images can only support still images, whereas MP4 format supports moving images. PNG is lossless compression whereas JPEG is not.

Hodder & Stoughton Limited © David Watson and Graham Brown 2022

11.2 Reduce file sizes for storage and transmission

Teacher's comments

a) The student has answered this question well, gaining all three marks. In a question like this, many students will submit a part of the answer and forget the name or extension.

b) This response would score 2 of the possible 6 marks. Marks would be awarded for PNG and JPEG *only* supporting still images and for MP4 supporting moving images. The student has omitted the detail of MP4 being a container which can also include other elements like still images. They are also incorrect in their statement that JPEG is not a lossless compression. The original JPEG images were saved with lossy compression but some JPEG standards now include lossless compression. There is scope for students to gain extra marks in the question by describing the differences between JPEG and PNG, for example: 'PNG was developed to replace JPEG and can contain images with a transparent background.' This answer lacks clarity because the student has not compared by identifying the similarities each of the file formats or contrasted by identifying the differences between these formats.

> **Tip**
>
> The only way to gauge the depth required in questions like on page 125 is to look at the allocated marks and space given to write the answer. In this case it is a question worth 6 marks so students should be aiming to write between 6 and 8 different mark points. Sometimes a number of mark points can be written into a single sentence.

11.2 Reduce file sizes for storage and transmission

REVISED

11.2.1 File compression

The need to reduce file sizes for storage or transmission

File sizes need to be as small as possible as all computer systems have a limited storage capacity and it is important to minimise any delays when data is transmitted (sent) between one device and another.

Reducing file sizes for storage or transmission

Often the largest files stored, or transmitted, are image files, especially video files which are a large number of still images. Still images can be reduced in size by resizing or resampling. Resampling is reducing the quality of an image. Resizing is reducing the width and height of an image. There are two recommended methods of resizing an image.

1. The first is to resize the image in a graphics package, for example reducing an image 800 pixels by 600 pixels to 400 by 300 pixels.
2. The second method of resizing is to remove part of the image using the cropping tool in a graphics package.

Using file compression

Completed documents containing lots of formatting or lots of images tend to have a large file size. One way of compressing a file is to convert it into Portable Document Format. When you have several files, it is more efficient to compress the files together in a single ZIP or RAR file.

Sample question and response

Explain **two** reasons why file compression is used. [2 marks]

Sample answer
Because files are too large and it takes too long to do anything.

> **Tip**
>
> Be specific with your answers; do not use phrases like 'it takes too long to do anything'. This should be phrased as, for example: 'It takes too long to open the web page using images with large file sizes', or 'It takes too long to transfer the data with such large file sizes.'

Teacher's comments

The student has answered this question poorly and would score no marks. Although they have identified large files as an issue, they have not been specific. The student should have identified the amount of storage capacity required to deal with large file sizes. They could have added that when the file is loaded or transmitted it will take considerably longer to load or transmit than a compressed file containing the same data.

It would have been better if the student had written that the transmission of smaller data files would mean less data packets transmitted which would lead to fewer transmission errors. This would also speed up the transmission time.

Exam-style questions for you to try

1. Some file types contain moving images. Identify **two** file extensions used with files containing moving images. [2]
2. Identify **three** file extensions used for generic text files. [3]
3. .rar and .zip are generic file extensions. Compare and contrast these file types. [4]

12 Images

Key objectives

The objectives of this chapter are to revise:
- resizing
- aspect ratio
- text wrap
- cropping
- rotation
- reflection
- brightness
- contrast
- layers.

12.1 Editing an image

REVISED

Images can be edited in many ways. They often have to be edited to fit into a predefined space or placeholder. How they are edited depends upon the task, but it is usual to make sure that the proportions of the image are not changed. Take care when considering the use of the image and its audience, for example if an image is to be included on a web page, a low-resolution image may be required. However, if an image is to be included in an enlarged publication, then a high-resolution image would be better to help reduce pixilation. Lowering the resolution of an image can reduce the file size of an image.

12.1.1 Resizing an image with aspect ratio maintained

Resizing changes the physical size of an image. Although resizing appears the easiest image editing skill, students often use the drag handles of an image without considering the loss of the **aspect ratio** of the image. It is better to use the 'Properties' window for the image and set the size there. This can help to make sure that the aspect ratio is maintained (some software requires you to tick the 'constrain proportions' check box). If an image size is specified on the question paper, resizing in this way makes sure that the image is exactly the right size, whereas using the drag handles is not always as accurate.

Common errors

REVISED

Error	Solution
Image is distorted when resized	The aspect ratio of an image should always be maintained when editing images, unless you have been told in the question not to do so

12.1.2 Wrapping text around an image

You can surround (wrap) an image with text. There are a number of different types of **text wrapping**, which are detailed as follows:

12 Images

Icon	Name	Notes
	In line with text	Image becomes an in-line graphic and is treated as a text character within the line of text. It will move if new text is inserted or deleted
	Square	Text flows around a rectangular placeholder
	Tight	Text flows all around the image, but not inside if it contains whitespace
	Through	Text flows all around and inside the image if it contains whitespace
	Top and bottom	Text flows above and below the image but not alongside it
	Behind	Image is placed behind the text, which is ideal for watermarks in documents
	In front	Image is placed in front of the text

12.1.3 Placing an image

Where possible use the 'Position…' tab to align an image to the margins. Marks cannot be gained for the placement of an image in the practical examinations unless it has been placed precisely so that the edges of the image match one or more margin/s. Dragging images to place them is less accurate.

12.1.4 Adding borders to an image

Image borders can sometimes be added to show the examiner that you have placed an image precisely, especially when the image has whitespace around the edges.

12.1.5 Rotating, cropping and reflecting an image

Rotating an image means to turn the image clockwise or counter-clockwise. When you **crop** an image, you remove part of an image by cutting one or more edges from it to create an image with a different size. Reflecting an image means to create a mirror image of itself, horizontally or vertically.

Original    Crop    Rotate    Reflect

Hodder & Stoughton Limited © David Watson and Graham Brown 2022

12.1.6 Adjusting the brightness and contrast of an image
The relative brightness of an image, as well as its contrast (i.e. the difference between an image's darkest and lightest areas) can both be adjusted.

12.1.7 Layer images
Layers are images placed in front of or behind each other. If a layer has transparent areas (seen with chequered patterns), the layer behind it can be seen through this layer. Layers can be grouped together so they can be manipulated as a single layer. Layers can also be flattened so that they become a single layer. Exporting layered images into .jpeg or .png format will flatten the layers.

Sample questions and responses

REVISED

An image has three layers. Layer A is at the back. Layer B has some transparent areas and is in front of layer A. Layer C has some transparent areas and is in front of layer B.
  a) Explain the term 'layer'. [2 marks]
  b) Explain the effect of changing the order of the layers so that layer A is the front layer. [2 marks]
  c) Explain what happens to the layers when this image is exported into JPEG format. [2 marks]

> **Tip**
> These single line answers would be too short for a 2 mark explain style question where you need at least two different marking points. If you make a point and add detail to it, sometimes a single sentence can be worth 2 or more marks.

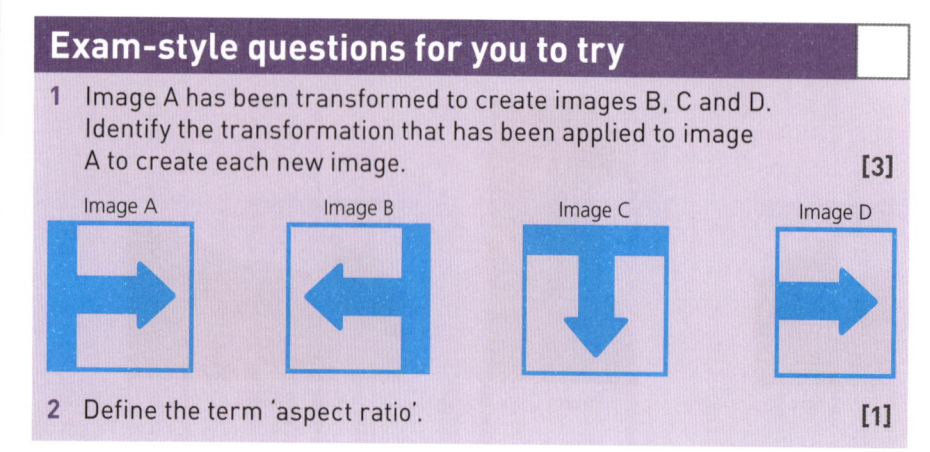

Sample answers
  a) A layer holds an individual picture. It sits in front of or behind other pictures.
  b) Layer A will be seen first with the other layers behind it.
  c) The layers are squashed.

Teacher's comments

> a) The student has answered this question well, although the use of the word 'picture' rather than 'image' is not correct; the image may contain text or numbers.
> b) This is correct; layer A will be seen first. This response would score 1 of the possible 2 marks as the student has not gone on to explain that the layers below will only be seen if layer A has some transparent areas.
> c) This response is very weak: the term 'squashed' is not the correct technical term for the flattening of the layers so would not get a mark. The student has only attempted one marking point for a question worth 2 marks so should have added that when the layers are flattened the individual layers can no longer be edited.

Exam-style questions for you to try

1. Image A has been transformed to create images B, C and D. Identify the transformation that has been applied to image A to create each new image. [3]

   Image A — arrow pointing right
   Image B — arrow pointing left
   Image C — arrow pointing down
   Image D — arrow pointing right

2. Define the term 'aspect ratio'. [1]

13 Layout

Key objectives

The objectives of this chapter are to revise:
- planning your document
- editing methods
- headers and footers
- automated fields
- aligning headers and footers
- tables.

13.1 Planning your document

REVISED

A document can be a piece of printed or electronic matter that provides information or evidence or that serves as an official record. Before starting a task, you must consider:

- What is the purpose of the document?
- Who is the target audience?
- How will I make it suitable for this audience?
- What is the appropriate medium?
- What is the appropriate package?

13.2 Create or edit a document

REVISED

13.2.1 Editing methods

Make sure that you know how to perform these operations on text and images:

- highlight text
- select an image
- **cut** and **paste**
- **copy** to **clipboard**, paste and delete the original text
- move, drag and drop.

Keyboard shortcuts for editing in *Microsoft Windows*:

- cut   <Ctrl><X>
- paste   <Ctrl><V>
- copy   <Ctrl><C>
- redo (the last action) <Ctrl><Y>
- undo (the last action) <Ctrl><Z>

13.3 Tables

REVISED

Tables of data may need to be inserted into your word-processed documents or presentations. A table can be edited in a number of ways. Rows and columns can be inserted or deleted. Individual cells can be merged together to create larger single cells either within one row or column, or across multiple rows or columns.

You can align data within individual cells horizontally and vertically. Horizontally you can align data left, right, centre or fully justified, while vertically you can align data to the top, centre or bottom of the cell. Other ways of formatting include choosing whether to show or hide gridlines, wrap text within a cell and add a shaded or coloured background to a cell.

Make sure that no tables are split over two columns or pages. Use a column or page break to make them fit the column or page. If they are so large that they will not fit, you are likely to have an error. Possible causes of these errors are:

- that the page size is smaller than specified in the question paper
- that the page orientation is not as specified in the question paper
- that the font size is larger than specified in the question paper
- that the line spacing is larger than specified in the question paper
- that the spacing before and after the style set for the table is larger than specified in the question paper
- if a table is the result of a database search, then there may be an error in the criteria used in the query
- you have not deleted the rows or columns specified in the paper.

13.4 Headers and footers

REVISED

Headers and **footers** are the areas at the top and bottom of every page in a document and are often used to display information like the author's name, the date of creation, a logo or the name of the document. Because headers and footers are often common to all pages, data only has to be entered once. This saves time and reduces the chance of data entry errors.

In some packages, it is possible to set different headers and footers for different pages or sections of a document. For example, you can choose not to display a header or footer on the first page. This is useful as, when books or booklets are being produced, facing pages may contain different information, using different settings for the left and right pages. Headers and footers can be found in word-processed documents, presentations, reports from spreadsheets and databases and in **web pages**.

13.4.1 Automated fields

Automated fields can be placed in many types of documents and are most commonly used to place items in the header or footer. This includes items like page numbering, an automated filename and file path, today's date and so on. Other automated fields can be placed elsewhere in documents.

Study the headers and footers used in this book and the *Cambridge IGCSE Information and Communication Technology Third Edition* Student's book. Do you think these contain automated fields?

13.4.2 Aligning headers and footers

For any word-processed document that you produce, it is essential that the margins on the header and footer match the margins of the page. If you are using *Microsoft Word*, change the positioning of the header and footer to align with the page margins using tab stops on the ruler (see page 298 in the *Cambridge IGCSE Information and Communication Technology Third Edition* Student's book for details on this).

13 Layout

Common errors

REVISED

Error	Solution
Contents are placed in a header or footer but not aligned to the page margin/s	Align all headers and footers to the page margins, especially when working within a word processor

Sample question and response

REVISED

A report of 68 pages has been created for a customer. The report contains headers and footers. Explain, using examples, why headers and footers are used. **[4 marks]**

Sample answer
Headers and footers are used to insert page elements that need to be present in all pages, like the page number.

Teacher's comments

This answer is worth 2 of the 4 available marks. It starts well, the identification that page elements are placed on all pages would gain credit, but the student could have included why it is an advantage to use this method rather than typing the elements on every page (less time required to enter/edit and less chance of errors). This would have turned the initial answer from a single mark into 3 marks. The page number on each page would also gain a second mark, but again there is scope for this student to identify other elements that may have been placed in the header or footer, like an automated filename and file path, the title of the report or the author's name.

> **Tips**
> Try to write your answer, then extend it a little showing the examiner that you understand more about this than the single statement. In the answer above, there are two points, the element on every page and the example of page numbering, but to get 4 marks you need to give more depth and more than one example.

Sample question and response

REVISED

List **two** items that would be appropriate to place in the header or footer of a report to show the storage capacities of solid-state drives (SSDs). **[2 marks]**

Sample answer
- page number
- the author's favourite football team
- the author's name
- the file name and path of the document.

Teacher's comments

This would only gain 1 of the 2 available marks. The page number would gain a mark. The second answer is clearly inappropriate for this task so would gain no mark. As this is a list question and has asked for two answers, all subsequent answers (even though they are correct) will not be marked.

> **Tip**
> If a question asks you to list, state, name or identify X number of items, credit will only be given for the first X answers given. This is to stop students listing lots of items in the hope that the examiner will find a correct answer among them.

Exam-style questions for you to try

1. Identify **four** items of information that it would be appropriate to place in the header or footer of a textbook. Do not include objects that would be placed using automated fields. **[4]**
2. Identify **four** items of information that it would be appropriate to place in the header or footer of a textbook using automated fields. **[4]**

14 Styles

Key objectives

The objectives of this chapter are to revise:
- corporate house styles
- font styles and sizes
- create and edit styles in a word-processed document
- using format painter
- using lists.

14.1 Corporate house style

REVISED

This is branding that makes a company recognisable. It can be used on something belonging to or sent from that company. House style often includes a logo, colour schemes, font styles and other features, and will be consistently applied to anything produced by the company. House style can be used on letterheads, websites, vehicles, posters, presentations, television advertising and other media.

As well as ensuring a uniform and professional look across a company's documents and media, a house style also helps give a company an identity, and can help with brand recognition. If styles are specified in questions, you must apply them using the predefined styles, especially in the document production, presentation authoring and website authoring questions.

14.1.1 Font styles

When you create a new style, you will be required to set font faces and sizes. Different packages use different named fonts, so (with the exception of website authoring) generic names will be used rather than specific font names. The generic names fall into two main categories: **serif** and **sans serif** (there are others but they are beyond the scope of IGCSE).

You will not find serif and sans serif as named fonts in your applications package, but **Times New Roman** is an example of a serif font, while **Arial** is an example of a sans serif font (as it does not have serifs on the letters).

Common errors

REVISED

Error	Solution
Students write a note on the exam paper saying 'My computer does not have a font called serif so I used ...'	Use **Times New Roman** as the serif font if you are using *Microsoft Office*
Students write a note on the exam paper saying 'My computer does not have a font called sans serif so I used ...'	Use **Arial** as the sans serif font if you are using *Microsoft Office*

134 Cambridge IGCSE Information and Communication Technology Study and Revision Guide Second Edition

14.1.2 Font sizes

Font sizes are measured in points; there are 72 points to an inch (just over 2.5 centimetres). If the question does not specify a point size, make the text readable for the audience specified, for example: a minimum of 10 points high for **body text**, 12 points high for older readers and at least 20 points for young children learning to read. Font face is the design of the typeface, for example Arial, Arial Narrow and **Arial Black** all have the same design for each letter but different widths.

The height of a font is measured from the top of the letter with the tallest **ascender** (often the letter 'h'), to the bottom of the one with the longest **descender** (often the letter 'f', though note that the typeface chosen for this book does not have a descender on the 'f'! Many do however: f, f, f, f, f).

14.2 Create and edit styles in a word-processed document

REVISED

When using *Microsoft Word*, styles are saved in a document's template file. Open the document and format one area of text within the document to match the required styles. Highlight this formatted area of text and use it to create a new style (see page 306 in the *Cambridge IGCSE Information and Communication Technology Third Edition* Student's book for details) with its own style name. Make sure that the style name matches that shown in the question, including the case (capitals and lower case letters) and any special characters (like the hyphen - or underscore _). Now highlight any other area/s where this text should be applied and click on the style you have defined, in the style section of the home tab. Use this tab to edit the styles defined for this document. Please note, *Microsoft Word* calls this Modify Styles rather than edit, as in the syllabus.

Common errors

REVISED

Error	Solution
When asked to show how styles have been defined, students screenshot only the first part of this process, that is, applying the individual style elements to the text	When asked to show how styles have been defined, show the whole of the Modify Style window for the specified style. Check that all of the style elements from the question paper can be seen in this window, including the spacing before and after the paragraph. These can often be seen in the text listing at the bottom of the Modify window

14.2.1 Using format painter

The **format painter** tool can be found in the Home tab in most *Microsoft Office* packages and is ideal for copying formatting from one part of a document to another. This works in packages like the spreadsheet *Microsoft Excel*, which do not allow you to use defined styles in the same way as *Microsoft Word*.

14.2.2 Bulleted and numbered lists

There are two types of list you need to know about: numbered lists (which can include lettering, roman numerals and so on) and bulleted lists. Make sure that you can change between the two types in both *Microsoft Word* and in *Microsoft Excel*. In the word processor, make sure that you are confident using tab stops on the ruler (see page 298 in the *Cambridge*

14.2 Create and edit styles in a word-processed document

IGCSE Information and Communication Technology Third Edition Student's book) so that you can indent the bullet points (or numbers) by a particular distance from the page or column margin.

Lists can have many levels, like this (note that when one list is placed inside another, this is sometimes known as a nested list):

- This is a first level list.
- This is a first level list.
  - This is a second level list.
  - This is a second level list.
    - This is a third level list.
    - This is a third level list.
  - This is a second level list.
- This is a first level list.
- This is a first level list.

Sample question and response

REVISED

Describe the lists used in this section of this document. **[6 marks]**

> **Topics covered so far in Chapter 14**
>
> While studying Chapter 14, I have learnt how to:
>
> 1 Create new styles for
>   a) Headers
>   b) Footers
>   c) Body text
>   d) Headings
>   e) Subheadings
> 2 Edit styles after they have been defined
> 3 Set font styles and sizes
> 4 Emphasise text
> 5 Use format painter
> 6 Use lists

Sample answer

There are two numbered lists, one inside another and no bulleted lists.

Teacher's comments

The student has correctly identified that there are two numbered lists and that they are nested. These elements would each gain one mark. The student has not mentioned that there are two different levels: the level 1 list being numeric; the level 2 list (while still technically a numbered list) being in lower case alphabetical order. The student could have identified the level 1 list as having bullet points indented 3 cm from the margin and the level 2 list indented a further 1 cm from the level 1 list (4 cm from the margin). Another element omitted by the student is that both list styles have the same font face and font size.

Tip

The question asks the student to describe the lists so it is acceptable and even desirable to extend the answer from the list styles set for each level to include the final statement of elements common to both lists. 'Describe' questions often lend themselves to answers that include similarities (which students often omit) as well as differences, especially where there is more than one element being described.

Exam-style questions for you to try

1. Describe the differences between a serif and a sans serif font. [2]
2. Define the term 'corporate house style'. [1]
3. Give **four** advantages of using a corporate house style. [4]

15 Proofing

Key objectives

The objectives of this chapter are to revise:
- spell check
- grammar check
- validation checks
- proofing techniques
- verification
- ensuring the accuracy of data entry.

15.1 Software tools

REVISED

15.1.1 Spell check

Spell check is usually found in word processing software. It compares each word in a document against those words held in its dictionary. If a word in the document does not match the dictionary it is flagged as a possible error using a red wavy underline like this: Speeling

Be aware that words that are spelled correctly but which are not included in the dictionary your spell check is using will still be flagged as possible errors. Examples of this are names or words from a different language.

Word processing software will often give you a list of alternative spellings to unknown words. These can be found by clicking the right mouse button on the word itself.

Sample questions and responses

REVISED

a) A student word processes the sentence: 'We visited the Tawara Beach Hotel.' The text is spell checked.
   Explain why the word Tawara is flagged as an error. **[3 marks]**
b) Write down an example of text that does not contain a spelling error, but may be flagged as a spelling error by the word processor. **[1 mark]**
c) Explain why your answer to part b is an error. **[2 marks]**

Sample answers

a) There is no such word as 'Tawara' so the spell check program cannot find it. It could be added to the dictionary by the user.
b) We did not not arrive at the hotel on time.
c) The repeated word would be shown as a spelling error even though it is an error in grammar.

15.2 Proofing techniques

Teacher's comments

a) The student has not identified that the word 'Tawara' does not exist *within the dictionary* because it is the name of a hotel, so the first sentence does not gain any marks. The second sentence does mention the dictionary but there is no link between the two parts of the answer. The second sentence is worth a mark as the student has recognised that the word is spelled correctly and should be added to the dictionary. It would have been a stronger answer if they had gone on to suggest that by adding the word 'Tawara' to their dictionary, this would not be flagged as an error again if this word was used.
b) This is a correct answer.
c) This answer would gain the marks as it clearly identifies the repeated word as the error and expands upon the answer to identify that it is a grammatical error rather than a spelling error.

15.1.2 Grammar check

A **grammar check** is usually found in word processing software. It reviews the entered text to see if it follows the accepted or expected rules for the grammar of the language used. A simple example is that each sentence should start with a capital letter. Possible errors in grammar are shown using a blue double underline like this: need to make sure

During practical examinations, do not attempt to correct any grammar errors unless they are in text that you have typed, for example in your answer to a theory question.

15.1.3 Validation

Validation is the process where data is checked to see if it satisfies certain criteria when being input. When designing files, it is important to consider field length, field name and data type. A data dictionary is used to show file structures, including any validation checks that may be carried out on the field data.

> **Tip**
>
> See Chapter 7 for more details on examples of validation.

15.2 Proofing techniques   REVISED

The term 'proofing' in printing means to make sure that the work is accurate. Carefully check all spelling, punctuation, grammar and page layouts. Page layouts should include:

- correct application of styles
- correct margin settings
- images placed with correct dimensions and no distortion
- text wrapped around images and other objects
- objects fitting within the boundaries of a page/column/slide and not overlapping
- no lists or tables split over two columns/pages/slides
- no blank pages or slides
- no **widows** or **orphans**.

Checking each of these carefully and correcting where necessary (often using page or column breaks) should help you to score higher marks on the practical papers. Consistent layout and consistent styles are very important.

15.2.1 Ensuring the accuracy of data entry

It is important to be accurate when entering data. Inaccurate data entry is one of the most significant reasons why students lose marks in their practical examinations. Check all data entry carefully!

Common errors

REVISED

Error	Solution
Placing upper or lower case letters in the wrong place	Check that all sentences start with capital letters and do not have capitals in the middle of a sentence. It is fine to have the word I, or names starting with capitals in the middle of a sentence
Numbers are transposed (they change places) as they are entered, for example the year two thousand and two entered as 2020 rather than 2002	Use visual verification to check that every character has been entered as it is in the original. Check the data entry, then check it again
Errorsin spacing in the sentence, either by missing spaces or adding too many	Use visual verification to check that every character has been entered as it is in the original. Check that spacing is consistent throughout the document

15.2.2 Verification

Verification can prevent errors when data is copied from one medium to another. It does not stop all errors, but reduces errors made when entering data into the computer by checking the accuracy of the data entry. There are two common verification checks:

- Visual verification: the person entering the data checks compares it to the original document. This is not the same as proofreading.
- Double data entry verification: data is entered twice, compared by the computer and if there is a difference the data is flagged as an error.

Together with validation, these checks help to reduce the number of errors in data entry, although they do not stop all data errors from occurring.

15.2.3 Proofreading

The term 'proofreading' is often used incorrectly by students. Proofreading is part of the proofing process; it is not a form of verification. It is the careful reading and re-reading of a document before printing to detect errors in spelling, grammar, punctuation or layout, even if they are not in the original document. Proofreading helps to remove errors by checking if the data is correct, not just that it has been accurately transcribed.

> **Tips**
> - If a question asks you to spell check and proofread your document, apply all of the techniques listed in this chapter to make sure that all spelling, spacing and style errors have been removed.
> - Always check the accuracy of all data entry.
> - Remember: check all data entry for errors, correct them, then check again.

Exam-style questions for you to try

1. This text was entered into a word processor:
   'The new airport will be constructed on marshhland on the outskirts of Tawara.'
   The spell check suggests there are two errors.
   Identify each suggested error and explain why it may or may not be an error. [4]

2. This text was entered into a word processor:
   'Mrs jones works an examiner. He marks examination papers.'
   Identify any errors in this text. [2]

16 Graphs and charts

> **Key objectives**
>
> The objectives of this chapter are to revise:
> - chart types
> - creating a chart
> - labelling a chart
> - secondary axes.

16.1 Chart types

REVISED

You may be asked to select an appropriate chart type to answer a question. For the IGCSE there are three types to choose from: a pie chart, a bar chart or a line graph. When considering which chart to use, you must first consider what the graph is supposed to show. Use a:

- **pie chart** to compare parts of a whole, for example the percentage of boys and girls in a class
- **bar chart** to show the difference between things, for example the number of times Ahmed, Ben, Carla and Dee went shopping in a week
- **line graph** to plot trends between two variables, for example plotting the distance a person travelled in 10 minutes recorded in 1-minute intervals.

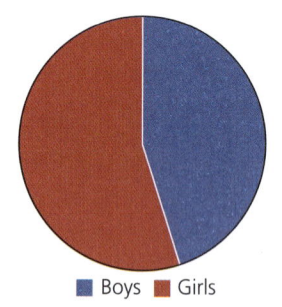

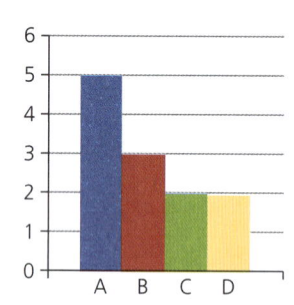

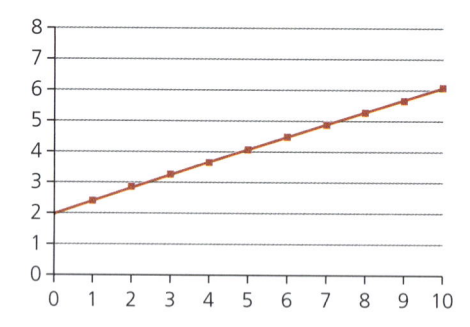

Sample questions and responses

REVISED

a) Identify the most appropriate graph or chart to display:
   i)   a comparison between distance travelled and time taken for a teacher to drive home
   ii) the number of oranges eaten this year by eight students
   iii) the percentage of people in a class with different hair colour
   iv) a comparison between the interest rate (shown as a percentage) offered by three banks. **[4 marks]**

b) The following data will be used to create a new graph or chart.

Time in seconds	0	1	2	3	4	5	6	7	8
Distance travelled in metres	0	2	5	8	12	16	16	12	6

   i) State the type of graph or chart that will be most appropriate.
   ii) Explain why this is the most appropriate type. **[2 marks]**

Sample answers

a) i) A line graph.   iii) A pie chart.
   ii) A bar chart.   iv) A pie chart.

b i) A line graph.
  ii) Because a distance–time graph plots the trends between two variables.

Teacher's comments

a) i) This is a correct answer.
  ii) This is a correct answer.
  iii) This is a correct answer.
  iv) This is not the correct answer. The student has not read the question carefully. Because this question mentions the word percentage (which would normally indicate a pie chart is suitable), that answer has been given. This question does not ask for parts of a whole but is comparing different rates from different banks. The correct answer to this question is a bar chart.

b) i) This is a correct answer.
  ii) This is an excellent answer identifying that this is a comparison between distance travelled and time, so therefore the line graph plots the trends between these two variables.

16.2 Create a chart

REVISED

Create a graph or chart by highlighting the data to be used for the graph or chart. Check if the data is **contiguous** or **non-contiguous**. If the data is non-contiguous then hold down the <Ctrl> key as you select the two (or more) ranges of data. Select the chart type, using the notes above on appropriate chart types to help you. Make sure that you fully label the chart.

16.3 Labelling a chart

REVISED

All charts must be fully labelled. Make sure that all the text in chart titles, sector labels and the legend are fully visible. It is usual to label a pie chart with segment labels *or* a legend but not both. Make sure that all labels are entered with 100% accuracy. The labels must give the user all the information about the data in the chart.

Sample question and response

REVISED

A trainee has created the following bar chart to show the director of a software company how many members of staff work in each job type within a branch:

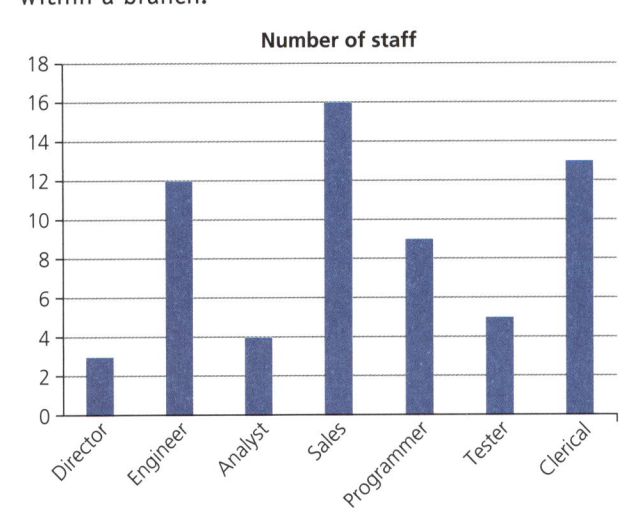

Discuss the suitability of this chart for this task. **[6 marks]**

Sample answer
This chart contains a chart title and both category and value axis labels but does not tell you what the chart shows. A category axis title and value axis title are both needed, as well as more detail in the chart title, so that the user can understand the data without referring elsewhere for its meaning.

Teacher's comments

This is the start of a very good answer worth 4 of the 6 marks. It identifies the title and axis labels as being present, then focuses on the omissions from the chart. To answer this 'discuss' question, a number of positive and negative points should be present. For example, that the title, category and value axis labels are not only present but fully visible, clear, easy to read and in appropriate font sizes for the audience. The chart type is also appropriate for the data being presented. One mark could also have been attained for a reasoned conclusion, gained by balancing the positive and negative points to suggest that the chart is suitable or unsuitable for its purpose, depending upon the strength of arguments for each side made by the student.

16.4 Secondary axes

REVISED

Secondary axes are added to a line graph (or combined line and bar chart) when two data sets are plotted on the same graph with very different sets of values. The chart shown here is an ideal example of this:

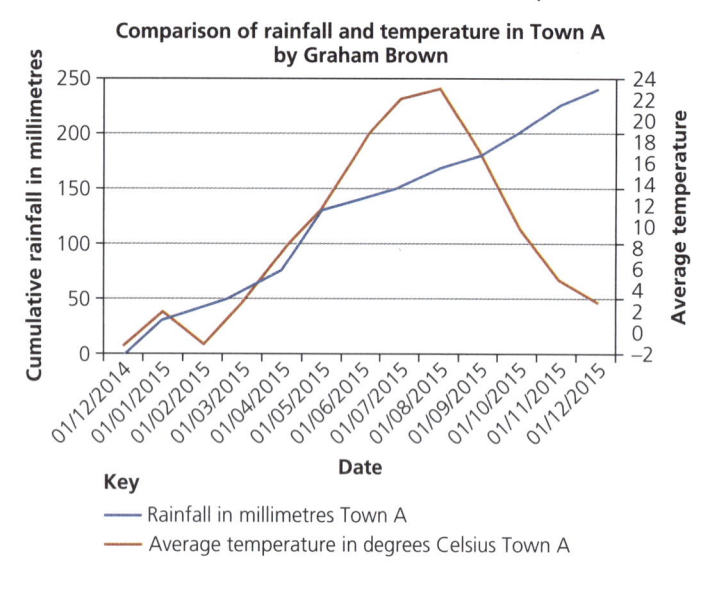

Comparison of rainfall and temperature in Town A by Graham Brown

Key
— Rainfall in millimetres Town A
— Average temperature in degrees Celsius Town A

The two sets of data show rainfall data between 0 and almost 250 millimetres and temperatures between −1 and 23 degrees Celsius. As these are very different sets of data, two value axes are required, a primary axis for the rainfall and a secondary axis for the temperature. In this example, these axes have also been edited to make them easier to read and compare.

If you are required to create a comparative line graph, check to see if the two data sets are the same type of data; if not, add a secondary axis to the graph.

16 Graphs and charts

Sample question and response

REVISED

Explain why three axes will be needed when creating a chart from this data:

2016 temperature and snowfall data for Keystone Colorado	January	February	March	April	May	June	July	August	September	October	November	December
Average minimum temperature °C	-18	-16	-11	-7	-3	1	4	3	-1	-6	-11	-16
Monthly snow (cm)	38	38	48	38	22	3	0	0	4	17	38	46

[4 marks]

Sample answer
The two sets of data are different.

Teacher's comments
This answer is too vague. The student should mention why the data sets that would be plotted against the category axis are very different: one is a temperature in degrees centigrade and the other is the number of centimetres of snow that had fallen in the town of Keystone. To obtain more marks the student should also identify that the temperature axis and snowfall axis could be scaled. An example of this could be: 'The minimum temperature axis should range from +5 to −20 in intervals of 5 degrees and that the snowfall should range from 0 to 50 in intervals of 10 centimetres.'

Common errors

REVISED

Error	Solution
Only partially labelling graphs or charts	Fully label all graphs and charts, taking into account the audience. Make sure the chart can be understood if presented to the audience without any explanation of supporting data/materials

Exam-style questions for you to try

1 **Bar chart** **Pie chart** **Line graph** **None of these**
   From the choices listed above, select the most appropriate way of graphically representing the following:
   a The percentage of a class of students who are boys and the percentage who are girls.
   b The distance travelled by a car over periods of time.
   c The height plotted against the weight for each student in a school.
   d The height of a student when the readings are taken every week for a year. [4]

17 Document production

Key objectives

The objectives of this chapter are to revise:
- page size
- page orientation
- page and gutter margins
- page, section and column breaks
- text alignment
- line spacing
- tabulation settings
- text enhancements
- bulleted lists.

17.1 Organise page layout

REVISED

17.1.1 Page size
Source files for document production questions are likely to be set to a different page size to that required for the final document, especially if they are in Rich Text Format (.rtf). Use the Layout tab and find the Page Setup section to change the paper size. The most commonly used page size is A4.

17.1.2 Page orientation
There are two types of page orientation, portrait and landscape. These are also selected from the Page Setup section in the Layout tab.

17.1.3 Page and gutter margins
The Page Setup section in the Layout tab also contains an area where settings for the margin (the border surrounding a page) can be changed. In any examination with document production questions this skill will be required. Take great care to set the margins as specified. The **gutter** size and position can also be changed here. A gutter may be required if a document is to be part of a bound book or booklet. If it is required, you will need to work out where the gutter will need to be on the page. For a traditional book (or booklet) it is often on the left of the first page, but if the document is to be bound at the top of the page (e.g. like some calendars) then select the top.

Common errors

REVISED

Errors	Solution
Setting the margin and/or gutter settings in the wrong units, for example in inches when centimetres are required	Check the units carefully, the computer that you are using may have its software set to work in inches rather than centimetres. You will need to set the margin/gutter settings in centimetres by typing the units in the drop-down box as well as the size
Setting the page margins correctly but not adjusting the margins in the header and footer to match	Edit the margin settings in the header and footer to match the page margins

17 Document production

17.1.4 Page, section and column breaks

A **page break** forces the text onto the start of a new page, leaving **white space** at the end of the previous page. It is particularly useful for removing widows and orphans from your document (see Chapter 15).

A **column break** forces the text into the top of the next available column, which may be on the same page or may be on the next page.

A **section break** can be used to split areas of a document with different layouts; it can force a page break (if selected) or be continuous which allows different layouts on the same page (e.g. a title across the whole page width when the text is placed in three columns). Columns can give a layout similar to a newspaper or magazine. You set the number of columns, their width and the spacing between them in the Layout tab.

17.2 Format text   REVISED

17.2.1 Text alignment

Text can be aligned in four basic ways:

- **Left aligned**: it is aligned with a straight left margin and a ragged right margin.
- **Centre aligned**: it is aligned to the centre of the page and has ragged left and right margins.
- **Right aligned**: it is aligned with a straight right margin and a ragged left margin.
- **Fully justified**: it is aligned with straight left and right margins.

Use these icons in the Paragraph section of the Home tab after highlighting the text:

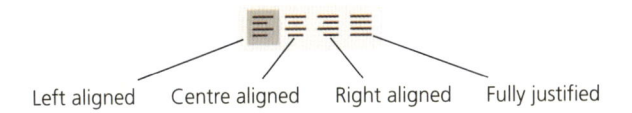

Left aligned   Centre aligned   Right aligned   Fully justified

17.2.2 Line spacing

Line spacing is usually set as part of a predefined style. The most commonly used layouts in the practical examinations are single line spacing, 1.5 line spacing and double line spacing. Spacing before and after paragraphs can be set within the predefined styles to give consistent spacing in a document. Use the [icon] icon in the Paragraph section of the Home tab.

Common errors   REVISED

Error	Solution
Not setting consistent line spacing throughout the document	Set the line spacing in your defined styles and apply these styles to all the text (of that type). There may be different settings for body style, headings, lists and tables

17.2.3 Tabulation settings

Tabulation, margins and column widths can all be set using the ruler. These settings affect how each paragraph appears on the page.

Hodder & Stoughton Limited © David Watson and Graham Brown 2022   145

17.2 Format text

Sample questions and responses

REVISED ☐

Here are some images showing the ruler in a word processing document:

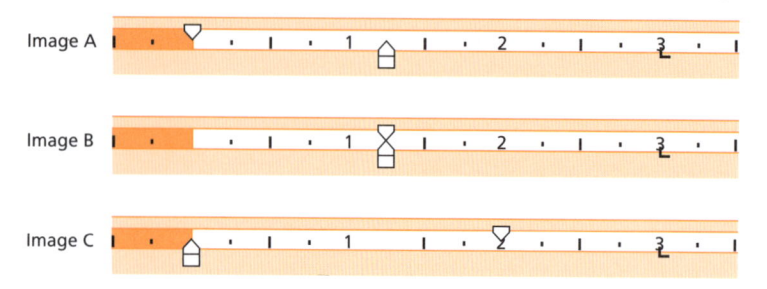

Image A

Image B

Image C

For each image, name and describe the type of paragraph that these tabulation settings produce. **[9 marks]**

Sample answers
a) Image A is a hanging paragraph.
b) Image B is a normal paragraph.
c) Image C is an indented paragraph.

Teacher's comments

All three answers have the correct names and each of these would gain this student a mark, so they would score 3 of the 9 marks. The question asks the student to name and describe, therefore two marks have been lost on each part as there is no attempt to describe each type of paragraph. Adding descriptions such as these would make this a stronger answer:
a) A hanging paragraph has the first line of each paragraph aligned to the left of the rest of the paragraph. The rest of the paragraph would sit to the right of the left margin. Only the first line of each paragraph will touch the left margin.
b) Each paragraph has the first line aligned with the rest of the paragraph; in this case both are indented 1.25 units from the left margin.
c) The first line of each paragraph is indented 2 units to the right of the other lines in each paragraph.

> **Tip**
> Note how in parts (b) and (c) of the teacher's comments, the sizes have been taken from the images. As the images give no units of measurement, like centimetres or inches, it is acceptable for the teacher to refer to them as units.

17.2.4 Text enhancements

Enhancements include bold, italics, underline and highlighting, which are used to make text stand out. **Subscript** and **superscript** reduce the size of the text and move it vertically above or below the baseline. For example, H_2O and CO_2 use subscript, whereas x^2 and $4\ cm^3$ use superscript.

17.2.5 Bulleted lists

Make sure that no bulleted or numbered lists are split over two columns or pages. Use a column or page break to make the entire list fit the column or page. If they are so large that they will not fit, you are likely to have an error. Possible causes of these errors are:

- that the page size is smaller than specified in the question paper
- that the page orientation is not as specified in the question paper
- that the font size is larger than specified in the question paper
- that the line spacing is larger than specified in the question paper
- that the spacing before and after the style set for the list is larger than specified in the question paper
- you have not deleted one or more list items specified on the paper.

> **Tips**
> - If you have checked and corrected all the possible causes listed above and the bulleted list still does not fit within a single column or page, remembering to make sure the text is still legible, change the font face used in your style definition to a narrower font. This will allow more characters on each line, which may help.
> - In a table, do not allow the text within the table to sit outside the column or page margins.

Exam-style questions

1 Explain what is meant by the term 'margin' within a document. [2]
2 Explain what is meant by the term 'fully justified text' within a document. [2]
3 Describe what is meant by a 'hanging paragraph'. [2]

18 Databases

Key objectives

The objectives of this chapter are to revise:
- what a database is
- flat-file and relational databases
- primary and foreign key fields
- advantages and disadvantages of flat-file and relational databases
- data types and subtypes
- form design
- searches
- calculations
- extracting summary data
- producing reports
- sorting data.

18.1 Database structure

REVISED

18.1.1 What is a database?

A **database** is a software program used to store data in a structured way. A database includes both the data itself, and the links between the data items.

All databases store data using **fields**, **records** and **files**.

- **Fields**: each is a single item of data and has a field name, which is used to identify it within the database. Each field contains one type of data, for example numbers, text or a date. All field names should be short, meaningful and contain no spaces.
- **Records**: each record is a collection of fields, for example all the information about one person or one item. These may contain different data types.
- **Files**: each file is an organised collection of records stored together. A file can have one or more tables within it.

There are two types of database: **flat-file databases** and **relational databases**.

18.1.2 Flat-file databases

A flat-file database has a simple structure where data is held in a two-dimensional table and is organised by rows and columns. This is stored in a single file.

A flat-file database is suitable for use with one type of data (e.g. data about customers, cars or CDs) that does not contain large quantities of duplicated data.

18.1.3 Relational databases

A relational database stores the data in more than one linked table, in a single file. It is designed to reduce duplicated data. A relational database is suitable for use with more than one type of data that are related (e.g. cars sold and customers), or with data that contains large quantities of duplicated data.

Primary key fields and foreign key fields

Each table has a key field. The relationships linking the tables use these key fields. Most tables have a **primary key** field that holds unique data (no two records are the same in this field) and is the field used to identify that record. Some tables will have one or more **foreign key** fields. A foreign key in one table will link to a primary key in another table. This makes relational databases more efficient when storing data, as an item of data is stored only once rather than many times. Storing the data only once reduces the time taken to add or edit data (and therefore the cost of employing workers) and reduces the chance of errors. It also means less storage capacity will be required, so it can reduce the initial hardware costs, especially for very large databases.

18.1.4 Advantages and disadvantages of using flat-file and relational databases

	Advantages	Disadvantages
Flat-file database	Ideal for small databases where there is little duplicated data Easier to create than relational database	Can take up more internal memory and external storage space Data may be duplicated so greater chance of errors when data is entered, edited or deleted
Relational database	Can use less internal memory and external storage space Data is not duplicated so fewer errors when data is entered, edited or deleted	More difficult to create efficiently than a flat-file database

Common errors

REVISED

Error	Why it is wrong
Relational databases can give search results more quickly than flat-file databases	The relative speed of the same search on the same data using a flat-file database and a relational database is dependent on the structures of the data tables in the relational database and the quantity of data being searched.

18.1.5 Data types and subtypes

When you create a new database, you will set a data type for each field. There are three main data types. These are:

- **Alphanumeric**: this is used to store text and numbers not used for calculations. In *Microsoft Access* this is called a 'text' field, or in later versions either 'short text' or 'long text'.
- **Numeric**: this is used to store numbers. In *Access* this is usually called a 'number' field and has several subtypes such as:
  - **integer**: which stores whole numbers. In *Access* it is better to use the 'long integer' subtype
  - **decimal**: which stores decimal numbers
  - **currency**: which displays local currency formatting. In *Access* this is called a currency data type, although it is technically a subtype
  - **date and time**: in *Access*, this displays the date in a recognised date format but stores the date and/or time as a number.
- **Boolean**: this is used to store data as 0 or –1 to represent Yes/No, True/False. In *Access* this is called a 'Yes/No' field.

Apart from these three main data types, *Access* also includes an 'autonumber' field. This is an automatically generated unique data field, which can be used to index and organise data.

18.1 Database structure

Sample question and response

REVISED

Anna is the principal of a college. She has employed a systems analyst to create a new database system to store records of her A level students.

Examples of the details of some students which will be stored are:

- Nadia Nowak, C3058, Female, 174, Not University
- Alfons Lisowski, C3072, Male, 177, University
- Nicola Menossi, F3888, Female, 173, Not University
- Giovanni Agnelli, D3012, Male, 192, University

Copy and complete the following data dictionary by entering the field names and most appropriate data type for each field. For any numeric field, specify the subtype. **[5 marks]**

Field name	Data type
Forename	
	Boolean
Height	

Sample answer

Field name	Data type
Forename	Text
Second name	Alphanumeric
Student_ID	Alphanumeric
Gender	**Boolean**
Height	Numeric – integer
Post_18	Boolean

Teacher's comments

The data type for the Forename field should have been identified as Alphanumeric, which is the correct name for this data type. However, as Text is the field type used in some software, examiners would be likely to credit the student with this mark. The field name that should have been Surname, Second_Name or Family_Name contains a space so would be unlikely to gain a mark. The data type for this field though is correct. Student_ID and its data type are both correct answers. The field name Gender is an appropriate field name for this Boolean data. The data type for Height is an excellent answer indicating both the data type and subtype. For the last row, field names such as Post_18 or After_College are fine, and the student has recognised that the data in the field has two possible conditions so it is Boolean.

Tips

- Take great care to follow the naming conventions for field names used in the question; if underscores are used instead of spaces continue this convention in your field names.
- Remember to keep all field names short, meaningful and containing no spaces. Examine the question carefully before attempting to answer the question.

18.1.6 Form design

Forms can include data capture forms, which are often created on paper to collect the data to add to a database, or online data entry forms. A good form should have the following features:

- a title
- instructions on completing the form
- appropriate font styles and sizes for the target audience
- clear, easy-to-read questions (**closed questions** where possible)
- boxes (or other indication of space) for the answers
- appropriate sizes for the answer boxes (not all the same size)
- similar fields grouped into blocks/categories (e.g. all address fields together)
- no crowding of fields (all should have white space between)
- the form fills the page
- no large areas of whitespace
- only relevant data collected.

Online data entry forms should also have navigation buttons: to submit/save the data (and move to the next record), clear the form, close the form, minimise the form, move to the first record, previous record, quit and so on. Where online forms are being designed, the use of radio buttons or drop-down menus should be used where possible.

18.2 Manipulate data

REVISED

18.2.1 Searching for subsets of data

Performing a database search allows you to select a subset of the data stored in the database. For example, a search could be used to find only the products that are red or blue from a database containing products with many different colours. In *Access*, a query is used to perform the search, usually using the Simple Query Wizard. This allows you to select the fields required and place criteria into some of these fields to perform the search. A query to find the red products may look like this:

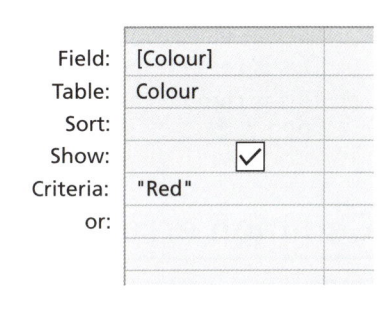

Field:	[Colour]
Table:	Colour
Sort:	
Show:	✓
Criteria:	"Red"
or:	

or one to find the red or blue products may look like this:

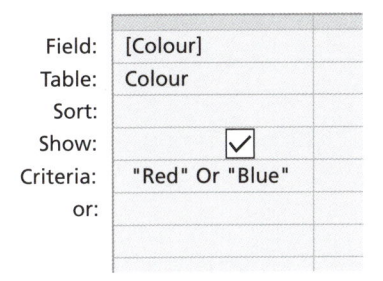

Field:	[Colour]
Table:	Colour
Sort:	
Show:	✓
Criteria:	"Red" Or "Blue"
or:	

Access queries are used to search for data. They can be simple queries using single criterion or more complex queries using multiple criteria. Queries can contain equalities: using = and LIKE or inequalities: using >, >=, <, =<, and <>. The three Boolean statements AND, OR and NOT can also be included in your queries. The * key will allow you to perform wildcard searches.

18.2 Manipulate data

Sample questions and responses

REVISED

A database contains the following data about meal costs at venues in England:

Meals				
Venue	Town	County	Meal_Cost	Guests
Flying Fox	ASHFORD	KENT	12.95	3
Freddie's	ASHFORDLY	YORKSHIRE	16.30	5
Korma Kurry	BRADFORD	YORKSHIRE	24.10	2
Yellow Goose	BRENTFORD	MIDDLESEX	23.00	2
Cricketer's Arms	FORDHAM	ESSEX	12.50	5
Patel's Pantry	SHEFFIELD	YORKSHIRE	9.65	16
White Swan	SKIPTON	YORKSHIRE	14.20	4

List the results which would be output when the following search criteria are used on the Town field:

a) *FORD
b) FORD*
c) *FORD*

[3 marks]

Sample answers
a) ASHFORD, BRADFORD
b) FORDHAM
c) ASHFORD, ASHFORDLY, BRADFORD, BRENTFORD, FORDHAM

Teacher's comments

a) The student has found the first two towns ending with the word FORD but has omitted the town of BRENTFORD.
b) This is correct: the student has found the only town starting with FORD.
c) This is correct: the student has found all the towns containing the word FORD.

> **Tip**
> This is a good example of a typical IGCSE answer where the student understands the question, yet in part (a) has missed out one of the answers. A good examination technique is to read the question, answer it, read the same question again, then check that the answer is correct. This technique can make a significant difference to your performance in the final examinations.

Common errors

REVISED

Error	Solution
The default setting in the query wizard (in some versions of *Access*) is to the last query or table that you used. Where two questions require independent queries, the results of the first query are selected as the source data for the second query, rather than selecting the original table	Make sure that you select the source data appropriate for the task you are completing. This often means that you need to change the source data back to being the original table. Don't leave the result of the previous query as your source data

18.2.2 Perform calculations

Calculations can be performed at run-time by creating a calculated field in your query, a calculated control in a report or by using built-in (summary data) functions in *Access*.

Calculated fields
Calculated fields can be added to a query. The name of the calculated field is defined and ends with a colon, and then is followed by the calculation to be performed.

You will need to remember the syntax for formulae used in your queries. If a calculated field is required (this is usually worded as 'calculated at runtime'), it must have the following syntax:

NameOfTheNewCalculatedField: [ExistingFieldname] Operator [ExistingFieldname]

or

NameOfTheNewCalculatedField: [ExistingFieldname] Operator Variable

In this example, for each record selected in the query, Tax of 20% will be calculated as the contents of the Price field multiplied by 0.2.

Field:	Tax: [Price]*0.2
Table:	
Sort:	
Show:	✓
Criteria:	
or:	

Extracting summary data
Selecting summary data does not show each data item when the query is run; it can be found in Summary options when using the query wizard. This option is only available if you have selected one or more numeric fields, as summary calculations cannot be completed on other data types. These allow you to perform calculations like sum and average on these numeric fields and to count the number of records.

Some of the summary functions available for this are:

Sum: the total value of the data selected

Avg: the mean value or average of the data selected

Min: the minimum value of the data selected

Max: the maximum or largest value of the data selected

Count: the number of records selected.

Sample question and response   REVISED
Create a field calculated at run-time called **Profit**

This field must calculate the Sales – Cost for each record.

Sample answer

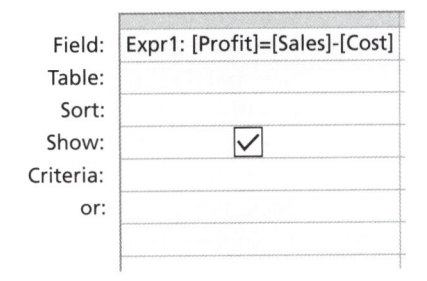

Field:	Expr1: [Profit]=[Sales]-[Cost]
Table:	
Sort:	
Show:	✓
Criteria:	
or:	

Teacher's comments
The student has attempted to use the formula, Profit = [Sales]–[Cost] to define the field. The error in this attempt is the use of = rather than a colon to define the field name. While the calculation part is correct, the = means that *Access* has added its own field name, in this case Expr1:

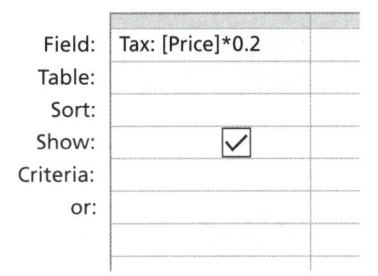

> **Tip**
> Make sure that you always check the syntax of any calculation used in databases or spreadsheets, then check the results to see if your answers appear to be correct.

Sample questions and responses

REVISED

Using fields from the Meals database table in the sample question on p.152, identify what would be entered to:

a) Create a new field called Total_Cost which is calculated at run-time. This field will show the Meal_Cost multiplied by the number of Guests. **[2 marks]**

b) Create a new field called Total_Plus_1 which is calculated at run-time. This field will show the Meal_Cost multiplied by the number of Guests multiplied by 2. **[3 marks]**

Sample answers

a) Total_Cost: [Meal_Cost]*[Guest]
b) Total_Plus_1: [Meal_Cost]*[Guests]*2

Teacher's comments

a) The student has gained 3 of the 4 marks. The correct field selection has been made for Total_Cost and the syntax of the ':' colon after it is correct. The [Meal_Cost] field is correct and enclosed in square brackets to indicate it is a field. The correct mathematical operator the '*' has been used but the student has called the last field Guest rather than Guests although the square brackets are correct to indicate it is a field.

b) This is the correct answer and is worth all 3 marks.

18.3 Present data

REVISED

18.3.1 Producing reports

When an examination question asks you to produce a report it does not always mean a report generated from *Access*. This is often the easiest method, but reports can be produced in a word processor by cutting and pasting the data from other places.

When creating reports in *Access*, make sure that you show all the data in the report; often students include all the fields and correct records but do not enlarge the control (often for the data but sometimes for the label) so that all of the data for every record is fully visible. Use the drag handle on the control to enlarge it when you are in Design view. Make sure that you use appropriate headers and footers within your database reports. Remember that report headers only appear once in the report and that page headers and page footers appear on every page of the report. If headers and/or footers are specified in a question, make sure you enter the data accurately.

18.3.2 Sorting data

Data can be sorted in either the query or the report. At IGCSE level it is easier to sort the data in the report. At this level you do not need to use grouping within your reports. Here are two examples of data being sorted in ascending order:

apple
ball
cake
dog

or

1
2
3
4

> **Tips**
> - Look at the query (or table) used to create the report and identify the longest data item for each field. Use these data items to check in the report that each control is wide enough.
> - If the question does not specify the page orientation, set this to landscape to allow more data to fit across each page.

Here are two examples of data being sorted in descending order:

dog
cake
ball
apple

or

4
3
2
1

Exam-style questions for you to try

1 Describe the following database features:
   a A record.
   b A field.
   c A file.
   d A table.
   e A report.
   f A query.
   g A calculated control. [7]
2 Explain the differences between a flat-file database and a relational database. [4]
3 My-Music-Inc sells many music DVDs. Below is a small selection of the DVDs stored on their database.
   The data has been sorted on two fields.

Artist	Album	Released	Price	Tracks
George Ezra	Staying at Tamara's	2018	£10.00	11
Taylor Swift	Fearless	2021	£10.00	13
Adele	30	2021	£10.00	15
Stormzy	Heavy Is the Head	2019	£7.00	16
Drake	Certified Lover Boy	2021	£7.00	21
Maroon 5	Jordi	2021	£6.00	12
Justin Bieber	Justice	2021	£6.00	17

   a Write down the field that was used as the primary sort in the database and the order in which it was sorted. [2]
   b Write down the field that was used as the secondary sort in the database and the order in which it was sorted. [2]
   c Tracy is the owner of My-Music-Inc and receives requests from customers about the music DVDs that are in stock. She converts these requests into search criteria.
   For example, a customer might ask for a list of DVDs that were released before 2016 and DVDs with more than 12 tracks. Tracy would write this as:
   Released < 2016 OR Tracks > 12
   Write down the search criteria for a customer who wants a list of all the DVDs that were released after 2015 that cost less than £10.00. [3]
   d Write down the names of the artists whose DVDs match the requirements of part c. [1]

19 Presentations

Key objectives

The objectives of this chapter are to revise:
- presentations, media and audience
- master slides
- presentation slides
- audience notes
- presenter notes
- hyperlinks and action buttons
- transitions
- animations
- display a presentation.

19.1 Create a presentation

19.1.1 Presentations, media and audience

A presentation is a series of slides used to give information to an audience, as shown in the two photos above. Methods of delivery can include a:

- large screen to teach or lecture
- monitor as a constant on-screen carousel.

Presentations are often used to give information or advertise products

Depending on the purpose of the presentation and the target audience for the presentation, you can select the:

- type of presentation
- medium for delivery
- **aspect ratio** of the presentation (often 4:3 or 16:9)
- styles used within the presentation.

Keep it simple and be consistent when creating your presentation using:

- one theme
- one simple colour scheme with good contrast
- one or two font styles and consistent sizes
- bulleted lists rather than sentences
- a master slide.

19.2 Master slides

A master slide allows you to design or change the layout of all slides with one action. It holds information on colours, fonts, headers and footers, effects and the positioning of objects on the slides, such as images, headings and bullets. Adding or changing master slide elements means that you do not have to change each slide individually.

To change all slides in *Microsoft PowerPoint*, always change the settings in the primary (top) master slide. This one overrides the slide masters for the other slide types which are found below the primary master slide.

19.3 Edit a presentation

REVISED

19.3.1 Presentation slides

Check carefully as you place objects on each slide that no object touches or overlaps the objects placed on the master slide (unless instructed to do so by the question paper). Make sure that the objects are clearly visible and that text has good contrast with the colours in the background/theme that you have selected.

Different types of slide layout will allow you to place text, images, lines, shapes, graphs and charts, video and audio clips on the slide. Select carefully the type of slide that you require each time you insert a new slide.

19.3.2 Audience notes

If a presentation is being used to teach or lecture to an audience, it is common for **audience notes** to be used. These are paper copies of the slides of a presentation that are given to the audience, so that they can add their own notes and take them away from the presentation. If you are required to print audience notes in *PowerPoint*, select the appropriate option from the 'Handout' section.

19.3.3 Presenter notes

Presenter notes are also used when teaching or lecturing to an audience. Presenter notes are a copy of the presentation's slides with prompts and/or key facts that need to be told to the audience by the person delivering the presentation. Presenter notes are added in the notes area of the presentation just below the slides. If you are required to print presenter notes in *PowerPoint*, selecting 'Notes Pages' is often the most appropriate.

19.3.4 Hyperlinks and action buttons

Hyperlinks can be used to link between slides or to other external documents, web pages and programs, for example to open an email editor so that you can prepare and send an email. Hyperlinks can be created from text or objects within a slide. Objects like rectangles can be used to create links from navigation buttons. Some buttons in *PowerPoint* are predefined, for example action buttons will allow you to move to the previous slide, next slide, first slide or last slide in the presentation.

19.3.5 Transitions

Transitions between slides are the methods used to introduce or move to a new slide. This can be simply replacing the existing slide with a new slide or using a number of different features to change from one to another. Transitions can be timed to run automatically (e.g. in a looped on-screen carousel) or set to be manually selected by clicking the mouse (a controlled presentation). For the practical examinations, always use the same transition throughout the presentation (unless told otherwise in the question paper). Use screenshots to show the examiner that you have used transitions, by selecting the Slide Sorter view, then the Transitions tab.

19.3.6 Animations

An animation effect is the effect used to introduce an object within the slide. Animations can be timed or manually selected by clicking the mouse. For the practical examinations, always use the same animation throughout the presentation (unless told otherwise in the question paper). Use screenshots of the Animation Pane to show the examiner your animations.

19.4 Output a presentation

REVISED

19.4.1 Display a presentation

Presentations can be displayed using the <F5> key. Always check the timings of your presentation if it is for an on-screen carousel. If timings are used, make sure there is enough time for a slow reader to read each slide. Slide shows can be made to loop continuously in the Set Up Show window by ticking the Play continuously until 'Esc' check box.

Sample question and response

REVISED

Discuss the statement:

'Sarah says "transitions and animations in a presentation are the same thing", but Brian disagrees.' **[6 marks]**

Sample answer
Brian is right because they are not the same thing.

Teacher's comments

This is a really weak answer; there is no evidence presented to the examiner why the student thinks that Brian is correct. As a 'discuss' question, arguments for and against would be expected; in this case, it would be a good idea to suggest that they were both very similar as they were 'actions' that are performed on slides and the objects placed on slides. They could enhance this by saying that both actions can be timed to run automatically and operate when the mouse is clicked. These factors would support Sarah's argument. However, transitions are actions performed on the slides whereas animations are on objects within the slides, which would support Brian's argument. A reasoned conclusion from these points would also allow the student to gain an extra mark.

> **Tip**
>
> Do not give short one-line answers to answer any 'discuss' question. Always look for two sides to the discussion, offering as many different points and detail to support these points for both sides before trying to use the points to come up with a reasoned conclusion.

Exam-style questions for you to try

1. A presentation will be delivered as a lecture and will use both presenter notes and audience notes. Explain why audience notes and presenter notes often contain different content. **[2]**
2. A presentation will be used in a shopping mall to advertise different shops and their products. Identify the feature added to the presentation to make sure that it never ends. **[1]**

20 Spreadsheets

Key objectives

The objectives of this chapter are to revise:
- spreadsheet models
- spreadsheet structures
- order of mathematical operations
- formulae
- absolute and relative cell referencing
- functions
- nested functions
- search data
- sort data
- format cells.

20.1 Create a data model

REVISED

20.1.1 Spreadsheet models

A spreadsheet is often used to create a model. This is sometimes called a data model. By changing the contents of one or more cells in a spreadsheet, different outcomes can be calculated and predicted. Sometimes data modelling is called making a 'what if scenario'. These models are often:

- financial
- mathematical
- scientific.

20.1.2 Spreadsheet structures

A spreadsheet is a two-dimensional table or grid consisting of rows, columns and cells and is used to perform calculations. Each cell has a cell reference like G5 (although this may not be seen if the cell has been given a name) which is the address for that cell. You can give an individual cell or a block of cells a name. These are called named cells and named ranges.

All spreadsheets store data using:

- **Rows:** each row is all the cells in one horizontal line in a spreadsheet. The row heading contains the number displayed to the left of the first cell.
- **Columns:** each column is all the cells in one vertical line in a spreadsheet. The column heading contains the letter displayed above the top cell.
- **Cells:** each is a single square/box within a spreadsheet into which only a single entry can be placed. A cell can hold a:
  - **label** (some text)
  - **number**
  - **formula** (that starts with an = sign).

Cells can be formatted to display data in different ways, so what a user sees in the cell is not always the actual content of the cell.

Sometimes more than one spreadsheet (which is sometimes called a worksheet) are stored together in a workbook.

> **Tip**
>
> Practice using named cells and named ranges. These are often required in the practical examinations. Make sure that you name the range exactly as it appears in the question paper (including case).

Hodder & Stoughton Limited © David Watson and Graham Brown 2022

20.1.3 Formulae

Formulae start with an = sign. Simple formulae can be used to:

- Refer to the contents of another cell, for example cell A2 contains the formula =B4. The formula copies the contents of B4 and displays it in A2. If the contents of B4 were changed, then the contents of A2 would also change.
- Perform calculations, for example cell A7 contains the formula =A5+A6. The formula adds together the contents of cells A5 and A6 and displays the result in cell A7. If the values held in either A5 or A6 were changed, then the contents of A7 would change.

The changing of cells to see the results is called modelling.

Arithmetic operators

Symbol	Operation
+	Addition
-	Subtraction
*	Multiplication
/	Division
^	Indices (to the power of)

20.1.4 Order of mathematical operations

The spreadsheet performs all calculations using the mathematical order of operations (BIDMAS). The rules are:

B	**B**rackets first
I	**I**ndices (i.e. powers and square roots etc.)
DM	**D**ivision and **M**ultiplication (left to right)
AS	**A**ddition and **S**ubtraction (left to right)

- Divide and multiply rank equally (and go left to right).
- Add and subtract rank equally (and go left to right).
- After you have done **B** and **I**, go from left to right doing any **D** or **M** as you find them.
- Then go from left to right doing any **A** or **S** as you find them.

Sample questions and responses

REVISED

Nicola tries the following formulae in her spreadsheet to model the total cost of some items:

	A	B	C
1	Number of items	Cost per item	
2	5	6	
3			
4	Total cost		
5	=5*6		
6	=A2*B2		

a) Calculate the answers that will be seen in:
   i) Cell A5.
   ii) Cell A6. [2 marks]
b) Explain, giving examples, why both formulae might not always provide the same answers. [3 marks]

Sample answers
a) i) 30
   ii) 30
b) Both give the same answer, so they are both correct.

Teacher's comments

Both parts of part (a) of this question are correct. For part (b), this is a very short answer for a 3 mark question, and contains an incorrect response, ignoring the help from the question suggesting it 'might not always provide the same answers'. Although the student has realised that for this set of data the correct answer would be gained in cell A5, they have not realised that, should the number of items or the cost of each item change, this cell would still give the total 30. As the question tells us that this spreadsheet will be used to model the total cost of some items, it is almost certain that the contents of either cell A2 or B2 (or both) are likely to change. When this happens, the answer in cell A6 will give the correct answer, but the formula in cell A5 is unlikely to do so. To gain the final mark for this question, a student would demonstrate this reasoning and then conclude that Nicola is not correct with her statement.

Tip
When asked to model data, design your spreadsheet so that you do not have to change your formulae. Referencing to other cells (like the formula in

20.1.5 Cell referencing

Absolute and relative cell referencing

Absolute cell referencing is a way of fixing the position of a cell within a formula. It is fixed using the $ key. For example, the formula =A3*$A$1 has the reference to cell A1 set as an absolute reference, while the reference to cell A3 is a **relative cell reference**. When the formula is replicated (copied), the reference to cell A1 will not change but the reference to cell A3 will change, like this:

	A	B
1	2	Times Table
2		
3	1	=A3*$A$1
4	2	=A4*$A$1
5	3	=A5*$A$1
6	4	=A6*$A$1
7	5	=A7*$A$1

Named cells and named ranges are automatically set as absolute references.

20.1.6 Functions

A function is a pre-set **formula** with a name. All types of spreadsheet software contain built-in functions. Make sure you are familiar with the use of each of these functions:

Function	Use and example
SUM	Adds two or more numbers together. =SUM(A3:A9)
AVERAGE	Calculates the average (mean) of a range of numbers by adding all the numbers together and dividing this total by the number of numbers that were added. =AVERAGE(A3:A9)
MAX	Displays the largest (maximum) number from a range of numbers. =MAX(A3:A9)
MIN	Displays the smallest (minimum) number from a range of numbers. =MIN(A3:A9)

20.1 Create a data model

Function	Use and example
INT	Calculates the integer (whole number) part of a number by removing all digits after the decimal point. =INT(B3)
ROUND	Calculates a number rounded to a number of decimal places. If 0 decimal places are specified, it rounds to the nearest whole number. This looks at the first digit after the decimal point and, if it is five or more, adds one to the whole number answer. =ROUND(B3,0)
COUNT	This looks at the cells within a given range and counts the number of these cells that contain numbers. =COUNT(A3:A9)
COUNTA	This looks at the cells within a given range and counts the number of these cells that contain labels and/or numbers. =COUNTA(A3:A9)
COUNTIF	This looks at the cells within a given range and counts the number of cells in that range that meet a given condition. The condition is placed in the function and can be a number, a label, an inequality or a cell reference. =COUNTIF(A3:A9,B3)
IF	This gives different actions/calculations/results depending upon the results of a given condition. If the condition is true, the first action/calculation/result is displayed/calculated. If the condition is false, the second action/calculation/ result is displayed/calculated. =IF(A1="Fred",0.5,A2*3)
SUMIF	This looks at the cells within a given range and if the cells in that range meet a given condition, it adds the value in a corresponding cell to produce the total. =SUMIF(A3:A9,4,B3:B9)
HLOOKUP	This performs a horizontal look up of data, by looking at each of the cells in the top row of a given range and comparing them with a given condition. The condition is placed in the function and can be a number, a string, an inequality or a cell reference. If the condition matches the contents of a cell, a value is looked up from the corresponding cell in a row below. The number of the required row is placed in the function (in the example shown, it is the second row in the range). The final parameter of the function can be 0 (or False), which forces an exact match when the data is compared, or 1 (or True) for an approximate match. =HLOOKUP(A3,C2:G3,2,0)
VLOOKUP	This performs a vertical look up of data, by looking at each of the cells in the left column of a given range and comparing them with a given condition. The condition is placed in the function and can be a number, a string, an inequality or a cell reference. If the condition matches the contents of a cell, a value is looked up from the corresponding cell in a column to the right. The number of the column to the right is placed in the function (in the example shown, it is the third column in the range). The final parameter of the function can be 0 (or False), which forces an exact match when the data is compared, or 1 (or True) for an approximate match. =VLOOKUP(A3,A5:C9,3,1)
XLOOKUP	This performs either a horizontal or a vertical look up of data. This is similar to HLOOKUP and VLOOKUP but is more powerful and flexible than either of these. It will also reference data stored in rows/columns before the lookup value. It therefore allows backward referencing within an array. The values to be looked up can be stored to either the right or left or above or below the lookup array. The look-up data can be stored either in the same file or in a different file. Using the example below, it works by comparing the condition given (contents of cell A3) with each of the cells in the first given range (which may be a row or column, in this case A5:A9). If the condition matches the contents of a cell, a value is looked up from the corresponding cell in the second range (which may be a row or column, in this case C5:C9). The text string "Not found" is displayed if there is no match. The next parameter of the function can be 0 which forces an exact match, −1 for an exact match or the next smaller item, 1 for an exact match or the next larger item, or 2 for a wildcard search. The final parameter can be 1 which searches (the range A5:A9) from the first cell to the last cell, −1 which searches from last to first, 2 which sorts the data and searches in ascending order, or −2 which sorts the data and searches in descending order. =XLOOKUP(A3, A5:A9, C5:C9,"Not found",0,1)

20.1.7 Nested functions

Sometimes examination questions will ask for formulae that are more complex. These types of question will often need one function inside another function. If three different conditions are needed, then nested **IF** functions are ideal. If there are lots of different conditions, using either **VLOOKUP** or **HLOOKUP** is a better option than lots of different nested **IF** statements.

Sample question and response

REVISED

Identify the formula that you would place in cell A10 to display the text Lower, Middle or Higher depending upon the contents of cell A3. If cell A3 contains a value:

- between 8 and 12 inclusive then display 'Middle'
- less than 8 then display 'Lower'
- greater than 12 then display 'Higher'. **[8 marks]**

Sample answer
=IF(A3<8, "Lower",IF(8=<A3=12,"Middle",IF(A3=<12Higher",0))

Teacher's comments

There is no single correct answer to this question. The student has started well by realising that nested IF functions would offer the best solution, but because there can be no other possible conditions for numbers held in A3 (it has to be less than 8, between 8 and 12 or greater than 12) only two IF statements are needed.

The student has also correctly identified that the data in the question is in an illogical order and has worked from the lowest value in A3 to the highest.

The initial **=IF(A3<8,"Lower",** is correct and would gain marks, but the next section contains a serious syntax error. The condition **IF(8=<A3=12,** would not be recognised by *Excel* as this contains two conditions and no logical operator like AND or OR to link them. The two conditions are not needed as anything less than 8 has already been trapped by the earlier function, so a single condition like **IF(A3<=12** would work. Because *Excel* would stop at this point, no further marks would be awarded for this formula.

This student's solution also contains another syntax error. There are three opening brackets and only two closing brackets.

There are many correct possible answers such as:

=IF(A3<8,"Lower",IF(A3<=12,"Middle","Higher"))

=IF(A3>12,"Higher",IF(A3>=8,"Middle","Lower"))

> **Tip**
> When given a question that requires nested IF functions, always work from lowest to highest (in order) or highest to lowest. Do *not* assume that the order of the question will give you the correct results.

20.2 Manipulate data

REVISED

20.2.1 Search data

Use the Custom AutoFilter tool (see page 463 in the *Cambridge IGCSE Information and Communication Technology Third Edition* Student's book) to search for subsets of data in your spreadsheet. This tool will allow you to present the examiner with evidence of your method by taking screenshots of the Custom AutoFilter window and placing this in your Evidence Document. Using the drop-down filter options does not always show the examiner the evidence of your method. This facility also allows you to use other features, like the use of the ? symbol to show a single wildcard character and the * symbol to show a wildcard selection of any length.

20.2.2 Sort data

Make sure that you select all the data for each item to be sorted. Make sure that you do not include the column headings in the data that is sorted.

Common errors

REVISED

Error	Solution
When a block of data needs to be sorted into a particular order, for example by name, only the single column of data that you are sorting by (the name column) has been selected	Highlight the whole block of data before performing the sort. Otherwise, when the data is sorted (by name column), the other data in the block would not be sorted with it and the integrity of the data would be lost
When all the data has been selected, the column headings are also selected so that these are sorted within the data	Highlight all the data apart from the column headings or select the tick box for 'My data has headers'

> **Tip**
>
> If more than one level of sorting is required on your data, always use 'Custom Sort...' to open the sort window. This allows you to add the different levels of sorting and also allows you to screenshot this window to place evidence of your method in your Evidence Document.

20.3 Present data

REVISED

20.3.1 Format cells

Cells can be formatted to enhance the contents and create, for example, titles and subtitles. Make sure to practise merging cells, applying bold, italic and underlining, changing the background and foreground (text) colours, and selecting different font sizes and styles, including serif and sans serif fonts.

Formatting cells containing numbers changes the way each cell is displayed but does not change the value held within it.

Common error

REVISED

Error	Solution
Where a question states 'Calculate … to 0 decimal places', you format the cell(s) as integers (to 0 decimal places) rather than using the INT or ROUND functions	If the question states 'Calculate … to 0 decimal places', use the INT or ROUND function

> **Tips**
> - If a question asks for '… rounded to one decimal place', this means the answer is both rounded and displayed to one decimal place. If a question asks '… displayed to one decimal place', the number in the cell is not changed but the cell is formatted to show only one decimal place.
> - If a question asks you to 'apply appropriate formatting to the spreadsheet', check the initial rubric as this usually indicates the type of currency or other formatting and number of decimal places. You will need to identify which cells should be, for example, currency/percentage and format these as appropriate.

Common errors

REVISED

Error	Solution
Currency format is applied to all numeric cells in the spreadsheet	Check what each cell represents. Only format it as currency/percentage, and so on, if it contains that type of data
The currency symbol can't be found in my regional settings so I will not format the cells	Scroll down the list of currencies available until the three letter ISO (international standard) codes appear. If the currency symbol for the country is not available, use the ISO code, for example for US dollars ($) it is USD, for pounds (£) sterling it is GBP (Great Britain pounds)

20.3.2 Change the size of the row and columns

Make sure that you set the column width and row height so that all data and labels are fully displayed.

Common errors

REVISED

Error	Solution
Producing printouts, particularly formulae printouts where all of the formulae are not fully visible	Check that each formula is fully visible. Don't just check the first row. Often the last row is much longer than the first. If it can't all be seen, make the row wider
Producing printouts where all the formulae are fully visible but are so small they are impossible to read	Do not leave lots of white space in each cell after the formulae. If the question does not instruct you to print on a single-width page, allow the formulae printout to run over more than one page

> **Tip**
> If the question does not state use portrait orientation, set the formulae printout to landscape.

20.3 Present data

Exam-style questions for you to try

1 The following spreadsheet shows the value of sales in a number of countries.

	A	B	C	D	E	F	G	H	I
1	Country	Code		Currency	Value		Date	Code	Sales
2	Brazil	BR		Real (R$)	940.00		15/12/2016	EC	200.50
3	Canada	CA		Dollar ($)	2050.50		16/12/2016	CA	320.20
4	Colombia	CO		Peso	62000.00		16/12/2016	PA	155.00
5	Ecuador	EC		Dollar ($)	746.50		17/12/2016	CO	12000.00
6	Mexico	MX		Peso	7650.00		18/12/2016	PA	200.00
7	Panama	PA		Balboa	885.00		20/12/2016	VZ	350.00
8	Venezuela	VZ		Bolivar	350.00		04/01/2017	EC	400.50
9							05/01/2017	CA	1020.00
10							09/01/2017	CO	30000.00
11							09/01/2017	MX	3150.00
12							10/01/2017	MX	2400.00
13							10/01/2017	PA	320.00
14							10/01/2017	BR	1210.50
15							11/01/2017	BR	940.00
16							12/01/2017	PA	210.00
17							14/01/2017	MX	2100.00
18							15/01/2017	CA	310.00
19							15/01/2017	CA	400.20
20							15/01/2017	CO	20000.00
21							16/01/2017	EC	145.50
22							No. products =		20.00

   a Cell E5 contains the formula:
      =SUMIF($H$2:$H$21,B5,$I$2:$I$21)
      Explain what this formula does. [4]
   b Write down the formula you would expect to see in cell E6. [3]
   c The formula in cell I22 refers to all the values in column I. Write down the formula you would expect to see in cell I22 to produce the value **20**. [2]

2 Two students use different formulae to calculate the whole number of dollars for products that they have sold.
Student A uses the formula:

=INT(A42*A43)
Student B uses the formula:
=ROUND(A42*A43,0)

Explain (using examples) why sometimes the two formulae give the same answer and other times they do not. [4]

3 a A cell contains the function =COUNTIF(ObjectTable,$A$3)
     Explain what this function does. [3]
   b Explain why $A$3 has been used rather than A3. [3]

21 Website authoring

Key objectives

The objectives of this chapter are to revise:
- web development layers
- web page structure
- predefined styles
- tables
- image, video and audio files
- bulleted and numbered lists
- bookmarks and hyperlinks
- absolute and relative file paths
- the head section
- metatags
- stylesheet structure
- CSS syntax
- font properties
- working with colour
- background colours and images
- table properties
- styles and classes
- CSS tables.

21.1 Web development layers

REVISED

21.1.1 What is a website?

A **website** is a collection of individual but related **web pages**, often stored together on a **web server**. The website can be created using a web-authoring package or text editor. It is displayed in software called a browser.

A **web page** is created using three layers:

- The **content layer**: contains the structure of the web page and its contents including text, images and hyperlinks. This is created in **HyperText Markup Language (HTML)**.
- The **presentation layer**: contains the styles and appearance of the web page. This is created in **Cascading StyleSheet (CSS)**.
- The **behaviour layer**: contains actions within the web page that often involve script languages. This is often created in JavaScript but is beyond the scope of the IGCSE course.

21.1.2 What is a web browser?

A web browser is application software that displays a web page allowing us to view and explore information, often on the web using http. To display a web page, it renders the page from all three layers to create the layout displayed for the user.

21.2 Create a web page

REVISED

21.2.1 Web page structure

This is completed in the content layer and is created in HTML. Whether you use a **text editor** like *Notepad* or a What You See Is What You Get (WYSIWYG) web-authoring package to develop a web page, it is always wise to add comments to your page. For the practical examination, these should include your name, centre number and candidate number. Comments are added using the following HTML syntax:

```
<!-- This is a comment in html -->
```

Make sure your HTML5 starts with `<!DOCTYPE html>` followed by `<html>` and ends with `</html>`.

Between the `<html>` and `</html>` **tags**, each web page is split into two sections: the **head** section and **body** section.

The head section is always above the body section and contains elements used in the page but these are **not displayed** on the page, for example the page title and attached stylesheets.

The body section contains the structure of the page, the contents placed within this structure and any hyperlinks. The contents of the body section are usually displayed in the browser. The structure of the web page you will create for the examinations will use tables.

> **Tip**
> Each time you make a small change to your HTML (or your CSS) save it, load the web page back into your browser (or press F5 to refresh it), then test the changes you have made. If you save and test after each change, it is easy to correct any errors that you may make.

21.2.2 Predefined styles

There are a number of predefined styles, including:

- p   paragraph style
- li   list styles (for bulleted or numbered lists)
- h1   heading style 1 (usually has the largest font size)
- h2   heading style 2
- h3   heading style 3
- h4   heading style 4
- h5   heading style 5
- h6   heading style 6 (usually has the smallest font size).

Your browser has default settings defined for each of these styles, but you can change how each one looks later in the presentation layer. Each of these styles is applied with an opening tag such as `<p>` and closed with `</p>`. The / tells the browser that this style has now finished. When you define any text in your web page, always use one of the style definitions above.

21.2.3 Tables

Tables can be used to structure the web page. They are used to organise page layout and are often used to define the structure with no borders visible, so that a page keeps a similar look even when a browser is resized. Each table can have a header with header data, footer with footer data, and body section with table rows and table data in each cell. These areas are defined by the tags `<table>`, `<thead>`, `<th>`, `<tfoot>`, `<tbody>`, `<tr>` and `<td>`, respectively. Again a / is placed after the < to close each section, for example `</table>`.

Table borders can be set as on with the **attribute** `<table border="1">` or off with `<table border="">`. They can also be made invisible in the presentation layer (CSS) attached to the web page. All other changes to table borders are made in the CSS, although this is sometimes placed in the HTML as an embedded style using the style attribute. An example of this is to merge all borders within a table where the CSS border-collapse element has been embedded in the HTML: `<table border="1" style="border-collapse:collapse">`.

See page 489 of *Cambridge IGCSE Information and Communication Technology Third Edition* Student's book for more detail on table structures.

> **Tip**
> Practise creating and editing tables including the use of the rowspan and colspan attributes `<td rowspan=…>` and `<td colspan=…>` to make table data appear over more than one row and/or column.

Sample question and response

REVISED ☐

Identify the HTML used to create a table structure, with no formatting, to look like this:

Cost table	
Item	Cost
Apple	$0.40
Banana	$0.80

List only the HTML for the table and one line of markup as a comment with your name. [6 marks]

Sample answer

```
<-- Graham Brown, table for sample question -->
<table border="1" style="border-width:2px">
  <tr>
    <td rowspan="2">
      <p>Cost table</p>
    </td>
  </tr>
  <tr>
    <td>
      <p>Item</p>
    </td>
    <td>
      <p>Cost</p>
    </td>
  </tr>
  <tr>
    <td>
      <p>Apple</p>
    </td>
    <td>
      <p>$0.40</p>
    </td>
  </tr>
    <td>
      <p>Banana</p>
    </td>
    <td>
      <p>$0.80</p>
    </td>
  </tr>
```

Teacher's comments

This markup contains a number of errors that would not allow the table to be displayed as shown in the question. The table data in the first row contains an error. This should show a colspan set to 2 rather than a rowspan set to 2. The final row of the table does not have a `<tr>` tag. The table has not been closed with a `</table>` tag. The markup for the table tag contains embedded CSS using the style attribute. The indented markup helps both the student and the examiner to check each pair of tags is present; notice how all `<tr>` and `</tr>` tags start at the same point on each line, and within each table row all the `<td>` tags also start from the same point as each other but are indented from the `<tr>` tags.

21.2 Create a web page

21.2.4 Images

Images are inserted into the framework of the table. The image (`<img>`) tag is used for this. This tag should always have (at least) two attributes, these are the:

- **image source** (`src`): which identifies the name of the file that will be used as the image
- the alternate text (`alt`): which is displayed instead of the image if the image cannot be displayed.

The image tag is one of the few tags that does not have a closing tag. An example of the syntax is:

```
<img src="img0047.jpg" alt="Image of a computer monitor">
```

You will notice that the image source does not have any file path. For this hyperlink to work, the image *must* be stored in the same folder as the saved web page (they will be uploaded from this folder to the host web server) or the image will not be displayed.

Bitmap graphics formats have always been used for websites, in particular JPEG (.jpg), GIF (.gif) and more recently PNG (.png). Vector graphics such as Scalable Vector Graphics (.svg) are now also used in some web pages but these are not suitable for all types of image.

For the purposes of this IGCSE, concentrate your answers on bitmap format graphics (not to be confused with .bmp format) such as JPEGs, GIFs and PNGs. Each of these can be resized in a graphics package (often to reduce the image and file sizes) or you can use embedded CSS in a style attribute of the image tag. To resize the image, img0047, to 200 pixels wide (and maintain its aspect ratio,) the example shown above will change to:

```
<img src="img0047.jpg" style="width:200px" alt="Image of a computer monitor">
```

> **Tip**
>
> Some of the errors identified here are typical of those found in students' answers. For example, not carefully reading the question, which specified no formatting, yet embedded CSS has been created by the student. Not closing each tag with its corresponding / tag. As almost all HTML tags work in pairs (there are a few exceptions like `<brk><img>`), check carefully that each tag is closed in the correct place.

21.2.5 Videos

Always use the `<video>` tag to place a video. There are other ways of doing this but many of these are now deprecated and will not work in all browsers. Add width and height attributes to the `<video>` tag for the video size and controls if required. A `<source>` tag is used to identify the source of the video, which is different to the attribute used for still images. An example of the syntax used for a video file is:

```
<video width="300" height="224" controls>
   Your browser does not support this type of video.
   <source src="wreck.mp4" type="video/mp4">
</video>
```

21.2.6 Audio files

Audio files are placed in the HTML in a very similar way to video files, but do not need width and height attributes. For example:

```
<audio controls>
   Your browser does not support this type of audio file.
   <source src="whale.mp3" type="audio/mpeg">
</audio>
```

21.2.7 Bulleted and numbered lists

The `<li>` tag is used to open each item in a list, and each item is closed with a `</li>` tag. There are two types of lists available in a web page. These are:

- An **ordered list** (can appear as a numbered or lettered list). Each ordered list (not each list item) starts with the `<ol>` tag and ends with `</ol>`.
- An **unordered list** (a bulleted list). Each unordered list (not each list item) starts with the `<ul>` tag and the list ends with `</ul>`.

Sometimes lists can be nested with bulleted, numbered (or lettered lists) placed inside another list.

Sample question and response

REVISED

The following HTML will be placed in the body section of a web page.

```
<h1>Holiday destinations</h1>
<ul>
  <li>Maldives</li>
    <ol>
       <li>relaxing beach holidays</li>
       <li>scuba diving</li>
       <li>wind surfing</li>
    </ol>
  <li>Austria</li>
    <ol>
       <li>skiing</li>
       <li>climbing</li>
       <li>mountain biking</li>
    </ol>
  <li>Iceland</li>
</ul>
```

Describe the results of this markup when seen in a web browser. **[6 marks]**

21.2 Create a web page

Sample answer
The title Holiday destinations has been placed above nested lists. There are three lists, one main list and two sub-lists.

Teacher's comments

> This is the beginning of a good answer. The student has identified that the initial text is in style h1 and is therefore a heading (although it would have been better for the student to also describe this to the examiner). They have also identified that there are three lists, one a main list and two sub-lists.
>
> The student has not identified the types of list used. For example: 'The main list is a bulleted or unordered list. It is not possible to identify the type of bullet points that would be seen because that depends upon the list styles applied in the stylesheet or on the browser's default list style setting.'
>
> For the two sub-lists, the student could identify: 'For two of the countries a numbered or lettered list of some popular activities that take place in these countries has been included. It is not possible to identify the format of these lists from the HTML as the presentation elements are covered in the stylesheet or in the browser's default ordered list settings.'
>
> Another good method is to use a diagram as an example, along with the text, for example: 'The browser may display this so it looks like the example shown here.' This could then lead into further detail like the sub-lists are indented from the main list, and so on. As it is a 6 mark question, more detail is required than this student has given.

Holiday destinations
- Maldives
  1. relaxing beach holidays
  2. scuba diving
  3. wind surfing
- Austria
  1. skiing
  2. climbing
  3. mountain biking
- Iceland

> **Tip**
> While a diagram can help to answer a question, the description will gain the marks, although sometimes a sketched diagram can help to make it clear to the examiner what you are describing.

21.2.8 Bookmarks and hyperlinks

A **bookmark** is a named reference point in an electronic document. It is set using an `id` attribute within a tag for example: `<li id="bkmrk1">`. Bookmarks are often used to hyperlink to that point from other locations.

A **hyperlink** is a method of accessing another document or resource from your current application. Hyperlinks can:

- move your position within a page
- open another page either locally or on the internet
- open your email editor so that you can send an email.

Each hyperlink is created using an `<a>` (anchor tag) and closed with `</a>`. These tags must surround the text or image that will be used for the hyperlink. The hyperlink is created by adding a `href` (hyperlink reference) attribute to the anchor which shows the place to move to (or action to perform).

172 Cambridge IGCSE Information and Communication Technology Study and Revision Guide Second Edition

21.2.9 Absolute and relative file paths

If the `href` is set to a file path, for example:

```
<a href="page33.htm">
```

this must be a **relative file path** (containing no references to any folder structure or local drives).

The use of an **absolute file path**, for example:

```
<a href="D:/myfiles/page33.htm">
```

may work on the machine you are using but is unlikely to work when uploaded to your web server.

Hyperlinks can be used to open web pages in the same browser window or a new browser window by setting the target attribute. The target attribute can be attached to an individual hyperlink like this:

```
<a href="page33.htm" target="_blank">
```

There are a small number of acceptable target extensions but for IGCSE `_blank` opens the new web page or document in a new window or tab and `_self` opens it in the current window or tab.

If all hyperlinks to linked web pages or documents are to appear the same, then this attribute can be set in the attached stylesheet as a default target window using:

```
<base target="_blank">
```

This *must* be placed in the `<head>` section of the web page. If the target attribute is not used, the browser will decide where to open a web page.

> **Tip**
> Do not use absolute references for any files, including attached stylesheets. Remember to set all file references to relative references, as absolute references are unlikely to work if your web page is opened on a different computer.

Sample questions and responses

REVISED

a) Describe what the following html does.

```
<a href="#mb1">mountain biking</a>
```
[2 marks]

b) Explain why the HTML in part (a) may not work. [1 mark]

c) Describe what the following HTML does.

```
<a href=https://www.hoddereducation.co.uk/ target="_blank"> <img src="bk.jpg" alt=""></a>
```
[2 marks]

d) Describe what the following html does.

```
<ahref="mailto:graham.a.brown@hotmail.co.uk?subject=Revision%20guide">here</a>
```
[2 marks]

Sample answers
a) When the user clicks on the text 'mountain biking' they are moved to an internal bookmark which has been called 'mb1'.
b) It is not there.
c) This hyperlink moves the user from the image called 'bk.jpg'. When it is clicked on it goes to a website.
d) This sends an email to the person with the address graham.a.brown@hotmail.co.uk

Teacher's comments
a) This is a sound student answer worth both marks, the first for identifying that the text is used for the link and the second for identifying that it moves the user to an internal anchor. It would have been even better if the student had used the word 'hyperlink' in their response.
b) This is a common type of answer. The response is not worth any marks because the student does not explain what is not there. A response such as, 'There may be no internal bookmark called "mb1" within the body text of the web page' would gain this mark.
c) This response starts well. The student has identified it is a hyperlink and has been very specific about the image and named it. The second part of this response is not as strong; the student has identified that it goes to a website but has not been specific enough in their answer. There is also no mention of the target window selected in this markup. This new web page would open in a new window called '_blank' and would, therefore, appear as a new tab in the browser.
d) This is a classic incorrect answer. The hyperlink does not send an email. When the hyperlink is clicked upon, it opens the default email editor and prepares an email to the recipient. In this example, it also places the text 'Revision guide' into the subject line of the email; the %20 forces a single space between the words.

> **Tip**
> Think carefully about the answers you give; for 'describe' questions give the examiner as much detail as possible. Do not assume the examiner knows what you are thinking ... put it down in your answer.

21.2.10 The head section
The head section is a container for all the head elements such as titles, stylesheets and metadata. The word metadata means data about other data. The head section is always placed between the `<html>` tag and `<body>` tag. The metadata about the HTML document is not displayed in the browser.

21.2.11 Metatags
A **metatag** is a tag that holds metadata. It uses the `<meta>` tag to open it and the `</meta>` tag to close it. We will use only three attributes with the `<meta>` tag; these are: charset, name and content.

- **Charset** is an attribute used to define the character set used by a web page and specifies the type of characters (called the character encoding) that are displayed, like this:

```
<head>
   <meta charset="UTF-8">
</head>
```

- Name is an attribute used to specify things like the author, description, keywords and viewport. Each time the name attribute is used, it is followed by a content attribute.
- Content is an attribute used with the name attribute and contains the value assigned to the name. This value is in the form of text, like this:

```html
<head>
  <meta name="author" content="Graham Brown">
  <meta name="description" content="Web page tips">
  <meta name="keywords" content="HTML, web page tips">
  <meta name="viewport" content="width=device-width, initial-scale=1.0">
  <meta charset="UTF-8">
</head>
```

21.3 Use stylesheets

REVISED

Using styles in your web pages helps you to be consistent in the way the pages look. Using styles is much quicker and easier than applying individual settings. Styles can be set for text, defining the same font face, font size, text alignment, font colours and so on, to every piece of text in each web page that you create. Styles can define page layout, colour schemes and default settings for other objects and links on the page.

Styles can be set with HTML tags. They are defined in the presentation layer of the web page in CSS format. You can embed CSS elements in the HTML using the style attribute. These are called in-line styles. Styles may also be defined in the head section of a web page or defined in an external **stylesheet**. These are attached to the web page in the head section. It is more efficient to write, edit and attach one or more common stylesheet/s to all the pages in a website. This collection of styles is saved in a different file in cascading stylesheet (.css) format. If a number of external stylesheets are applied to a web page, the first stylesheet has the lowest priority and the last stylesheet has the highest priority, so if the same style was defined differently in two different stylesheets, the style defined in the last attached stylesheet will be used.

21.3.1 Stylesheet structure

This is completed in the presentation layer and is created in CSS. Whether you use a text editor like *Notepad* or a WYSIWYG package to develop a web page, it is always wise to add comments to your stylesheet. For the practical examination, these should include your name, centre number and candidate number. Comments are added using the following HTML syntax:

```
/* This is a comment in css */
```

21.3 Use stylesheets

Styles can be applied by using:

- embedded styles, where styles are placed using a style attribute within the HTML, but these have to be defined for each element
- attached stylesheets, where styles are placed in a document that is loaded by the browser. The style definitions from the document are applied to all elements on the web page.

Embedded styles overrule attached styles and are placed in the HTML like this:

```
<table style="background-color: #0000ff; color: #ff0000">
```

In this example, the table would have a blue background colour and yellow text, which may be different from the styles set in the attached stylesheet.

Attached stylesheets contain all the styles that may be needed for a web page. Using these saves a lot of work as the styles only need defining once, then the stylesheet can be attached to a number of pages. These web pages will then all have the same presentation features. This is very useful for showing corporate house styles. A number of different stylesheets can be attached in the `<head>` section of each web page. The bottom stylesheet has the highest priority, then the one above it and so on, hence the name 'cascading' stylesheets as each one flows towards the bottom (like a series of cascading waterfalls, the last one being the largest and most powerful). The stylesheet is attached like this:

```
<link rel="stylesheet" href="style1.css">
```

The hyperlink reference must be a relative file path containing no references to any folder structure or local drives. If not, the stylesheet is unlikely to be found when uploaded to your web server, unless the computer using the web page has an identical file name and file structure to your computer.

If both attached stylesheets and embedded styles are included on a web page, the embedded styles override the attached stylesheet.

21.3.2 CSS syntax

All CSS rules have a selector and a declaration block like this:

```
h1      {color:#ff0000; font-size:14px;}
```

Selector: h1 (HTML element)
Declaration: {color:#ff0000; ...} — Property: color, Value: #ff0000
Declaration: font-size:14px; — Property: font-size, Value: 14px

> **Tip**
> Practise creating styles in a stylesheet attached to a web page. Edit each style to see what difference it makes. Remember to save the stylesheet in CSS format after each change and to refresh the web page for the changes to take effect.

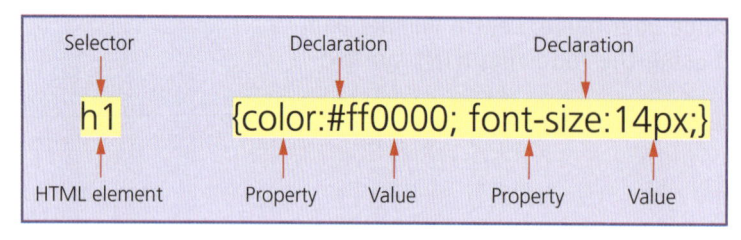

- Each element has one or more declarations, each separated by a semicolon.
- Each declaration has a property name and a value, separated by a colon.
- Each declaration block is surrounded by curly brackets.

21.3.3 Font properties

Font families

Setting font families in your stylesheet often needs you to specify three different values for each declaration. One of these is usually a *Microsoft Windows* font, one an *Apple* font and the third is usually a generic font family in case neither of the font faces selected is available. An example of this is:

```
h1      {font-family: "Times New Roman","Times",serif}
```

The browser looks at the font list and tries to find the first named font family in its stored font list. If it is present, it displays this. If not, it looks at the next named font, with the same results. If none of the named fonts are available, it displays its default serif or sans serif font.

Sample question and response

REVISED

Define style h1 as Trebuchet. If this is not available, then Trebuchet MS. If neither of these fonts are available, then the browser's default sans serif font.   **[4 marks]**

Sample answer

```
h1      {font-family: "Trebuchet"}
```

Teacher's comments

> This student has probably got a font called Trebuchet installed in their computer, so they have selected this as the only font required as it works for them at this moment in time. The correct answer should have been:

```
h1      {font-family: "Trebuchet","Trebuchet MS",sans-serif}
```

Font size

Having dealt with setting font families, let us move on to consider font size. Font size can also be set when text styles are defined, for example:

```
h1      {font-family: serif; font-size: 60pt}
```

The `font-family` has been reduced to a single generic font so that it all fits on one line, and the `font-size` property value has been set to 60 points high.

Font sizes can be set as **absolute values**, for example 72pt which would appear approximately 25 mm high (depending upon the size and resolution of the monitor), or as **relative values**, for example 2em, which would enlarge this text to twice the size of the current font.

> **Tip**
>
> Read the question carefully, especially where font size is concerned. Font sizes are likely to be specified in either points, picas or pixels (although other types of measurement are possible). Marks are unlikely to be awarded if the correct type of measurement is not present. There must also be no space between the `60` and the `pt`.

21.3 Use stylesheets

Text alignment

Text alignment is set with the `text-align` property. The possible values that can be added to this are shown here:

```
h1      {text-align: left}
h2      {text-align: center}
h3      {text-align: right}
h4      {text-align: justify}
```

Text can be bold, italic or underlined. Each uses a different property for the declaration. These are:

```
h1      {font-weight:bold;
         font-style:italic;
         text-decoration:underline}
```

21.3.4 Text colour

Text can be coloured using the `color` property followed by a hexadecimal RGB value, such as:

```
h1      {color: #ff0000}
```

Colour is always defined in the presentation layer (using CSS), usually in an external stylesheet. Colour codes are usually referred to using hexadecimal numbers and are always listed in RGB order. RGB are the primary colours for light: Red, Green and Blue. Each hexadecimal colour code has six digits, two for red, then two for green, then two for blue.

21.3.5 Background colour

This CSS will produce a web page with a red background:

```
body    {background-color: #ff0000}
```

The `#` tells the browser that the number is in hexadecimal and the American spelling of 'color' must be used. The `ff` for the red component turns on full red light for each pixel on the screen or projector, and each `00` for green and blue turns off these colours. If all colours are `00` (so it becomes `#000000`), then the screen would be black as no colour is projected, and if they were all fully on (`#ffffff`), then the screen would be white as mixing red, blue and green light gives white light.

21.3.6 Background colours and images

Background colours and images are defined in CSS with the body selector. The background image is added with a value using **URL** syntax like this.

```
body    {background-color:#0047fc;
         background-image: url("image3.png");
         background-repeat: no-repeat;}
```

The background repeat declaration is set to repeat if you wish to have 'tiled' images. If there is no background repeat, you can define the position of the background image in the window.

178 Cambridge IGCSE Information and Communication Technology Study and Revision Guide Second Edition

21.3.7 Table properties

Table definitions can be set in external stylesheets. This is very useful if web pages contain a number of tables. Different selectors can be used to format different parts of tables in different ways, for example the body of the page, tables and table headers can have different background colours that complement each other. Table borders can also be defined in the stylesheet, for example:

```
body    {background-color:#90ee90;}
table   {background-color:#2eb757;
         border-collapse:collapse;
         border-style:solid;
         border-width:6px}
td      {border-style:solid;
         border-width:3px}
```

This defines different background colours for the table and body of the page and sets the table to have a six-pixel-wide border around it and three-pixel-wide gridlines within the table.

21.3.8 Styles and classes

Styles are defined and applied to all web pages to give consistency through all the pages in a website. There are times when some element of a page needs to be different or stand out from the rest. Adding a class can be an easy method of making, for example, one paragraph red.

A class is defined in the attached stylesheet using the dot or full stop (.) symbol like this:

```
.red            {color:#ff0000;}
```

This is then applied to the style in the HTML, like this:

```
<p>This text is black</p>
<p class="red">This text is now red</p>
```

> **Tip**
>
> A common error is to include a full stop, like `<p class=".red">`. There should be no full stop here; it is only used when defining the style.
>
> Classes define different subtypes within an element. A class is defined using a dot (full stop) before the style name. Some WYSIWYG packages automatically use classes rather than defining styles. In these examples:
>
> ```
> h1      {color: #ff0000}
> .h1     {color: #0000ff}
> ```
>
> the top line defines the style h1 and the second line defines the class h1.

Common errors

REVISED

Error	Solution
When asked to 'create the following styles …' in a question, students generate all the correct declaration properties and values for a series of classes rather than defining the styles	When a question asks for styles, check your WYSIWYG package has not defined classes

21.3.9 CSS tables

Table definitions can be set in external stylesheets. The selector can be set for the whole table or for elements, such as the table header, table rows and individual cells of table data, and can be made to stand out from other elements on the page like this:

```
body      {background-color: #aeb6bf;}
table     {background-color: #f9e79f;}
thead     {background-color: #f1c40f;}
```

You may be asked to set internal gridlines and/or external table borders for tables. To set the border width of internal gridlines you must adjust the border width of the table data (or table header); for the external borders set the border for the table, like this:

```
table     {background-color: #aeb6bf;}
           border-collapse: collapse;
           border-style: solid;
           border-width: 4px;}
td        border-width: 2px;}
```

> **Tip**
>
> Remember that borders have to be switched on in the HTML as well as defined in the CSS.
>
> Tables can also be positioned within the browser window (if they are smaller than 100% of the window width), for example to centre align all tables within the window, this could be added to the attached stylesheet:
>
> ```
> table     {margin-left:auto; margin-right:auto;}
> ```

Exam-style questions for you to try

1. Explain the term 'web browser'. [2]
2. The following shows a cascading stylesheet created by a student. It contains a number of errors. Identify each of these errors and suggest a way to correct them.

```
h1        {colour:#00006f;
           font-family:Arial,sans serif:
           font-size:20px;
           text-align:center}

h2        {colour:000040:
           font-family:Times New Roman,serif;
           font-size:24px;
           text-align:centre}

table     {border-collapse:collapse;
           border-width:6px;
           border-style:"solid";
           border-color:#004040}

td        {border-width:4px;
           border-style:solid;
           border-colour:#004040}
```

[8]

3. Describe the use of the content and presentation layers in a web page. [6]

Practice Paper 1: Theory

Time allowed: 2 hours   **Maximum number of marks:** 100   **Answer all questions**

1 Data can be entered into a computer using direct data entry.

   Use one of the following input devices to complete the following table; use the **most suitable device** in all cases. Each device may be used once, more than once or not at all.

barcode reader	light sensor	optical mark reader
camera	magnetic stripe reader	QR code reader
chip and PIN reader	microphone	RFID reader
keyboard	optical character reader	trackerball

Statements	Most suitable input device
The device used to read the data from a contactless debit card	
The device used to convert characters in a photograph of a car's number plate into machine-readable format	
The device used to read a block of black and white squares	
The device used to read dark and light lines of varying thickness	
The device used to read an embedded smart card microchip	

[5]

2 Tick (✓) whether the following are examples of application software or systems software.

	Application software (✓)	Systems software (✓)
Spreadsheet		
Control software		
Antivirus software		
Device driver		
Audio editing software		

[3]

3 Circle **two** of the following items that use NFC technology:

   contactless cards   barcode reader   QR code reader
   ANPR system   passports   GPS121   [2]

4 Circle **two** of the following items that are examples of utility software:

   compiler   printer driver   antivirus
   screensaver   worms   linker   [2]

5 Indicate, by placing a tick (✓) in the appropriate box, whether the following statements refer to dot matrix printers, laser printers or inkjet printers:

Statements	Dot matrix printer (✓)	Laser printer (✓)	Inkjet printer (✓)
Makes use of dry ink (powder) toner cartridges			
Can make use of continuous and two-part stationery			
Can produce ozone and ink particulates in the air during operation			
Uses a print head, stepper motor and colour ink (liquid) cartridges			
Makes use of thermal bubble and piezoelectric technology			

[5]

Practice Paper 1: Theory

6 a Explain the term 'artificial intelligence'.

....

....

.... [2]

b Describe **two** features of augmented reality (AR) and give **one** use for AR.

....

....

....

.... [3]

c Describe **two** features of virtual reality (VR) and give **one** use for VR.

....

....

....

.... [3]

7 a Describe **two** components that make up an RFID tag.

....

....

.... [2]

b There are two types of RFID tag.
Name the **two** types of RFID tag and explain the differences between them.

....

....

....

.... [3]

8 a Explain what is meant by Geographic Information Systems (GIS).

....

....

.... [2]

b Give **two** advantages of using GIS.

....

....

.... [2]

c Give **two** disadvantages of using GIS.

....

....

.... [2]

9 Five features of network devices are given in the table below. For each feature, tick (✓) the appropriate box to indicate whether it refers to a router, switch or hub.

Statements	Router (✓)	Switch (✓)	Hub (✓)
Used to connect devices together to form a local area network (LAN)			
It looks up the destination MAC address before sending a data packet to the correct network device			
Used to connect LANs to other external networks			
Uses both MAC and IP addresses to enable data packets to be sent to the correct device on another network			
It sends all data packets to all the devices on a network			

[5]

10 The diagram below shows a traffic junction controlled by a set of traffic lights.
A computer model has been written to simulate the traffic flow.

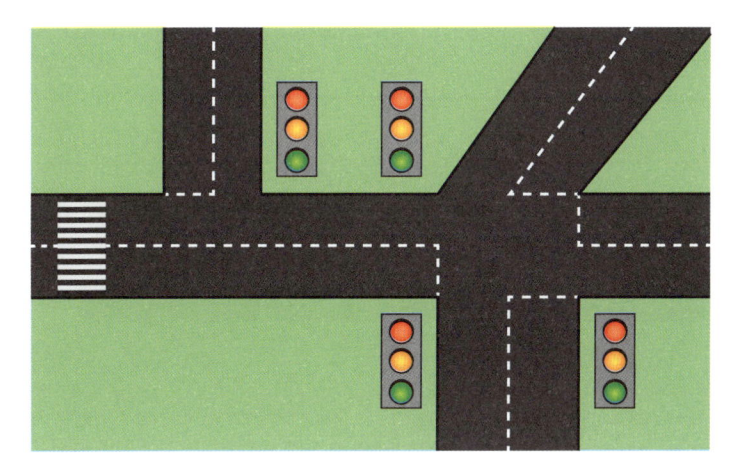

a Describe what real life data needs to be collected to be input into this model.

....

....

....

.... [3]

b Describe how the simulation would be carried out.

....

....

....

.... [3]

c Give **two** advantages and **two** disadvantages of using models to predict the behaviour of a real-life situation.

....

....

....

....

.... [4]

11 a Describe the changes in technology that have led to the disappearance of the hard disk drive (HDD) as the main backing store on a computer.

....

....

.... [3]

b Describe the changes in technology that have led to the reduction in the use of CD and DVD drives being installed on modern laptop computers.

....

....

....

.... [3]

12 In the table that follows, five ICT descriptions have been given. Write in the column on the right which ICT term is being described.

Description	ICT term
Embedding malicious code within QR codes	
Used in wireless networks to allow access to a network at various points using wireless technology	
A small file sent to the user's web browser when they visit a website; the file stores information about the user which is accessed each time they visit the website	
Hardware address that uniquely identifies each device connecting to a network	
A command used in HTML to instruct a web browser how to display text, images or other objects; they are not displayed with the web page	

[5]

13 Six descriptions are shown on the left and six network terms are shown on the right. By drawing arrows, connect each description to its correct network term.

Description	Network term
1. Discussion website consisting of discrete diary-style entries; displayed in reverse chronological order	A. Netiquette
2. Collection of articles that multiple users can add to or edit; users can use a web browser to edit or create the website	B. Extranet
3. Code of good practice that should be followed when using the internet or writing emails	C. Blog
4. Software application for accessing information on the World Wide Web; retrieves and translates HTML embedded in a web page	D. Wiki
5. Type of intranet that can be partially accessed by authorised external users	E. Search engine
6. Software that does a systematic trawl of websites to find websites that match a given criteria	F. Web browser

[5]

14 Give an application for each of the following input and output devices. In each case, give a justification for your choice of application.

Name of device	Application	Justification
Dot matrix printer		
QR code reader		
Microphone		
Radio frequency identification (RFID)		

[8]

15 Hubs and switches are both used to enable devices to communicate with each other on a network.
   a Describe the differences and similarities in the use of hubs and switches in a network.

   ....

   ....

   ....

   .... [3]

b A bridge is another device used in network connectivity. Describe the function of a bridge.

....

....

.... [2]

c Routers are used to allow local area networks (LANs) to connect to external networks. Local area network 'A' is in Europe and local area network 'B' is in India.
Describe how routers are used to enable a computer on network 'A' to send data and emails to a computer on network 'B'.

....

....

....

.... [3]

d Describe the main differences between routers and bridges.

....

....

.... [2]

16 A program is being written that only accepts numbers in the range 1 to 100 (inclusively) to be input. Validation rules are being used to check the data input.
  a Name two validation routines that could be used to check the input data in this program. Give a reason for your choice in each case.

....

....

.... [2]

  b Test data can be normal, abnormal or extreme. Explain the differences between these three types of test data. Use examples to illustrate your answer.

....

....

....

.... [3]

Practice Paper 1: Theory

c For this program being written, indicate by ticking (✓) the appropriate box, whether the following input data is normal, abnormal or extreme.

	Normal (✓)	Abnormal (✓)	Extreme (✓)
52			
1			
104			
100			
twenty-five			
99			

[3]

17 Online shopping and banking are both becoming increasingly popular.

Discuss the benefits and drawbacks of using online shopping and banking to customers.

[7]

Answers to exam-style questions

Chapter 1

1   a   An input device is hardware used to enter data into a computer. Input devices turn entered data into a format understood by the computer. Examples include a keyboard, sensors, direct data entry devices and so on.

   b   An output device shows the result of a computer's processing in a form understood by a human or for use by another electronic device. Examples include printers, monitors (screens), loudspeakers and so on.

   c   A dialogue-based interface uses the human voice to give commands to a computer system. It will use microphones to pick up a human's voice which will then be converted into a computer-readable format. Examples include voice activation devices in the car (e.g. to operate the radio or satnav system) or the home (to turn on lights or close shutters by a simple word command) and so on.

   d   A gesture-based interface relies on the movement of a hand, head or foot, for example to send an input to a computer. Sensors and cameras are used to provide a computer vision and image processing interface. Examples include rotating a finger to increase the output volume of a radio, moving a foot under the bumper of a car to open the boot or waving the hand near a window to open it and so on.

2

Statement	CLI (✓)	GUI (✓)
The user is in direct communication with the computer	✓	
All commands need to be typed in using the correct format	✓	
Needs a complex OS and large memory requirement to operate		✓
Allows computer configuration settings to be directly changed	✓	
Makes use of pointing devices (such as a mouse) or finger (if using a touchscreen)		✓

3   1 → C   5 → G
    2 → F   6 → B
    3 → E   7 → D
    4 → A

4   Advantages:
    ○ very small and lightweight thus easy to carry round with you (in a pocket)
    ○ can connect to either a cellular network or to WiFi
    ○ longer battery life than a laptop computer.
    Disadvantages:
    ○ small screen size can make it difficult to see all the detail
    ○ virtual keyboards can be difficult to use
    ○ relatively small memories, therefore slower data transfer rates.

5   a   A phablet is a hybrid of a smartphone and a tablet; they have larger screens than a smartphone but have all the features of both types of device, for example a device with screen size 14 cm to 18 cm.

   b   An accelerometer is a sensor that detects movement and orientation of a device, for example moving a display from portrait to landscape when a device is turned through 90°.

   c   Fast battery drain refers to the reduction in power levels of a battery, for example through the use of apps and surfing the internet, which require more than normal power usage.

   d   An app store is an online facility where users can download items for free (or by paying a monthly fee), for example downloading a game.

6

Statement	True (✓)	False (✓)
Desktop computers are easier to upgrade/expand than laptops	✓	
Laptop computers use a touchpad, as part of the keyboard, as a pointing device	✓	
Phablets and tablets require the use of plug-in keyboards to allow them to be used to write emails		✓
Tablets don't allow the use of Voice over Internet Protocol (VoIP) or video calling		✓
The built-in cameras on smartphones and tablets can be used to read QR codes	✓	
Desktop computers must use a wired internet connection; they cannot connect to WiFi		✓

7   VR → A, D and E
    AR → B, C and F

Chapter 2

1

Input device	Tick (✓) if suitable device
Microphone	
pH sensor	✓
Keypad	
Oxygen gas sensor	✓
Touchscreen	✓
Joystick	
Remote control	
Light pen	
Trackerball	✓

2 a In a computer game or driving simulation. The wheel allows for a natural interface between human and computer since turning the wheel will give input to the software indicating turning the vehicle left or right.

b For use with voice activation software. For example, a person with disabilities could use their voice to switch lights on/off or close/open window blinds.

c At an information kiosk in an airport. By simply touching a symbol this will activate information for the user; they don't need to be language specific, which is a huge benefit in an international airport and have no need to be manned by airport staff.

d Reading QR codes using a mobile phone. Since QR codes only require a photo image and QR software to interpret the image, then a QR code could easily be read and understood by a smartphone camera.

3 a QR code
  b optical mark reader/recognition (OMR)
  c scanner
  d remote control
  e RFID reader.

4 a
  – Each book will have a unique barcode identifying it.
  – Each person using the library will have their own library card with a barcode identifying the library user.
  – When a person takes out a book, they take it to the librarian who scans the barcode in the book – this now updates the book file showing the book has been borrowed (the system will look up the barcode on the book file and change the 'borrowed field' to 'on loan', change the date book was borrowed and will also link to the borrower file).
  – The librarian also scans the barcode on the customer's library card – the borrower file is now updated with date book borrowed and barcode of book borrowed.
  – Assuming books can be borrowed for seven days, the computer system will cross-check both files and inform the customer that the book needs to be returned on dd/mm/yyyy.
  – Once the book is returned, both the book's barcode and customer's barcode will be scanned again and both files will be updated.

b Advantages:
  – book tags can be read from a distance (thus preventing somebody walking out of the library with a book without scanning it first)
  – several books can be booked out at the same time automatically
  – very fast read rate (important in a large, busy library).

Disadvantages:
  – impossible to tamper with the RFID tag (unlike barcodes)
  – tag collisions are possible
  – more expensive technology than barcodes
  – RFID signals can be jammed by other devices.

5

Application	OCR	OMR	QR reader
Reading the number plate on a vehicle entering a pay car park	✓		
Reading and counting the voting slips in an election		✓	
Reading the data on a passport at an airport security desk	✓		
Used in augmented reality at a car showroom to give the customer an immersive experience			✓
Reading embedded website addresses written in a matrix code on an advertising poster			✓
Digitisation of ancient books and manuscripts	✓		
Marking multi-choice exam questions automatically		✓	

6 a Dot matrix printer:
  – these printers can withstand dirty environments and noise won't be an issue
  – they can also produce multi-copies for filing information.

b i) Dot matrix printer:
  – can print 'hidden text' since they are impact printers and can print inside sealed envelopes by using carbon paper inside
  – can use continuous stationery so that a print run of all wage slips can be done overnight without any need to replace paper trays.

ii) Touchscreen monitor:
- allows operator in the office to find information quickly if a query is received
- silent systems in an office environment.

iii) 3D printer:
- can produce prototypes quickly and cheaply when developing new products.

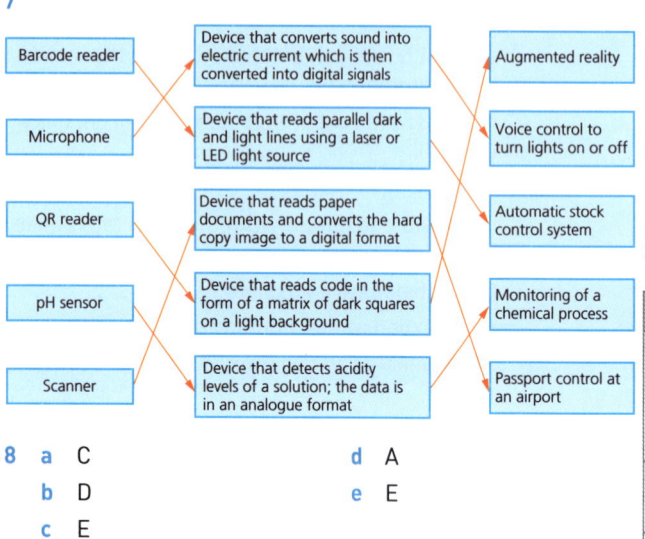

7

Barcode reader	Device that converts sound into electric current which is then converted into digital signals	Augmented reality
Microphone	Device that reads parallel dark and light lines using a laser or LED light source	Voice control to turn lights on or off
QR reader	Device that reads paper documents and converts the hard copy image to a digital format	Automatic stock control system
pH sensor	Device that reads code in the form of a matrix of dark squares on a light background	Monitoring of a chemical process
Scanner	Device that detects acidity levels of a solution; the data is in an analogue format	Passport control at an airport

Matches:
- Barcode reader → Device that reads parallel dark and light lines using a laser or LED light source → Automatic stock control system
- Microphone → Device that converts sound into electric current which is then converted into digital signals → Voice control to turn lights on or off
- QR reader → Device that reads code in the form of a matrix of dark squares on a light background → Augmented reality
- pH sensor → Device that detects acidity levels of a solution; the data is in an analogue format → Monitoring of a chemical process
- Scanner → Device that reads paper documents and converts the hard copy image to a digital format → Passport control at an airport

8
a C   d A
b D   e E
c E

Chapter 3

1

	Magnetic	Optical	Solid state
Blu-ray reader/writer player		✓	
Portable hard disk drive	✓		
Flash drive			✓
CFast card			✓
DVD-RW drive		✓	
Pen drive			✓

2 a i)
- Blu-ray discs use blue laser light for read/write operations whereas DVDs use red laser light.
- Blu-ray discs have much greater capacity than DVDs and have a much faster data transfer rate.
- Blu-ray discs have built-in secure encryption systems.

ii)
- Blu-ray application: storing of HD movies.
- DVD-RW application: recording music and movies (using the capability to write to the DVD many times).

b i) Three points from the following:
- SSDs have no moving parts whereas HDDs use rotating platters and moveable read/write heads
- SSDs use solid-state transistor technology to read/write data (control the flow of electrons) whereas HDDs use magnetic properties of certain metal oxides to store 0s and 1s
- SSDs are very lightweight and also consume considerably less power than HDDs
- HDDs suffer from latency whereas SSDs don't suffer from this.

ii) Two points from the following:
- SSDs are much more robust/reliable than HDDs (no moving parts)
- SSDs consume much less power than HDDs (makes them very suitable for use in laptops/notebooks)
- SSDs are very thin and much smaller than HDDs so they can easily fit into devices such as tablets and smartphones.

3

Statement	True (✓)	False (✓)
SSDs suffer from high latency due to the time it takes for disks to spin round to the read/write head		✓
Blu-ray discs only allow data to be read		✓
Platters in an HDD can be recorded on both the bottom and top surfaces	✓	
The data transfer rate is the time it takes to locate data on an HDD		✓
Both DVDs and Blu-ray discs use dual-layer technology	✓	
SSDs have a shorter working life than the equivalent HDDs	✓	
One advantage of flash drives is that old data can be permanently deleted	✓	
CD-RW can act as a ROM		✓
Solid-state drives have many complex moving parts that makes them wear out quickly		✓
Blu-ray discs use laser light with a shorter wavelength than DVDs	✓	

4 a
- control gate/floating gate
- floating gate/control gate
- voltage
- 1s and 0s.

b
- blue laser
- dual-layering
- Blu-ray discs.

c
- platters
- aluminium/glass/ceramic
- read-write
- latency.

5
- Optical disks have a much lower storage capacity than flash memories.
- It is more difficult to save data on optical media.
- Optical disks can be damaged quite easily (scratch the surface).
- Optical disks require fairly bulky read-write devices unlike SSD devices (leading to the development of MP3 files that use SSD technology).
- Using cloud storage is reducing the need for optical media (and other recording media).
- Streaming of music and videos has also reduced the need for recording media).

6
- Introduction of solid-state technology has led to thinner and lighter devices.
- Touchscreens are now commonplace on devices which means they now use post-WIMP interfaces (no need for a mouse as pointing device) and they can use a stylus to select options.
- Use of cloud storage means that modern devices no longer come equipped with read-write devices built-in.
- WiFi and Bluetooth connectivity means that recent devices can be taken anywhere to access the internet and there is no longer the need for trailing wires between devices and, for example, printers; this also means that only one USB port is supplied.
- New devices run cold unlike their 2012 counterparts and they also have much better battery life.

Chapter 4

1 a
- The cloud is a method of data storage using physical remote servers.
- Data is frequently stored on more than one cloud server in case maintenance or repairs need to be carried out (this is called data redundancy).
- There are three common types of cloud storage:
- public cloud: a storage environment where the client and cloud storage provider are different companies/entities
- private cloud: storage provided by dedicated servers behind a firewall; client and cloud storage provider act as a single entity
- hybrid cloud: a combination of public and private clouds where sensitive data is stored on a private cloud and other data is stored on a public cloud.

b Three points from the following:
- Client files stored in the cloud can be accessed at any time, from any device, anywhere in the world, provided internet access is available.
- There is no need for a customer/client to carry an external storage device with them, or even use the same computer, to store and retrieve information.
- The cloud provides the user with remote backup of data with obvious advantages to alleviate data loss/disaster recovery.
- If a customer/client has a failure of their hard disk or backup device, cloud storage will allow recovery of their data.
- The cloud system offers almost unlimited storage capacity.

2 a Devices needed include: computers, servers, printers, switches, bridges and all necessary cabling and desks.

b Routers, telephone lines or satellite links; alternatively, private communication lines could be used to link the LANs together.

c They will need access points (APs) throughout all eight floors to allow for WiFi connectivity; these APs will be hardwired into the LAN to give maximum data access/transfer speed and bandwidth.

3

Statements	Router (✓)	Switch (✓)	Hub (✓)
Device that can cause unnecessary LAN traffic and can reduce effective bandwidth			✓
The destination MAC address is looked up before the data packet is sent to the correct device		✓	
Used to connect LANs to other external networks	✓		
Uses both MAC and IP addresses to enable data packets to be sent to the correct device on another network	✓		
All data packets are sent to all the devices on a network			✓
Data packets are sent only to a specific device on the same network		✓	

4
- Switch: this allows the devices in each network to be connected together; this would be better than a hub since it is more secure.
- Server: this would allow a central database of information to be used which could be accessed by any device on the network and it could also include software for use by all company staff.
- Wires and cables: although the network connections would probably be wireless, there

Answers to exam-style questions

is still a need for some cables to connect devices together to create the actual network structure.
- Network interface cards: all devices on the network would require an NIC so that they could be connected to the network
- Printers and other shared hardware: centralisation on each floor would reduce costs (since only one or two devices needed instead of each computer requiring its own printer, for example).
- Bridge: to connect the LANs on each floor so they are joined together to form one large single network.
- Router: to allow the computers on the networks to communicate with external networks in the company.

5 - Wide area networks (WANs) cover a large area geographically (e.g. a whole country or even larger).
- WANs are actually a number of LANs connected together by a series of routers (e.g. the network of ATMs is a WAN as is the internet).
- Due to the large geographical distances, WANs make use of public communications infrastructure (e.g. telephone lines and satellites) but sometimes use private dedicated lines if greater security is needed.
- An example is the internet.

6 a (physical) token
   b zero login
   c smart card
   d video conferencing
   e antivirus.

7 a Zero login allows users to log in without passwords. Zero login relies on smart technology and the ability to recognise a user by biometrics and behavioural patterns. The system builds up a complex user profile based on biometrics (e.g. fingerprints or face recognition) and unique behaviour (e.g. where you normally use a device, how you swipe a screen and so on), thus eliminating the need to key in a password. There are problems, such as 'How do you know when you've logged out?', 'How secure is the system?' and so on.
   b Web conferencing is sometimes referred to as a webinar or webcast. Multiple computers in various locations using the internet hold conferences in real time. The only requirement is a computer and a high-speed, stable internet connection. To carry out web conferencing, each user either downloads an application or logs on to a website from a link supplied in an email from the conference organiser. Delegates can leave or join the conference as they wish. The organiser can decide on who can speak at any time using the control panel on their computer. If a delegate wishes to speak, they raise a flag next to their name. Delegates can post comments using instant messaging for all delegates to see at any time.

c Antivirus software is essential to protect computers on a network from attack by viruses. Antivirus software runs in the background and constantly looks for known viruses or potential viruses. All antivirus software has the following features:
- All software or files are checked before they can be run or loaded.
- They use a database of known viruses as the first check (which is why antivirus software should be kept up to date since this database is constantly updated).
- They do heuristic checking (this is the checking of software for types of behaviour that many viruses emulate).
- If a virus, or potential virus, is detected it is first quarantined and then automatically deleted or the user is invited to delete it (sometimes software isn't actually infected in spite of the antivirus warning – this is called a false positive).

Chapter 5

1 a and b   Three points form the following for health risks and one mitigation for each risk listed:
- Back and neck strain:
  - use fully adjustable chairs to give the correct posture
  - use footrests to reduce posture problems
  - use tiltable screens to ensure the neck is at the right angle.
- Repetitive strain injury (RSI):
  - ensure correct posture is maintained (e.g. correct angle of arms to the keyboard and mouse)
  - make proper use of a wrist rest when using a mouse or keyboard
  - take regular breaks (and exercise)
  - make use of ergonomic keyboards
  - use voice-activated software if the user is prone to problems using a mouse or keyboard.
- Eyestrain:
  - if necessary, change screens to LCD if older CRT screens are still used
  - take regular breaks (and exercise)
  - make use of anti-glare screens if the room lighting is incorrect (or use window blinds to cut out direct sunlight)
  - users should have their eyes tested on a regular basis (middle vision glasses should be prescribed if the user has a persistent problem with eye strain, dry eyes, headaches etc.).
- Headaches:
  - make use of anti-glare screens if the room lighting is incorrect (or use window blinds to cut out reflections which cause squinting, leading to headaches)
  - take regular breaks (and exercise)

Cambridge IGCSE Information and Communication Technology Study and Revision Guide Second Edition

- users should have their eyes tested on a regular basis (middle vision glasses should be prescribed if the user has a persistent problem with headaches).
- Ozone irritation:
  - proper ventilation should exist to lower the ozone gas levels to acceptable values
  - laser printers should be housed in a designated printer room
  - change to using inkjet printers if possible.

2   Devices in the home fall into two categories: labour-saving and other devices. The benefits of using microprocessor-controlled devices include:
- People no longer have to do manual tasks at home.
- They give people more time for leisure activities, hobbies, shopping and socialising.
- There is no longer a need to stay home while food is cooking or clothes are being washed.
- It is possible to control ovens and automatic washing machines, for example, using smartphones – a web-enabled phone allows devices to be switched on or off while the owner is out.
- Automated burglar alarms give people a sense of security and well-being as they give a very sophisticated level of intruder warning at all times.
- Smart fridges and freezers can lead to more healthy lifestyles (they can automatically order fresh food from supermarkets using their internet connections) as well as prevent food waste.

The drawbacks of using microprocessor-controlled devices include:
- Labour-saving devices can lead to unhealthy lifestyles (because of the reliance on ready-made meals).
- They tend to make people rather lazy since there is a dependence on the devices.
- People can become less fit if they just lie around at home while the devices carry out many of the tasks that were previously done manually.
- Tasks carried out by people in the past are now done by the microprocessor-controlled devices, which means there is a potential to lose these household skills.
- As with any device which contains a microprocessor and can communicate using the internet, there is the risk of cybersecurity threats.

General benefits of using microprocessors in household devices include:
- Microprocessor-controlled devices save energy since they are far more efficient and can, for example, switch themselves off after inactivity for a certain time period.
- It is easier 'programming' these devices to do tasks rather than turning knobs and pressing buttons manually (e.g. QR codes on the side of food packaging can simply be scanned and the oven automatically sets the cooking programme).

General drawbacks of using microprocessors in household devices include:
- The devices lead to a more wasteful society – it is usually not cost-effective to repair circuit boards once they fail; the device is then usually just thrown away.
- They can be more complex to operate for people who are technophobes or who are not very confident around electronic devices.
- Leaving some devices on stand-by (such as televisions or satellite receivers) is very wasteful of electricity.

3   Benefits:
- safer because human error is removed, leading to fewer accidents
- better for the environment because vehicles will operate more efficiently
- reduced traffic congestion (humans cause 'stop-and-go' traffic (known as 'the phantom traffic jam'); autonomous vehicles will be better at smoothing out traffic flow and reducing congestion in cities)
- increased lane capacity (research shows autonomous vehicles will increase lane capacity by 100% and increase average speeds by 20%, due to better braking and acceleration responses together with optimised distance between vehicles)
- reduced travel times (for the reasons above) therefore less commuting time
- stress-free parking for motorists (the car will find car parking on its own and then self-park)
- more frequent and reliable bus services.

Drawbacks:
- very expensive system to set up in the first place (high technology requirements)
- the ever-present fear of hacking into the vehicle's control system
- security and safety issues (software glitches could be catastrophic; software updates would need to be carefully controlled to avoid potential disasters)
- the need to make sure the system is well-maintained at all times; cameras need to be kept clean so that they don't give false results; sensors could fail to function in heavy snowfall or blizzard conditions (radar or ultrasonic signals could be deflected by heavy snow particles)
- driver and passenger reluctance for the new technology (especially public transport)
- reduction in the need for taxis and buses could lead to unemployment.

4   a   Advantages:
- Smart motorways constantly adapt to traffic conditions, reducing traffic jams and minimising everyone's journey times.
- Transport systems are more efficient: more cars, trains and aeroplanes can use the transport network, allowing for more regular services.
- Using ANPR technology in the motorway signs, traffic offences can be automatically penalised and stolen cars can be easily spotted.

Answers to exam-style questions

- Computerised control systems minimise human error, which reduces the rate of accidents.
  b Risks:
  - A hacker could gain access to the computerised system and cause disruption.
  - If the computer system fails, then the whole transport system could be brought to a standstill.
  - Poorly designed systems could compromise safety and, in some cases, even make the system less efficient.
  - ANPR systems mean that innocent people's movements can easily be tracked (who has access to such data?); criminals using false number plates could easily 'fool' such systems.

Chapter 6

1 Advantages (three points from the following):
   ○ they can contain moving images and music/voice-overs
   ○ they are much easier to update
   ○ cheaper to produce since there is no need to print out books and magazines and to distribute them
   ○ there is the potential for more advertising revenue (since the reader audience is potentially much larger)
   ○ there is no unsold stock at the end of the week/month which wastes money and also requires disposal
   ○ the books and magazines can be interactive.
   Disadvantages (three points from the following):
   ○ the need to pay for website time
   ○ the need to pay for development and maintenance
   ○ the risk of malware attacks
   ○ it can be more difficult to read since the user has to navigate between pages
   ○ outdated software on a device may make it impossible to download the e-publication
   ○ if the user has slow internet or a poor connection, download speeds may prevent videos and sound from loading up.

2 1 → E   4 → B
   2 → C   5 → D
   3 → A

3 a - Number of vehicles passing the junction in all directions.
     - Time of day also needs to be recorded for each vehicle being counted.
     - Build-up of traffic at different times of day and how long it takes to clear.
     - Other road factors that can affect traffic (e.g. a pedestrian crossing nearby).
     - Time it takes the slowest vehicle to pass through the junction.
     - Other factors, such as accidents, filtering and emergency vehicles.

- Once the data has been collected and is fed into the model, different scenarios can be tried out to optimise traffic light timings and to determine where to place traffic sensors in the road.
- The final version will receive live data and a central control box can compare actual traffic data with simulation data allowing the model to be fine-tuned.

  b - road sensors collect data about all vehicles travelling through the junction (in all directions)
    - this data is sent to a control box
    - the live data is compared to stored data from the simulation and signals are sent to the lights to change colour as necessary

4 Four points from the following:
  ○ It prevents double-booking (which could happen in paper-based systems that didn't update the system fast enough).
  ○ The customer gets immediate feedback on the availability of cinema seats and whether or not their booking has been successful.
  ○ The customer can make bookings at any time of the day.
  ○ The customer's email allows the booking company to connect 'special offers' to their email and inform them of such offers automatically.
  ○ It is usually easier to browse the cinema seating plans to choose the best seats available at the price.
  ○ It is possible to 'reserve' a seat for a period of time. This allows a customer to make up their mind before finalising the booking of the seat (this was difficult to do with the older paper-based systems).
  ○ Very often there are no printed tickets which saves postal costs and also allows impulse bookings only a few hours in advance.
  ○ Online booking allows the use of modern smartphone and tablet apps technology; the customer is sent a QR code which contains all the booking information necessary (this QR code is stored on the smartphone or tablet and just needs to be scanned at the cinema).

5 a Three points from the following:
    - robots can work in environments harmful or dangerous to human operators
    - robots can work non-stop (24/7)
    - robots are less expensive in the long term (although expensive to buy initially, they don't need wages)
    - robots have a higher productivity (don't need holidays etc.)
    - robots have a greater consistency (e.g. the robot sampling will be identical each time)
    - they can do boring, repetitive tasks leaving humans free to do other more skilled work (e.g. drilling for rock samples is a task that could best be done by a robot under computer control)

Cambridge IGCSE Information and Communication Technology Study and Revision Guide Second Edition

- to carry out different tasks, robots are fitted with different end effectors (attachments), for example drill bits for different types of rock.

b Two points from the following:
- robots find it difficult to do 'unusual' tasks (e.g. unusual terrain or rock formations could cause problems)
- they can cause higher unemployment (replacing skilled labour)
- since robots do many of the tasks once done by humans, there is a real risk of certain skills (such as searching for suitable rocks) being lost
- the initial set-up and maintenance of robots can be expensive.

6 ○ The first step is **called out clearing** when the payee's bank is presented with the cheque; the cheque is fed into a reader which takes a photograph of the cheque and built-in OCR software turns the image into an electronic record.
○ The payee's bank now creates a digital record containing money to be paid in, sort code on the cheque and account number shown on the cheque.
○ All transactions relating to the payer's bank during the day are added to a file (which includes the electronic record relating to this cheque) and the file is sent to a central facility (other banks will have their own separate files containing cheque transactions relating to their bank).
○ The file containing cheques drawn on the payer's bank is now processed and a 'request to pay' message for each cheque is made and a stream of 'request to pay' images (for all cheques) is sent to the payer's bank; if the cheque hasn't been signed or fraud is suspected, then a 'no pay' message is created for each affected cheque.
○ The central facility routes all 'request to pay' and 'no pay' responses to the payee's bank and the payment shown on each cheque is carried out; essentially, at this stage, the recipient is debited with the amount from the payer's bank account.

7 a

Statement	True (✓)
Smart cards prevent students signing in for each other	
It is possible to determine whether a student is on the premises in case of a fire	✓
It is possible to determine a student's attendance record over the whole year	✓
It is not possible to clone smart identity cards, making the system very secure and accurate	
Data stored on a card is the name of the school, name of the student, student's date of birth and their unique ID number	✓
Using a PIN only works if the identity card is fitted with an embedded microchip	

b

Statement	True (✓)
Students can learn at their own pace	✓
Students must complete the whole session on a particular topic before moving on to the next topic	
CAL frees up teachers to do other things since it can replace trained teachers in the classroom	
CAL lessons can include multimedia and animations	✓
It is not possible for CAL to be interactive since no teachers are involved in the CAL process	
CAL allows for micro-learning where topics are broken down into manageable modules	✓

8 a
- car approaching barrier picked up by a sensor; sensor data sent to a microprocessor
- microprocessor 'instructs' camera to photograph front of car
- OCR software recognises individual characters in number plate and creates an electronic file
- this file is used to check a database containing permitted number plates
- if a match is found, the barrier is raised
- if no match is found, motorist is denied access to the car park.

b
- tags embedded in the badge can be read from a distance (thus allowing them access automatically)
- several visitors can be serviced at the same time in a large group
- very fast read rate (important in a large, busy company)
- impossible to tamper with the RFID tag (unlike barcodes)
- tag collisions are possible, thus preventing some people access
- more expensive technology than barcodes
- RFID signals can be jammed by other devices, for example some electronic devices might interfere with the tags on the badges.

c
- the QR code could contain embedded URLs automatically sending visitor to the company's website
- by pointing their smartphone at the QR code, the built-in camera takes a photo and the QR app allows the photo to be interpreted by the smartphone browser
- the browser then automatically contacts the company website
- other data embedded in the QR code (such as menus for the restaurant) would be automatically downloaded to the smartphone screen.

Answers to exam-style questions

9 Award a ½ mark per correct answer up to a maximum of 6 marks (marks can be rounded down if less than 11 correct):
- ○ tokenisation
- ○ wallet
- ○ built-in camera
- ○ wallet
- ○ debit card
- ○ randomly generated
- ○ tokens
- ○ smartphone
- ○ random numbers
- ○ transaction
- ○ change

10 a

Statement	Correct (✓)
They contain a knowledge base made up of attributes and objects	✓
They are part of the 3D printing process	
They refer to inference rules in a rules base	
They make use of near field communication technology	✓
Each question asked is based on the response to a previous question	✓
They can be used in tax and financial planning	✓
They make use of a tokenisation system	
They are examples of a search engine	

b – gather information from expert sources regarding plant features
   – this information is put into the knowledge base using plant attributes and objects that will show how to identify each plant
   – a rules base and inference rules are then created
   – the inference engine is then developed
   – a user-friendly human computer interface is now developed
   – the system is then tested using plants with known outcome
   – if the expert system produces incorrect results for the known test data, then it has to be modified and then tested again until it is 100% accurate.

c – first of all an interactive screen is presented to the user
   – the system asks a series of questions about the TV fault(s)
   – the user answers the questions asked (either as multiple choice or Yes/No questions)
   – a series of questions are asked based on the user's responses to previous questions
   – the inference engine compares the fault descriptions entered with those in the knowledge base looking for matches
   – the rules base (inference rules) is used in the matching process
   – once a match is found, the system suggests the probability of the TV fault(s) being identified accurately

   – the expert system also suggests possible solutions and remedies to solve the problem or recommendations on what to do next
   – the explanation system will give reasons for its diagnosis so that the user can determine the validity of the diagnostics
   – the diagnostics can be in the form of text or it may show images of the TV circuitry to indicate where the problem may be
   – the user can request further information from the expert system to narrow down even further the possible reasons for the fault and how to solve it.

11 a – NFC is a subset of RFID technology
      – NFC can be used by smartphones to make payments; it can also be used in car key fobs (when the driver approaches his vehicle, the NFC device 'talks' to the car and the doors are automatically unlocked).

   b – peer-to-peer mode:
      – used by smartphones
      – allows two NFC-enabled devices to exchange data
      – both devices switch between being active (when sending data) and being passive (when receiving data)
      – for example, two smartphones sharing data, such as photos
      – read/write mode:
      – one-way data transmission
      – a passive device links to another device and reads data from it
      – for example, when an active tag is sending out advertising data to other devices in close proximity (e.g. as you pass a restaurant it advertises its menus automatically)
      – card emulation mode:
      – NFC device can function as a smart or contactless card
      – allows the card to make payments at an NFC-enabled terminal
      – for example, when entering public transportation system (e.g. metro), the NFC-enabled card is read and allows access.

12 1 → F   4 → J
    2 → K   5 → H
    3 → D   6 → B

Chapter 7

1 a i) normal data:
       – this is data that is acceptable/valid and has an expected (known) outcome, for example, the month of a year can be any whole number in the range 1 to 12
   ii) extreme:
       – this is data at the limits of acceptability/validity, for example the month can be either of the two end value, that is 1 or 12

196 Cambridge IGCSE Information and Communication Technology Study and Revision Guide Second Edition

Answers to exam-style questions

iii) abnormal:
- this is data outside the limits of acceptability/validity and should be rejected or cause an error message, for example none of the following values are allowed as inputs for the month: any value <1 (e.g. 0, –1, –15)
- any value >12 (e.g. 32, 45)
- letters or other non-numeric data (e.g. July) non-integer values (e.g. 3.5, 10.75).

b In this scenario, examples would be:
- normal: 21, 30.4, 15.6 and so on
- extreme: (assuming max recorded value is 44°C and the lowest recorded value is 11°C) 44, 11
- abnormal: 560, –500, fifty.

2

Input scenario	Length check	Presence check	Range check	Format check	Type check
Input a post code/zip code, such as LA21 4NN, in the correct layout				✓	
Entering a number that must be greater than 0, but not greater than 100			✓		✓
In an online form, a mandatory field, email address, must not be left empty		✓			
Check that a telephone number must contain exactly 11 characters	✓				✓
Input data that can only be numeric and no other characters are permitted					✓
A date must be entered as DDMMYY, for example 11 10 23 or as 3 6 21				✓	✓

3 a Analysis → Design → Development/testing ↓
Evaluation ← Documentation ← Implementation

b Interviews
Advantages:
- it gives the opportunity to motivate the interviewee into giving open and honest answers to the questions
- the method allows the analyst to probe for more feedback from the interviewee (questions can be extended)
- it is possible to modify questions as the interview proceeds and ask questions more specific to the interviewee
- the analyst can watch body language and facial expressions.

Disadvantages:
- it can be a rather time-consuming exercise
- it is relatively expensive since a team of interviewers and an analyst are needed
- the interviewee can't remain anonymous with this method, and may hide information or not be honest with their answers
- the interviewee can give answers they think the interviewer wants to hear
- interviewees may not be available at times to suit the analyst.

Questionnaires
Advantages:
- the questions can be answered fairly quickly
- it is a relatively inexpensive method
- individuals can remain anonymous if they want (therefore might be inclined to give more honest answers)
- allows for a quick analysis of the data
- interviewees can fill in questionnaires in their own time
- allows a greater number of people to take part.

Disadvantages:
- the number of returned questionnaires can be low; not always a popular method
- the questions are rather rigid since they have to be generic; it isn't always possible to ask follow-up questions
- no immediate way to clarify a vague answer to a question; not possible always to expand an answer on the questionnaire
- users tend to exaggerate their responses as they are anonymous and they may not take it seriously.

Observations
Advantages:
- the analyst obtains first-hand and reliable data
- it is possible to get a better overall view of the existing system
- relatively inexpensive method since it only involves the analyst
- all inputs and outputs to the current system are seen.

Disadvantages:
- people are generally uncomfortable being watched and may work in a different way to normal (the Hawthorne effect)
- if workers perform tasks that normally contravene standard procedures, they are unlikely to do this while they know they are being watched.

c The best method would be immediate (direct) implementation. For safety reasons, it is best to changeover to a new air traffic control system totally rather than having parallel or phased implementation – these latter two systems could lead to different data being generated. If the air traffic control system is part of a chain of airports, then using a pilot scheme could be the best option. This could be introduced into the smallest airport and test the system over a number of months (to iron out any problems) before introducing the new system to all airports.

4 For example:

[Form mockup: Name of phone (dropdown); Date phone refurbished (boxes); New/Used (radio buttons); Price: $ (boxes); Condition: excellent/good/poor (radio buttons); Description (text boxes); buttons: Next record, SAVE, Previous record]

5

Description of component	Technical documentation (✓)	User documentation (✓)	In both types of documentation (✓)
How to save files on the system		✓	
The meaning of error messages			✓
Programming language used	✓		
How to do a printout		✓	
List of variables used	✓		
Software requirements			✓
Screen and report layouts			✓

Description of component	Technical documentation (✓)	User documentation (✓)	In both types of documentation (✓)
FAQs		✓	
Known limitations of the system			✓
Minimum memory requirements	✓		

6 a Presence check
   b Validation
   c Live data
   d Technical documentation
   e Observation

Chapter 8

1 Health → A, D, E, G
   Safety → B, C, F

2 a – A copy of the data on the magnetic stripe of a credit/debit card is made using a skimmer; this is a data capture device that allows criminals to read all data on the magnetic stripe and then copy it to a fake card.
      – Smart cards that use a microchip were brought in to combat card cloning; however, the use of a shimmer allows the microchip to be read as well as the magnetic stripe. A shimmer contains a chip and flash drive in a paper-thin shim that is almost invisible when inserted into an ATM.

   b Fingerprint scans are an example of biometrics; fingerprints are essentially unique and can be used to identify somebody; an electronic copy of a person's fingerprints are stored on a computer and when a finger is placed on the scanner, the fingerprint is compared to the ones stored. They are used on many smartphones to activate the phone and protect it from being used by someone else.

   c Encryption is the 'scrambling' of data (using an encryption key) into a format that makes it unreadable unless a user has the necessary decryption key; the original text (plain text) is put through an encryption algorithm to produce cypher text.

   d Secure Sockets Layer (SSL) is a type of protocol that allows data to be sent and received securely over a network (e.g. the internet); when a user logs on to a website, for example, SSL encrypts the data using a public encryption key; an SSL session is denoted by https or a green padlock in the browser address window.

   e This is voicemail phishing and is a form of phishing where the cybercriminal uses a voicemail message to trick the user into calling a number (e.g. pretending to be anti-fraud department at a bank).

3 Award a ½ mark per correct answer up to a maximum of 5 marks (marks can be rounded down if less than nine correct):
   - ○ e-safety
   - ○ sensitive data
   - ○ privacy settings
   - ○ hacking
   - ○ smishing
   - ○ encrypted
   - ○ cypher text
   - ○ authentication
   - ○ two-factor authentication.

4 a Tasks carried out by a firewall (four points from the following):
   - Examines the 'traffic' between user's computer (or internal network) and a public network (e.g. the internet).
   - Checks whether incoming or outgoing data meets a given set of criteria.
   - If the data fails the criteria, the firewall will block the 'traffic' and give the user (or network manager) a warning that there may be a security issue.
   - The firewall can be used to log all incoming and outgoing 'traffic' to allow later interrogation by the user (or network manager).
   - Criteria can be set so that the firewall prevents access to certain undesirable sites; the firewall can keep a list of all undesirable IP addresses.
   - it is possible for firewalls to help prevent viruses or hackers entering the user's computer (or internal network).
   - The user is warned if some software on their system is trying to access an external data source (e.g. automatic software upgrade); the user is given the option of allowing it to go ahead or request that such access is denied.

   b Firewalls can be hardware or software; when the firewall is a hardware interface between computer and internet, it is known as a gateway.

5 a Data protection acts are designed to protect the public regarding data stored about them on systems. They set up principles that should be followed to protect a user from misuse of their data and to protect it from being stolen

   b Data protection act principles (three points from the following):
   1 Data must be fairly and lawfully processed.
   2 Data can only be processed for the stated purpose.
   3 Data must be adequate, relevant and not excessive.
   4 Data must be accurate.
   5 Data must not be kept longer than necessary.
   6 Data must be processed in accordance with the data subject's rights.
   7 Data must be kept secure.
   8 Data must not be transferred to another country unless they also have adequate protection.

   c Personal data (two points from personal data and two from sensitive data):
   - name and address
   - email address
   - passport number
   - IP address
   - date of birth
   - bank details
   - cookie IDs
   - photographs.

   Sensitive data:
   - ethnicity/race
   - political views
   - sexual orientation
   - criminal record
   - medical history
   - genetic data
   - biometric data
   - membership of trades union or political party.

6 B → E → C → A → D

7 ○ Trojan horse
   ○ skimmer
   ○ hacking
   ○ worm
   ○ ransomware
   ○ phishing
   ○ vishing
   ○ shoulder surfing
   ○ adware
   ○ virus.

Chapter 9

1 a Language used:
   - no vulgarity or use of inappropriate language since this can easily offend people
   - the use of technical terms should be reserved for an experienced or technical audience.

   Multimedia used:
   - use of sound, video and animation will always catch the attention of the audience
   - it is important not to over-do sound, video and animation in case the message gets hidden because of too many distractions in the presentation
   - a young audience is more likely to respond to loud music and embedded video clips
   - complicated descriptions are often better explained using graphs and/or animations.

   Length of presentation:
   - long presentations will only work if they are interesting and engage the audience
   - a very young audience would quickly get bored and start to become restless.

   Interactive presentation:
   - asking questions or getting the audience to 'try' things is always a good strategy
   - always be aware that not everyone wants to take part.

Examples used:
- when using examples to illustrate ideas, remember to be considerate (e.g. don't refer to meat products if the audience is vegetarian or to alcohol if the group contains people who could be offended by its reference).

b - Product keys or unique reference numbers: when software is being installed, the user will be asked to key in a unique reference number or product key (a string of letters and numbers) which was supplied with the original copy of the software (e.g. 4a3c 0efa 65ab).
- The user will be asked to click 'OK'/'I AGREE' or put a cross in a box to agree to the licence agreement before the software continues to install
- The original software packaging often comes with a sticker informing the purchaser that it is illegal to make copies of the software; the label is often in the form of a hologram indicating that this is a genuine copy.
- Some software will only run if the CD-ROM, DVD-ROM or memory stick is actually in the drive; this stops illegal multiple use and network use of the software.
- Some software will only run if a dongle is plugged into one of the USB ports.

2 a product key
   b hologram/holographic image
   c dongle
   d copyright (laws)

3 a We need to consider:
- The ages of the users (the kiosk needs to have very clear text and an easy-to-understand interface that appeals to young people as well as older people).
- If the kiosks are to supply general information in the area, the designers need to consider the kind of interests that would match various visitors to Bucharest.
- The designers need to be wary of people with disabilities (these could include people who use wheelchairs, people unable to use their hands properly or those who are visually impaired – consider the height of the display, type of interface and use of colours and large fonts etc.).

   b - If the user group is made up of older people, or people with disabilities or those who have sight problems, then it is important to make sure the kiosk has clear-to-read fonts.
- Complex language can be a real turn-off to potential kiosk users, for example if English is the passenger's second language, the text needs to be clear and easy to read for these reasons.
- It is necessary to hold the attention of the users (i.e. the information displayed should be interesting and relevant to all age groups), otherwise they will give up using the kiosk and quickly walk away.

- Good and attractive screen designs will attract users to make full use of the kiosks.
- Keeping the user interfaces clear and easy to use attracts people; lots of typing is a real 'put off' and it is better to adopt touchscreen and icons rather than text since this also helps people who don't necessarily speak good Romanian or English.

   c - Use 'real' people to test out the kiosks once they have been set up and use their feedback to improve the final system.
- Interview a number of people at the railway station and get their views on how well the kiosks work and check they meet their audience's needs.
- Give out short questionnaires to people visiting the railway station and check out what they would like to see on automatic information systems.
- Compare the functionality with parallel manually operated information systems and make any changes if necessary.

4 Four points from the following:
○ It is illegal to make copies of the software and give it away.
○ It is illegal to use coding from the copyrighted software in your own software and then pass on the software as your own without permission.
○ It is illegal to rent out the software without permission from the copyright holders.
○ It is illegal to use the name of the copyrighted software without agreement to do so.
○ It is illegal to use software on a network or in multiple user computers unless a licence has been acquired to allow this to happen.

Chapter 10

1

Statement	True (✓)	False (✓)
Only those in the Cc box of an email can see the name of all of the intended email recipients		✓
Email addresses are often grouped together for the purposes of marketing	✓	
The use of too many emoticons in an email can often annoy the recipients	✓	
Passive attacks on emails involve the changing or harming of the recipient's system		✓
Emails (and their attachments) are not subject to the copyright laws		✓

2 a Any unsolicited email is regarded as spam.
   b Software, known as spambots, is used to collect email addresses from the internet and build up

Answers to exam-style questions

spam mailing lists (emails can be gathered from websites, forums, chat rooms, social networking sites and so on).

c A security breach in which the system is not harmed but messages, settings or data (such as password data sent in an email) are read by an unauthorised third party.

d A security breach that involves changing or harming a system (e.g. malware that deletes files).

e Emails are electronic messages send by electronic means from one computer user to one or more recipients (frequently via the internet).

3 a Emails are often grouped together for the following reasons (three points from the following):
- it is easier to send out multiple emails if all the email addresses are grouped together under a single name
- marketing purposes where companies send out the same emails to target groups according to age, interests, financial status and so on
- 'spammers' use email grouping to target many users at the same time
- when setting up meetings, grouping people together makes sure everyone gets the same information, meeting invites and so on.

b Although spam can appear harmless, it causes the following issues (three points from the following):
- use up a person's time and is annoying
- use up valuable bandwidth on the internet, slowing it down
- can contain viruses and other malware
- clog up a user's inbox.

c - Companies need to set guidelines that all employees should follow when sending out emails; companies need to enforce these rules or face potential legal action.
- The rules and guidelines should cover:
- emails must be related to the company's business and sent out using specified, registered devices.
- the content and style of emails should be specified (this is often done using templates stored on the user devices)
- confidentiality should be clear as should the security of emails used and stored on the system
- protection using anti-malware must be used at all times; data traffic to and from company devices should always pass through a firewall
- regular training should take place to ensure that all employees are aware of the rules, confidentiality and security of emails.

4 a Three points from the following:
- intranet has restricted access/internet is worldwide
- intranet is used only within a company/organisation
- intranet access has more control of data whereas internet access is public and has no control
- intranet is policed/moderated/managed
- intranet has reduced unauthorised access to material whereas internet has general material
- intranet can restrict access to some websites/internet has no restrictions on websites
- data on intranet is more likely to be reliable/relevant/anyone can add material on internet
- intranet sits behind a firewall
- intranet protected by passwords/extra security layer/more chance of hacking on internet
- intranet used to give information relating to company whereas internet is general information
- internet has much more information.

b Extranets can link to an intranet through:
- mobile phones (a number of safeguards permit certain users only to have access)
- virtual private network (VPN): this uses the internet and makes use of secret keys to encrypt all communications between extranet user and the intranet).

c - they have a HOME page
- they have the ability to store a user's favourite websites/pages
- they keep a history of the websites visited by the use
- they give the ability to go backward and forward through websites opened
- they have hyperlinks that allow users to navigate between web pages; these hyperlinks are shown as blue underlined text or use a small picture, such as a pointed finger, under a phrase or image; by clicking on these hyperlinks the user is sent to another website or web page.

5 a
i) - short for web log
- personal online diary/journal
- owner's opinions/single author
- others can post comments
- frequently updated by owner
- postings tend to be in reverse chronological order
- blog is a website.

ii) - allows users to create/edit web pages using a browser
- many people can contribute/edit/update entries
- members of group can contribute
- holds information on many topics
- posting not in chronological order

Hodder & Stoughton Limited © David Watson and Graham Brown 2022

201

- structure determined by users/contents
 - wiki is website or software
 - wiki is usually objective.

iii) Social networking sites focus on building online communities of users who share the same interests and activities; they enable people to share photos, videos and music, hobbies, favourite eating places and so on; the members do this by creating public profiles and thus form 'relationships' with other users.

iv) Moderated forums are online discussion groups/forums under the control of an administrator who determines what is allowed to be posted; this gives greater protection from spam and from inappropriate material being posted.

b Microblogs are similar to blogs but are most often used on social networking sites to make short, frequent posts; the posts can be done using instant messaging, emails or use other social networking vehicles (such as tweets); social networking sites use microblogs to allow members to update their personal profiles, for example.

c An unmoderated forum is owned by no one and therefore isn't 'policed'; essentially the internet is an unmoderated forum relying on voluntary co-operation between users.

6 Arguments in favour of policing the internet:
- it would prevent illegal material being posted on websites (e.g. racist comments, pornography, terrorist activities and so on).
- people find it much easier to discover information which can have serious consequences (e.g. how to be a hacker, how to make a bomb and so on); although this can be found in books, it is much easier for a novice to find the required information using a search engine
- some form of control would prevent children and other vulnerable groups being subjected to undesirable websites, including criminal material
- some form of control would stop incorrect information being published on websites.

Arguments against policing the internet
- material published on websites is already available from other sources
- it would be very expensive to 'police' all websites, and users would have to pay for this somehow
- it would be difficult to enforce rules and regulations on a global scale
- it can be argued that policing would go against freedom of information/speech
- many topics and comments posted on websites are illegal and laws already exist to deal with the offenders
- who is to decide what is illegal or offensive – many things are only offensive to certain people (e.g. religious comments) but not necessarily to the majority.

Concluding argument, for example:

While policing the internet sounds like a good idea, who would do this (all countries have different ideas about what is acceptable and what isn't) and how would you 'police' seven billion people? It could create a 'dark internet' where people would carry out illegal acts with almost no way of detecting what they are doing. It is better to simple educate people about internet use (netiquette) and remember laws already exist to combat crime (normal and cybercrime).

7   1 → C   4 → F
    2 → D   5 → B
    3 → A   6 → E

Chapter 11

1 .mp4 and .gif
2 .txt, .rtf and .csv
3 ○ Both file types are containers.
   ○ Both file types can hold a number of files with different types.
   ○ Both file types contain compressed data … and are used to reduce the number of bytes needed to save a file … to save storage space/reduce transmission time.
   ○ .rar file extension is an acronym for Roshal ARchive/developed by Russian software engineer Eugene Roshal.

Chapter 12

1 Image B Reflection/rotation through 180 degrees
   Image C Rotation through 90 degrees clockwise
   Image D Cropped
2 Aspect ratio: the ratio of the width to the height of an image.

Chapter 13

1 Author's name; Document title; Chapter title; Publisher's name/email/website.
2 Page numbering; Section numbering; Date of publication; File name and path.

Chapter 14

1 A serif font is a font style where the ends of characters contain small strokes called serifs. If these strokes are not present, then it is a sans serif font.
2 Corporate branding/a method of recognising a company through elements like its logo/colour scheme and so on.
3 ○ To give consistency to documents and other materials.
   ○ To save time in planning/setting up/creating/formatting documents.
   ○ Creates brand recognition.
   ○ Reduces the risks of mistakes in documents.

Chapter 15

1. 'marshhland': two h's suggest it is not a word, nor the name of a place or object. This is a spelling error.

   'Tawara': this appears to be the name of a place so is unlikely to be held in the dictionary of the spell check program. The capital T also gives us a clue to this, suggesting it is a name.

2. 'Mrs jones' should have a capital letter for her name ('Mrs Jones').

   The first sentence suggests a female examiner and the second suggests a male examiner. The spell check and grammar check would not identify these errors.

Chapter 16

1.
   a. Pie chart
   b. Line graph
   c. None of these (it would be a scatter diagram)
   d. Line graph

Chapter 17

1. The area between the edge of a page...

   ... and the main content of the page.

   This is usually whitespace.

   Text flows between the page margins.

2. Text which aligned...

   Text which displays straight (not ragged) margins...

   ... to both left and right margins

3. The first line each paragraph is aligned to the left margin. All other lines are left hanging/indented from the margin. It is useful for short headings followed by blocks of text. This is set using hanging indent and first line indent markers on the ruler.

Chapter 18

1.
   a. A record is a collection of fields containing information about one data subject, usually one person or object.
   b. A field holds a single item of data.
   c. A file is a logically organised collection of records.
   d. A table is a two-dimensional grid of data organised by rows and columns within a database.
   e. A report is a document that provides information. In a database, it is designed to make the data presented easy to understand.
   f. A query is a request for information from a database/search to interrogate a database.
   g. A calculated control is a special field in a database report that is calculated as the report is run.

2. Four points from the following:

   A flat-file database contains a single two-dimensional table ...

   ... which holds data about one subject/type of item.

   A relational database has more than one table ...

   ... each table holds data about one subject/type of item.

   These tables are linked together ...

   ... through common data elements ...

   ... using a system of primary key and foreign key fields.

3.
   a. Price; descending order.
   b. Tracks; ascending order.
   c. Released > 2015 AND Price < 10
   d. Emile Sande, Phil Collins, Michael Buble.

Chapter 19

1. Presenter notes often contain more content than shown on the slides. Presenter notes can include greater detail than the audience notes. Presenter notes can contain anecdotes to 'hook' the audience.

2. Continuous looping.

Chapter 20

1.
   a. Looks through the contents of cells H2 to H21. Checks to see if contents are equal to contents of cell B5. The contents of the corresponding/matching cells from I2 to I21 are added to the total/summed, which gives the value 746.50.
   b. =SUMIF($H$2:$H$21,B6,$I$2:$I$21)
   c. =COUNT(I2:I21)

2. Four points from the following:

   When the result of A42*A43 gives a response ...

   ... that has a decimal part of 0.5 or greater ...

   ... then different answers will occur.

   The INT function will remove the decimal part.

   The ROUND(...,0) function will round up to the next whole number ...

   ... if the decimal part is greater than or equal to 0.5.

   Any two suitable examples of data in A42 and A43.

3.
   a. It counts the number of times the contents of cell A3 ...

      ... is stored in the named range ObjectTable ...

      ... which has already been defined by the user.
   b. $A$3 is an absolute cell reference.

      This cell reference will not change when the cell is replicated/copied.

      If a relative cell reference like A3 was used, the reference would change when it was replicated/copied.

Chapter 21

1. A web browser is software that allows a user to display a web page on a computer screen; it interprets html from a web page. It shows the results as text/images/sound/video.

2.
   h1 colour should be color

       sans serif should be sans-serif

       20 px should be 20px (i.e. no space between 20 and px)

   h2 000040 should be #000040

       Times New Roman should be "Times New Roman"

       centre should be center

table "solid" should have no quotes

td   border-colour should be border-color

3 Content layer
   - Is used to create the page structure/layout.
   - Is usually HTML/uses HTML tags/saved in HTML format.
   - Contains text, images and hyperlinks.

   Presentation layer
   - Is used to set display features/parameters of the page.
   - Is usually CSS/saved in CSS format.
   - Presentation layer can be attached as an external stylesheet, set as an internal stylesheet or as embedded tags within the HTML.

Answers to Practice Paper 1

1 l RFID reader
   - OCR
   - QR code reader (not camera unless states it is digital)
   - barcode reader
   - chip and PIN reader

   ☞ 2 marks for column 1 and 1 mark for column 2.

	Application software (✓)	Systems software (✓)
Spreadsheet	✓	
Control software	✓	
Antivirus software		✓
Device driver		✓
Audio editing software	✓	

3 - contactless cards
   - passports
4 - antivirus
   - screensaver

5

Statement	Dot matrix printer (✓)	Laser printer (✓)	Inkjet printer (✓)
Makes use of dry ink (powder) toner cartridges		✓	
Can make use of continuous and two-part stationery	✓		
Can produce ozone and ink particulates in the air during operation		✓	
Uses a print head, stepper motor and colour ink (liquid) cartridges			✓
Makes use of thermal bubble and piezoelectric technology			✓

6 a Artificial intelligence:
   – AI is a machine or application which carries out a task that requires some degree on intelligence.

   b Augmented reality (two points from the first four and an example of a use):
   – user experiences relationship between digital (virtual) and physical (real) worlds
   – virtual data and objects are overlaid
   – user can experience AR world through special goggles or via a smartphone/tablet
   – the user is not isolated from the real world and can still interact
   – example of use: in a car showroom to give a user a 'feel' for a new car without taking it out onto the open road.

   c Virtual reality (two points from the first three and an example of a use):
   – technology has the ability to take the user out of the real world into a virtual, digital environment
   – the user is fully immersed in the simulated world
   – users wear a VR headset which a gives 360° view of the virtual world
   – examples of use: can be used in medicine/surgery, construction, education and military applications.

7 a – a microchip that stores and processes information
   – an antenna which is used to receive and transmit data/information.

   b – passive or active
   – passive tags use the RFID readers radio wave energy to relay back the information
   – active tags have their very own battery power and can work from a much greater distance.

8 a – GIS is a system that allows a user to map, model, query and analyse large amounts of data according to a location.
   – GIS allows the following:
   – amalgamation of information into easily understood maps
   – performance of complex analytical calculations and then presentation of the results as a map, table or graphics

- use by many groups, such as geographers, scientists and engineers, to see data in different ways.
  b Two points from the following:
  - allows the exploring of both geographical and thematic components in a way which shows them to be intimately interconnected with each other to form a single entity
  - allows the handling and exploration of huge amounts of data (massive number crunching)
  - allows data to be integrated from a wide range of very different sources (which appear at first to be totally unconnected).
  c Two points from the following:
  - the learning curve on GIS software can be very long
  - GIS software is very expensive
  - GIS requires enormous amounts of data to be input (thus increasing the chances of errors)
  - it is difficult to make GIS programs which are both fast and user-friendly; GIS require very complex command language interfaces to work properly.

9

Statements	Router (✓)	Switch (✓)	Hub (✓)
Used to connect devices together to form a local area network (LAN)		✓	✓
It looks up the destination MAC address before sending a data packet to the correct network device		✓	
Used to connect LANs to other external networks	✓		
Uses both MAC and IP addresses to enable data packets to be sent to the correct device on another network	✓		
It sends all data packets to all the devices on a network			✓

10 a Three points from the following:
- collect the number of vehicles passing the junction in all directions
- time of day also needs to be recorded for each vehicle being counted
- observe the build-up of traffic at different times of day and how long it takes to clear
- consider other road factors that can affect traffic (e.g. a pedestrian crossing nearby)
- record the time it takes the slowest vehicle to pass through the junction
- consider the effect of other factors, such as accidents, filtering and emergency vehicles.

b - Once the above data has been collected and is fed into the model, different scenarios can be tried out to optimise traffic light timings and to determine where to place traffic sensors in the road.
- The modeller will try different traffic densities at different times of the day and see how it affects the traffic light timings: does the timing of the lights cause hold-ups and how will different light timings affect traffic flows?
- Should priority be given to traffic in certain directions to maintain good traffic flow and so on?
- The final version will receive live data and a central control box can compare actual traffic data with simulation data allowing the model to be fine-tuned.

Advantages (two from the following):
- using computer models is less expensive than having to build the real thing (e.g. a bridge)
- on many occasions it is safer to use a computer model (some real situations are hazardous, for example chemical processes)
- when using computer modelling, it is much easier to try out various scenarios in advance
- it is nearly impossible to try out some tasks in real life because of the high risk involved or the remoteness (e.g. outer space, under the sea, nuclear reactors, crash testing cars etc.)
- it is often faster to use a computer model than do the real thing (some applications would take years before a result was known, e.g. climate change calculations, population growth etc.).

Disadvantages (two from the following):
- a model is only as good as the programming or the data entered; the simulation will depend heavily on these two factors
- although building the real thing can be expensive, sometimes modelling is also a very costly option, and the two costs need to be compared before deciding whether or not to use modelling
- people's reactions to the results of a simulation may not be positive; they may not trust the results it produces (modelling can never mimic real life and there will always be a difference between the results from modelling and reality).

Answers to Practice Paper 1

11 a Three points from the following:
- SSDs are very lightweight and also consume considerably less power than HDDs
- HDDs suffer from latency whereas SSDs don't suffer from this
- SSDs are much more robust/reliable than HDDs (no moving parts)
- SSDs consume much less power than HDDs (makes them very suitable for use in laptops/notebooks)
- SSDs are very thin and much smaller than HDDs so they can easily fit into devices such as tablets and smartphones.

b Any three from the following:
- optical disks have a much lower storage capacity than flash memories
- it is more difficult to save data on optical media
- optical disks can be damaged quite easily (scratch the surface)
- optical disks require fairly bulky read-write devices unlike SSD devices (leading to the development of MP3 files that use SSD technology)
- using cloud storage is reducing the need for optical media (and other recording media)
- streaming of music and videos has also reduced the need for recording media.

12

Description	ICT term
Embedding malicious code within QR codes	Attagging
Used in wireless networks to allow access to a network at various points using wireless technology	(Wireless) access point
A small file sent to the user's web browser when they visit a website; the file stores information about the user which is accessed each time they visit the website	Cookie
Hardware address that uniquely identifies each device connecting to a network	Media access control (MAC) address
A command used in HTML to instruct a web browser how to display text, images or other objects; they are not displayed with the web page	Tag

13 1 → C   4 → F
      2 → D   5 → B
      3 → A   6 → E

14

Name of device	Application	Justification
Dot matrix printer	Printing out of wage slips at the end of the month	Can use continuous carbon paper for overnight printing
QR code reader	Supplying tourist information at a railway station for arrivals	Most people now have smartphones, website for area can be embedded in QR code
Microphone	Automatic control of switching lights off and on using voice commands	People with disabilities may have difficulty getting about and this requires no input apart from use of the voice
Radio frequency identification (RFID)	To track parts in a large distribution warehouse	Movement of goods is automatic throughout the process from warehouse to delivery

15 a Similarities:
- both devices are used to exchange data packets within their own LANs
- neither device can exchange data with external networks
- either device can be used to connect devices in a network together.

Switches:
- switches send data packets to a specific device on the network
- security using switches is better than security using hubs
- switches use MAC addresses to locate devices on the network
- switches use a look-up table to find the MAC address of the device intended to receive the data packet.

Hubs:
- hubs send data packets to every device connected to the network.

b Bridges (two points from the following):
- the main objective of a bridge is to connect LANs together
- bridges scan a device's MAC address
- data is sent out using data packets
- connect networks together that have the same protocols
- bridges don't make use of routing tables
- a bridge only has two ports.

c – routers are used to route data packets from one network to another network (using IP addresses)
 – routers are used to join a LAN to the internet or to other external networks:
 – When a computer on network 'A' wants to send data outside its own LAN, the data is split into packets and the router connected to the LAN sends the data packets to the outside network.
 – Routers use a routing table that contains information about the router's immediate network and information about routers in the immediate vicinity; this allows routers to establish how to deal with each data packet.
 – Each data packet will be directed to network 'B' via its own route.
 – When a data packet is received, the router inspects the IP address of the recipient and determines whether the data packet is intended for its own network or for another network; if the IP address indicates another network, the data packet is sent to the next router.
 – Routers don't store MAC addresses (only IP addresses are stored so it knows where to send the data packet in the next stage of its journey).
 – Once all the data packets have been received by the router connected to network 'B', they are assembled in their correct order then sent to the appropriate device (using the MAC address which was part of the original message sent by the computer on network 'A').

d Routers:
 – the main objective of a router is to connect various types of network together
 – routers scan a device's IP address
 – data is sent out using data packets
 – connected networks use different protocols
 – a routing table is used to direct data packets to the appropriate device
 – a router has several ports.

 Bridges:
 – the main objective of a bridge is to connect LANs together
 – bridges scan a device's MAC address
 – data is sent out using data packets
 – connect networks together that have the same protocols
 – bridges don't make use of routing tables
 – a bridge only has two ports.

16 a Range check: numbers <1 or numbers >100 should be rejected.
 Type check: only numeric values should be input; non-numeric data should be rejected.

 b Normal data: this is data that is acceptable/valid and has a known outcome, for example the month can be any whole number in the range 1 to 12.

 Extreme data: this is data at the limits of acceptability, for example the month can be either 1 or 12 only.

 Abnormal data: this is data outside the limits of acceptability and should be rejected or cause an error message, for example the following values input for a month should be rejected: –2, 0.34, 100, July and so on.

 c

	Normal (✓)	Abnormal (✓)	Extreme (✓)
52	✓		
1	(✓)		✓
104		✓	
100	(✓)		✓
twenty-five		✓	
99	✓		

17 Benefits of online shopping and banking:
 ○ There is no longer a need to travel into the town centres thus reducing costs (money for fuel, bus fares etc.) and wastage of time; it also helps to reduce town centre congestion and pollution.
 ○ Users now have access to a worldwide market and can thus look for products that are cheaper; this is obviously less expensive and less time-consuming than having to shop around by the more conventional methods; they will also have access to a much wider choice of goods.
 ○ People with disabilities and elderly people can now access any shop or bank without the need to leave home, which is of great benefit to them; it helps to keep them part of society since they can now do all the things taken for granted by non-disabled people.
 ○ Because it is online, shopping and banking can be done at any time on any day of the week (i.e. 24/7, which is the term now used); this is particularly helpful to people who work as the shops/banks would normally be closed when they finished work.
 ○ People can spend more time doing other things, for example going shopping at the supermarket probably took up a lot of time; by doing this online (e.g. setting up repeat items) people are now free to do more leisure activities.
 ○ Many people find it less embarrassing to ask for a bank loan using the internet rather than enduring a face-to-face discussion with bank staff.
 ○ There are often long queues at banks or checkouts at the shops, so internet banking saves time.
 ○ The shops and banks save money by not having as many staff working for them (reduced wage bill) or hiring of high street premises (reduction in rental costs); these savings are often passed on to the customer in the form of lower interest rates, cheaper goods or higher rates of interest for savers.

Answers to Practice Paper 1

Drawbacks of online shopping and banking:
- There is the possibility of isolation and lack of socialisation if people stay at home to do all their shopping and banking.
- There are possible health risks associated with online shopping or banking because of lack of exercise; if people physically go shopping then they are getting some exercise.
- Security issues are a major concern (e.g. hacking, stealing credit card details, etc.) as are viruses and other malware (e.g. phishing, pharming and so on).
- Accidentally using fraudulent bank or shopping websites is always a risk and this is linked to security issues.
- It is necessary to have a computer and to pay for the internet to be able to do online shopping and banking.
- Unlike high street shopping, it is only possible to see a picture of the goods, which might not portray the exact colour of a dress for instance (nor can you try something on to see if it fits), before buying them; you also have to wait several days for the goods to arrive; returning goods is expensive.
- High street shops and banks are closing because of the increase in online shopping and banking and this is leading to 'ghost towns' forming.
- It is easier to make errors with online banking and transfer money to the wrong account.

Answers for Practice Paper 2 and 3 are online along with the source files that are required for the tasks.

Index

3D printers 20, 67–8

A
absolute cell referencing 161
absolute file paths 173
access points (APs) 34, 36
accuracy 139
actuators 20
analogue data 2
analogue sensors 12
analysis stage 81–4
antivirus software 40, 97
applications software 2
artificial intelligence (AI) 8–9
ATMs 10, 11, 14, 18, 36, 63
attached stylesheets 176, 179
attagging 16
audiences 107–9, 110
audio conferencing 41–2
audio files 125, 171
augmented reality (AR) 8–9, 16
authentication 39–40, 43, 64, 98, 102
automated number plate recognition (ANPR) 47, 73–4
autonomous transport 47–8

B
backing storage *see* storage devices
banking systems 63–5, 72
barcodes 11, 14, 16, 70
basic input-output system (BIOS) 3
biometrics 39, 60–1, 75, 99–100, 102
blogs 117
Bluetooth 34
Blu-ray discs 27
booking systems 62–3, 65–6
bookmarks 172
boot files 3
bridge design 55
bridges (in networks) 34, 37
building design 55

C
calculations 152–3, 160
card fraud 98
Cascading StyleSheet (CSS) 125, 167, 168, 170, 175–80
cathode ray tube (CRT) monitors 18
CDs 26, 27
cells 159–61, 164–5
central processing unit (CPU) 1, 3
changeover 88–9
charts 140–3
cheques 64, 65
chip and PIN readers 10, 14, 64, 71
classes 179
cloud storage 35, 101
colours 178
columns 159, 164, 165
command line interfaces (CLI) 4

communication
   of information 51–3
   mobile 53–4
   satellites 77
   social interaction 46
   via emails 112–15
complementary metal oxide semi-conductor (CMOS) 3, 28
computer-aided learning (CAL) 61
computer-controlled systems 58–61
computer modelling 54–7
contactless cards 14, 39, 75
control gate transistors 28
copyright 109–10, 113
corporate house style 134
credit/debit cards 14, 63, 64, 98

D
data
   data types 84–5, 149–50
   manipulation 151–4, 164
   personal/sensitive 94–5
   presentation 154–5, 164–5
   security issues 96–103
   sorting 154–5, 164
databases 148–55
data capture forms 85–6, 151
data flow diagrams (DFDs) 83
data models 54, 159–63
data packets 33, 34
data protection act (DPA) 94
design stage 84–6
desktop computers 7
dialogue-based interfaces 4, 5
digital cameras 11
digital certificates 100
digital data 2
direct data entry (DDE) devices 14–17
documentation stage 89
documents 131
   layout 131–3, 144–5
   production 144–7
   proofing 137–9
   styles 135–6
dot matrix printers 19
driving wheels 11
DVDs 26, 27

E
electronic funds transfer at point-of-sale (EFTPOS) 63, 64, 71
electronic funds transfer (EFT) 63
email 95, 100, 102, 112–15
embedded styles 176
encryption 98, 101–2, 120
e-publications 53
e-safety 95–6, 103–4, 121
evaluation stage 89
expert systems 68–70, 77–8

extended reality (XR) 8
extranets 117

F
fields 84, 148
file compression 125, 126–7
file formats 124–6
file management 124–6
file structures 84–5
firewalls 102, 116
flash memory 29
flat-file databases 148, 149
floating gate transistors 28
flood water management 55–6, 57
fonts 134–5, 177–8
footers 132–3
foreign key fields 149
forms 85–6, 151
formulae 160
forums 118
functions 161–2

G
geographic information systems (GIS) 76–7
gesture-based interfaces 4
global positioning system (GPS) 76
grammar checking 138
graphical user interface (GUI) 4
graphs 140–3

H
hard disk drives (HDDs) 1, 3, 25
hardware 1
headers 132–3
head section 174
health risks 49
hotspots 34, 36
hubs 33, 35, 37
human-computer interfaces 4–5
hyperlinks 157, 172
HyperText Markup Language (HTML) 125, 167
   see also web pages

I
images 51, 128–30, 170, 178
implementation stage 88–9
inkjet printers 19
input devices 3, 10–13
internet
   functionality 118–19
   policing 121
   protocols 120
   safety 95
   using 116–18
internet banking 72, 101, 102
Internet Protocol (IP) address 32–3, 34
Internet Service Providers (ISPs) 102, 118
intranets 116–17

Index

J
joysticks 11

K
keyboards 10

L
laptops 7
laser printers 19
layer images 130
layout 131-3, 144-5
Light Detection and Ranging (LiDaR) 48
light pens 12
lists
　in documents 135-6, 146-7
　on web pages 171-2
local area networks (LANs) 33, 34, 35-6

M
magnetic storage devices 24-5
magnetic stripes 14, 39, 60
magnetic tapes 24-5
malware 40, 97-8
master slides 156
media access control (MAC) address 32, 33
medicine, computers in 67-8, 70
memory cards 29
memory sticks 28-9
metatags 174-5
microphones 11
microprocessor-controlled devices
　in the home 45-6, 49-50
　transport systems and 47-8
microprocessors 1, 3
mobile computers 7
modelling *see* computer modelling; data models
monitors 18
mouse/mice 10
multimedia projectors 19

N
near field communication (NFC) 71, 75
nested functions 163
netiquette 113-14, 115
network interface cards (NICs) 1, 32
networks 32-7, 39-40
newsletters 51
notebooks 7
numeric keypads 10

O
online gaming 96
online shopping 72, 101, 102
operating system (OS) 2, 4
optical character recognition (OCR) 15, 65, 73
optical mark recognition (OMR) 15, 73
optical storage devices 26-7
output devices 3, 18-22

P
passwords 39, 102-3, 113
pen drives 28-9
personal finances 54
personal/sensitive data 94-5, 103-4
phablets 7
physical safety 93
physical tokens 40, 43
piracy 110
plotters 20
point-of-sale (POS) terminals 10, 70-1
portable hard disk drives 25
posters 51
presentation layer 167, 168, 175, 178
presentations 52, 107, 110, 156-8
primary key fields 84, 148-9
printers 19, 20
production control 59-60
proofing 137-9
proofreading 139
protocols 120

Q
queries 151-3
quick response (QR) codes 16-17, 62

R
radio frequency identification devices (RFIDs) 14, 15, 74-5
random access memory (RAM) 1, 3
read-only memory (ROM) 1, 3
recognition systems 73-5
records 84, 148
relational databases 148-51
relative cell referencing 161
relative file paths 173
remote controls 11
repetitive strain injury (RSI) 10, 49
reports 154
retail industry, computers in 70-2
robots, in industry 58-60
routers 34, 37
rows 159, 165

S
safety issues 93-6
satellite navigation (satnav) 76
satellites 76-7
scanners 11
school management systems 60-1
search engines 119
secure sockets layer (SSL) 100-1, 120-1
security, of data 96-103
sensors 12-13, 47, 48, 56, 60, 73
smart motorways 47
smartphones 7, 16-17, 53-4, 71
smart televisions 29, 46
social networking sites 95, 102, 103-4, 118
software 1-2
solid-state drives (SSDs) 1, 3, 27, 28
solid-state technology 27-9
sorting data 154-5, 164
spam 114

speakers/loudspeakers 20
spell checking 51, 137-8
spreadsheets 2, 54, 159-65
stock control systems 70-1
storage devices 3, 24-30
streaming 29, 52
styles
　corporate house style 134
　documents 135-6
　web pages 168, 175-80
stylesheets 175-80
subscriber identity module (SIM) cards 53
switches 33, 35, 37
systems life cycle 81-90
system software 2
system specifications 83-4

T
tables
　in documents 131-2
　on web pages 168-9, 179, 180
tablets 7
testing 86-8
text
　formatting 145-7
　wrapping 128-9
tokens 40, 43, 71
touchpads 10
touchscreens 4, 11, 18
trackerballs 10
traffic management 56
transport systems 47-8
two-factor authentication 102

U
uniform resource locators (URLs) 118-19
user interfaces 4-5

V
validation 85, 138
verification 139
video conferencing 40-1
video files 125, 170
virtual reality (VR) 8
Voice over Internet Protocol (VoIP) 53, 101

W
weather forecasting 56
web browsers 118-19, 167
web conferencing 42
web pages 167-75
websites 52, 120, 167-80
wide area networks (WANs) 36-7
WiFi 34
wikis 117
windows icons menu and pointing (WIMP) interfaces 4
wireless local area networks (WLANs) 36
word processors 2, 51
　see also documents
World Wide Web 116, 121-2